Communal Utopias and the American Experience

Communal Utopias and the American Experience

RELIGIOUS COMMUNITIES, 1732–2000

Robert P. Sutton

Westport, Connecticut
London

Library of Congress Cataloging-in-Publication Data

Sutton, Robert P.
   Communal utopias and the American experience : religious communities, 1732–2000 /
Robert P. Sutton.
      p. cm.
   Includes bibliographical references and index.
   ISBN 0–275–97554–1 (alk. paper)
   1. Utopias—United States—History.   2. Utopias—United States—Religious aspects—
History.   I. Title.
   HX653 S88   2003
   335′.973—dc21   2002032991

British Library Cataloguing in Publication Data is available.

Library of Congress Catalog Card Number: 2002032991
ISBN: 0–275–97554–1

First published in 2003

Praeger Publishers, 88 Post Road West, Westport, CT 06881
An imprint of Greenwood Publishing Group, Inc.
www.praeger.com

Printed in the United States of America

The paper used in this book complies with the
Permanent Paper Standard issued by the National
Information Standards Organization (Z39.48–1984).

10 9 8 7 6 5 4 3 2 1

Man seeketh in society comfort.

—Francis Bacon

Contents

Introduction

Communal Utopias and the American Experience: Religious Communities, 1732–2000 is the first of a two-volume history of communal utopias describing these communities from the first religious cloister at Ephrata, Pennsylvania (1732–1813), through the modern intentional communities. Its companion volume, *Communal Utopias and the American Experience: Secular Communities 1824–2000*, is scheduled to appear in 2004.

Until now, American communalism has been studied in fragments, either in monographs on individual communities, in anthologies such as Donald E. Pitzer's *America's Communal Utopias* (Chapel Hill: University of North Carolina Press, 1997), or in historical dictionaries such as Robert S. Fogarty's *Dictionary of American Communal and Utopian History* (Westport, Conn.: Greenwood Press, 1980). Equally significant, all of these histories, with the exception of Timothy Miller's *The Sixties Communes: Hippies and Beyond* (Syracuse, N.Y.: Syracuse University Press, 1999), stop at mid-twentieth century, if they go that far. This is true even for Yaacov Oved's *Two Hundred Years of American Communes* (New Brunswick, N.J.: Transaction, 1988). The result is that, as Paul S. Boyer puts it in his foreword to Pitzer's anthology, our understanding of our communal tradition when "remembered at all . . . tends to be in a confusing and disjointed fashion as free-floating bits of cultural ephemera."

These two volumes, which cover 65 communities and bring the story of American communalism into the twenty-first century, will rectify this fragmented perception of our utopian past. They will show that the utopian tradition is an unbroken motif, not an erratic and fragmented experience. There was never any extended period of time when an important experiment, or experiments, was not underway, from the Ephrata Cloister to today's more than 500 intentional communities. True enough, there were times when community building flourished and times when it was less vigorous, but the quest for utopia has never ceased.

The first volume, on religious communities, begins with the Ephrata Cloister and then discusses the Shakers and the Separatist colonies. Next, in sequence, it examines Oneida, the Hutterite Brethren, Jewish agricultural colonies, and California's exotic brotherhoods. The final chapter discusses religious utopias built during the twentieth century. The second volume begins with Robert Owen's New Harmony. Then it discusses the Fourierist phalanxes followed by a treatment of Icaria, Gilded Age socialist cooperatives, and the Great Depression experiments. The last chapter deals with the modern hippie colonies and intentional communities.

Though each communal utopia was unique in purpose, membership, and length of existence, together they shared a number of common features. Whether religious or secular, they showed a persistent dichotomy between a full commitment to communal goals and assertive self-interest. Consequently, high ideals such as brotherhood, fraternity, and cooperation were constantly challenged by chronic individualism. Power structure was based on equality and democratic participation, but often a strong-willed individual ruled the community. Values of communal ownership of property and communal work were undermined by the economic opportunities available outside the community, such as high wages and cheap land. Cultural life sometimes reached impressively high levels of accomplishment, as in the Ephrata Cloister, Brook Farm, and the Icarian colonies; but often it was regimented—in Icaria, even censured—in order to have it conform to community values. Many utopias promised a new, emancipated role for women but still kept them in traditional women's jobs and in subordinate roles vis-à-vis men. Communal utopias insisted that children be treated with understanding, tenderness, and compassion, but some adults saw them as dangerous enticements for parents to have special love for their progeny rather than unfettered devotion to the community. When utopias pushed education for the children (most religious ones did not), they had advanced ideas, such as the same curriculum for both sexes and preschool training. But in practice they sometimes just indoctrinated their youth with communal values. Last, many utopian communities before the 1960s perceived themselves as paradigms, as perfect models of a new and better way of living, which outsiders would want to emulate. However, except for the Shakers and Brook Farm, they never proselytized and they remained largely isolationist and sometimes xenophobic.

Religious utopias, except for some of the most recent ones, were millennial societies founded on the belief that a purified fellowship must gather quickly to await an imminent Second Coming of Christ. They usually viewed marriage and sexual intercourse as the most disturbing examples of the moral wretchedness of a degenerate, sinful world. Spiritual goals took priority over economic ones, and they usually adopted common ownership of property as an economic necessity. Charismatic individuals, many claiming direct contact with God, around whom the community coalesced, led them all. Sometimes, when he or she died, the bonds of loyalty weakened, and the community declined.

I am especially grateful to the libraries and special collections across the country that quickly responded to my seemingly endless requests. Of special importance to this history is the collection of over 200 taped and transcribed interviews with members of modern intentional communities. Timothy Miller and Deborah Altus collected this primary-source material during a year of travel to communities all over the United States. It is called "The 60s Communes Project" and can be found in the archives at the University of Kansas; it was funded by a grant from the National Endowment for the Humanities. Finally, I should like to express my appreciation to Western Illinois University for a sabbatical leave of absence during the fall semester of 1998 that made it possible for me to begin research on this manuscript.

CHAPTER 1

The Ephrata Cloister

Before Conrad Beissel founded the Ephrata Cloister in 1732 at a site 10 miles north of present-day Lancaster, Pennsylvania, only four briefly lived religious utopian communities had appeared in the English colonies. Horekill, begun by Pieter Cornelius Plockhoy in 1663 near Lewes, Delaware, survived only a year. The Bohemian Manor, established in Maryland in 1683 by Labadist refugees from Holland, allowed its devotees to continue their life of isolated "inward illumination of the spirit" until 1727. In 1694, 40 German Pietists, all men and led by the young mystic Johannes Kelpius, built the Woman in the Wilderness Community on 175 acres just west of Philadelphia; a millennial commune, it held together until Kelpius's death in 1708 and then rapidly disintegrated. In 1697, also near Philadelphia, Bernhard Köster, who had lived in the Woman in the Wilderness, organized the Brethren in America at Plymouth, west of Germantown. Here, Köster and his followers constructed a communal tabernacle called House of Peace (Irena). But because of Köster's divisive personality and his return to Germany in 1699, the community dissolved.[1]

Then, in the nadir of the winter of 1732, Conrad Beissel arrived at Cocalico Creek, a desolate area of the Pennsylvania frontier. There, he created the Ephrata Cloister (named after the Hebrew word for Bethlehem), the first in a long line of religious communal utopias; it lasted until 1814 and left a rich legacy. Its mystical poetry was unsurpassed, even by English writers. Its hand-decorated, illuminated manuscripts, or *Frakturschriften*, were masterpieces, exquisite expressions of spiritual devotion. It ran the largest printing and publishing operation this side of the Atlantic Ocean. It produced the most important body of religious music in the colonies, and Beissel wrote the first treatise on music in America. Most significant, Ephrata was not just a prototype for later religious utopias, it was the first counterculture community. E. Gordon Alderfer, writing in 1985, maintained that in its historical setting Ephrata "emphasized the relationships of its inner life and drama to events, ideas, and movements in the world around it." And, he went on, "what it represented in the eighteenth century has too many correspondences to counterculture movements of our own era to ignore."[2]

Beissel, the son of Mathias Beissel, a poverty-stricken alcoholic, was born in 1691 in the Palatine town of Eberbach. His father died before Conrad was born, and at the age of seven, when Conrad's mother passed away, his older brothers raised him. These early experiences evidently produced a lonely, introverted child and "undoubtedly contributed to his search for spiritual solitude and his rejection of the natural family as an institution."[3] Apprenticed to a baker as a teenager, Beissel learned not only a trade but also how to play the violin. From that point on, music was a major influence in his life.

While still serving his apprenticeship, he underwent a religious experience that made him abhor conventional Lutheran worship and its clergy. As he later recalled, he saw that "preachers themselves are, for the most part unconverted, natural, and carnal men, who live in pride and love of the world, and do the will of the flesh and of the reason in evil works; who have not the eternal, living, and self-sustaining Word of God."[4] Beissel soon began to seek out groups that shared his convictions, especially Anabaptist dissenters. He was fascinated with their life of primitive asceticism and their condemnation of private property; and he particularly was taken with their view of a church as a community of saints.

In 1709, Beissel moved to Strasbourg, and then to Heidelberg, where he became a journeyman baker. But he detested the ribald vulgarity of the guild members. The good bakers, on the other hand, soon tired of his diatribes on their immorality and wanted him expelled from the town as a radical Pietist. In 1716, when the city court ordered his arrest, Beissel fled to Wittgenstein, a town with a reputation as a haven for religious refugees, and then to other towns across southern Germany. He became involved with the Schwarzenau Brethren (later known as the Dunkers, or the Church of the Brethren) and then the Inspirationists (later the Amana Society). These sects repudiated infant baptism and believed in the perfection of life in this world, spiritual instead of sexual marriage, and inspired ministry. Their emphasis on the "gift of prophecy" apparently encouraged Beissel to proselytize, to wander from place to place, preaching in disjointed exhortations, an "unbridling of the Spirit," as he called it. Committed to a life of poverty, he survived, barely, by spinning wool for a pittance. By the age of 29, though, for reasons he never fully explained, Beissel despaired of ever finding enduring spiritual solace in Germany. In 1720, when he learned about the Woman in the Wilderness, he and some friends left for America to join that community in a search for religious peace.

When he arrived at the commune, he discovered that the community of Christian hermits had been scattered for a dozen years and that many of them had married. He moved to Germantown, in Pennsylvania, and found work as an apprentice weaver. In 1724, he was baptized by a Dunker minister. Nearby, at Mühlback Creek, he and a companion named Jacob Stuntz built a cabin. Over the next several years Beissel attracted a growing number of followers with his erratic sermons about observing the Saturday Sabbath, his demands for celibacy as a replacement for marriage, and his insistence upon observing Old Testament dietary laws. Some of the celibate built their own log cabins to be near him all the time. They were committed, like Beissel, to celibacy and to abjure the ways of the world. From that time on, contemporaries used the name "Solitary" to identify the community.[5]

Beissel's sermons were mystical tirades in which he spoke in a trance, eyes closed, without a Bible. According to an Ephrata chronicle, he spoke "with astonishing strength of spirit . . . so that . . . its delivery might not be weakened by written knowledge" because, Beissel said, the revelations came directly from God and should replace Scripture.[6] Dunkers began to resent Beissel's criticism of their beliefs, and, despite several efforts at reconciliation, the gap widened. When, in 1728, he published a tract, *Mystyrion anomias* (The Mystery of Lawlessness), the Germantown Dunkers disowned him.[7]

In *The Mystery of Lawlessness* Beissel claims that observance of a Saturday Sabbath separated the holy from the unholy and that celebrating it created a spirit of love and redemption. He insists that all sex, even in marriage, was an abomination, an insult to God. He elaborated on this tenet in his second book, *Die Ehe Das Zuchthaus fleischlicher Menschen* (The Imprisoned Marriage of Carnal People), published in 1730. Marriage, he claimed, at best provided the discipline to avoid illicit sex, nothing else; men and women must be united only in a union of celibate souls and live together as friends. Two years later, without any explanation, Beissel moved to Cocalico Creek. The Solitary quickly followed him there. He christened a small hill above a creek "Zion" and started to build his communal utopia. Donald F. Durnbaugh, an authority on early Pietist sects in America, concludes that by the end of 1732, "the Ephrata Cloister could be said to have taken form."[8]

Women were among Beissel's first converts at Ephrata, and soon, throughout the area, husbands began to dread his seemingly persuasive ideas on celibacy. For example, Maria, the wife of Germantown printer Christopher Sauer, abandoned her husband for a life of abstinence with the Solitary. Christina Höhn refused all further sexual relations with her husband, and after his death moved to Ephrata. When a farmer's wife stayed at Cocalico Creek for extended periods, her irate husband physically assaulted Beissel and dragged the woman home. But when the man died, she rejoined the community and remained there the rest of her life. Men, too, were attracted to the celibate life, and by 1730 several of them had joined Ephrata. Over the next five years a steady stream of new pilgrims arrived at Cocalico Creek, some of them intellectuals such as Peter Miller, a graduate of Heidelberg University. Since celibacy was the sign of a true believer, only "Brethren" and "Sisters" were considered full members of the cloister. From the start, however, Beissel allowed married adults to join as "Householders"; most of them continued marital relations and had children. By 1740, there were 36 Brethren and 35 Sisters at Ephrata, and nearly 300 Householders were living close by. Beissel constructed a dormitory for the Brethren called the *Burghaus* and used it for religious ceremonies. Later he built the *Kedar* with men's rooms on the first floor, the women's cells on the third floor, and large rooms on the middle floor for meetings and services. But the *Burghaus* and *Kedar* proved inadequate, and, so, in the meadow below Mount Zion, they put up the *Bethania* for the Brethren and the *Saron* for the Sisters. The *Saron* also had rooms for married couples who had adopted celibacy and an attached chapel called the *Saal*. Beissel lived in a small, two-room stone house about 30 yards from the *Saal* and *Saron*. All Ephrata structures conformed to building specifications found in Scripture. Walls were one foot thick, no iron tools or nails were used, and door hinges were made of wood.

The *Kedar, Bethania,* and *Saron* were enormous structures—three and four stories, each with tiny, one-window sleeping cells and meeting rooms. Cloisterites coated the interior walls with a hard loam and straw plaster and decorated them with large linen sheets covered with ink paintings and Gothic-letter quotations from the Bible. The *Saron* had two special writing rooms: one for drawing the wall decorations, the other for transcribing Beissel's preachings. In the meeting rooms they placed spinning wheels, looms, carding reels, candle molds, chests, and other craft items.[9]

Ephrata had no constitution and operated on the rules that Beissel laid out in his rambling sermons. Salvation, he said, came as a gift of God and not from good works. Observe the original Sabbath because only God could change the Scriptural order for observing the seventh day as sanctified. Anyone who joined the cloister had to surrender his or her private property, which Beissel condemned as "Ananias's sin." However, he did not require the Householders to turn over ownership of their farms. Many of them, though, donated land, money, or personal possessions to Beissel. All proceeds from work done at Ephrata, either by the celibates or the Householders, he kept in the name of the community. His Apostolic baptism required the individual to stand knee-deep in Cocalico Creek. Then Beissel grabbed the supplicant by the back of the neck and plunged the person into the water. Anyone who showed signs of resistance while submerged he forcibly held underwater for an extended spiritual experience.[10]

By all accounts, Beissel was an eccentric, agitated yet compelling leader. A mystic, he "inhabited a celestial world in which there were many mountains, and the loftiest of these, a giddy, isolated peak, was reserved for him."[11] He saw himself as a prophet, the equal of Christ, and insisted that everyone call him *Vorsteher,* meaning "director" or "chief." He said that other Christs had followed the first Messiah and he was the last in that line. On Friday evenings he had the cloisterites give him written confessions of their weekly faith, called lections, which he read aloud at the Sabbath worship.

This service was at first held in the open or in cabins, but after 1741 Beissel and the cloisterites worshiped in the *Saal* chapel. There, Beissel sat between the celibates in the front of the main-floor sanctuary, while the Householders perched on benches in the rear. Then, with contortions and facial expressions of pain and anguish, he opened with a hymn. After the singing, a Brethren read from Scripture and Beissel delivered a rapid-fire sermon accompanied by more gestures of his arms and legs. In a shrill voice and in ungrammatical German, he shrieked about the irrepressible conflict between the flesh and the spirit. He ranted about having to wage eternal war against the vulgarity of the material world. Life, he squealed, was but a painful pilgrimage to a union with God that would come only to those who renounced corruptions of the flesh and obliterated all evil desires. He claimed that exhausting labor from dawn to dusk—felling trees, planting and harvesting crops—would help to banish sin. Hard work, he said, brought a "deep silence" called the "great All of God" through which perfection could be reached. The Deity, he explained, "is an incomprehensible Being; therefore He cannot be found in comprehensible things," whatever that meant. Finally, "holy obedience" to the *Vorsteher* would bring peace on earth and salvation afterward.[12]

Under Beissel's unfriendly persuasion a strict daily routine of denial and simplicity took shape. Everyone rose at six in the morning, voluntarily without any bell or alarm, for an hour of meditation and hymn singing called a *matin*. Then they went to their assigned tasks until a nine o'clock breakfast of bread and water. After breakfast they went to work again until eleven o'clock, when they gathered for meditation. At noon, a few individuals took lunch, but most of the devout avoided it altogether as a sign of holiness. Following an afternoon of more work, they gathered for a meager meal of bread and a plate of pumpkin mush and barley. Sometimes they had cabbages, roots, greens, and cheese. Only rarely did Beissel permit meat on the table, but never pork. Water and milk were the only beverages. At irregular intervals Beissel celebrated special meals called *agape*, or "love feasts," at which the men and women, separately, sat down to bread, apple butter, pickles, and coffee. At the agape they exchanged a handshake and the "holy kiss" (essentially a peck on the cheek), received communion of bread and wine, and washed each other's feet.

The daily supper began with a Brethren reading from Scripture, followed by silent meditation. Then each person took a knife and wooden spoon from his or her pocket and ate in total silence. After eating, they licked clean the knives and spoons and observed another period of Bible reading and meditation. In the evening, from seven to nine o'clock, they devoted themselves to writing, reading, drawing, and more meditation. At midnight they went to the *Nachtmetten*, or watch meetings, where, if appropriate, they initiated new members into the cloister. These gatherings were penitential. The first thing Beissel did was to make everyone apologize to anyone he or she might have offended during the day; and that person, in turn, had to forgive the offense. Afterward, they prayed and marched in a procession around the compound for two hours, in all kinds of weather, singing polyphonic hymns. Then it was off to bed until six the next morning when the regimen started all over again.[13]

On the Sabbath Beissel handed out the week's work assignments, both to the celibates and the Householders. He mandated strict separation of the sexes. The women did the spinning, sewing, quilting, embroidering, canning, and they split firewood. They made household items such as candles, sulfur matches, wax tapers, and paper lanterns. They tended the gardens. The men did the heavy work of running the communal farm—planting, cultivating, and harvesting crops of corn, wheat, and barley. In the first years, before they had acquired domestic animals, the men dragged the plows with a rope. They tended a vineyard and a small orchard of apple, cherry, and peach trees. They quarried stone for their buildings and fences. They cut pine and oak trees for lumber and firewood. Inside the buildings they made clothing and shoes, wove fabrics, cooked the meals, baked bread, and did the laundry.

The Brethren and Sisters wore a monastic habit of cloaks and hoods that exposed as little as possible of the body, which Beissel called "that humiliating image revealed by sin." The *Talon* was a long coat of wool in winter and linen in summer. The tonsured men donned a pointed cowl reminiscent of the Capuchin order. The women's cap hung down to their feet in front and down to their waist in the back. The Sisters covered their foreheads with this hood so that only their eyes and mouths were visible. At religious services both sexes wore a mantle or scarf. They went barefoot, except in cold weather when they wore leather shoes. Householders wore the habit only on the Sabbath; at all other times they dressed as ordinary German colonists.

Beissel required that the celibates adopt new names. For example, he called himself Father Friedsam. Under him, as supervisor of the cloister, Israel Eck-erling became Brother Onesimus. Beissel's successor as head of Ephrata, Peter Miller, was Brother Jabez. Other men took names such as Gottrech (German for "right with God") and biblical ones such as Amos, Gideon, and Haggar. Sisters called themselves Anastasia, Etigena, Abigail, Amalia, Esther, Ketura, Miriam, and so on.[14] Most visitors described communards as friendly, although a trifle thin and wan, and as having a "smiling innocence and meekness" on their faces. One outsider remarked on the "softness of tone and accent" in their conversations. Their behavior, overall, was "gentle and obliged."[15]

In the beginning Beissel welcomed almost everyone to Cocalico Creek. But sometime after 1734 he imposed a probation year of testing during which he told the applicants what he expected of them and noted any deviation from the discipline. For example, an inspector reported to Beissel anyone who slept through, or was late for, the midnight or six o'clock meetings. They had to abjure breakfast and lunch and surrender some of the time allowed for sleep.

During the day, they were watched for any loud talking, whistling, or daw-dling. After 1739, when a group called the Zionic Brethren joined the cloister, Beissel added a new requirement: every candidate had to endure 40 days of physical hazing until he or she felt reborn. Only then was the individual given a charter of admission with the Shield of David drawn on it and inscribed with "Lord of Hosts, The Eckerling Yews." On the other hand, after joining, if anyone tired of the discipline, Beissel did not expel the person but sent him or her on a temporary exile among the Householders. If the person had a change of heart and wanted to come back, he or she had to submit two separate requests for readmission at intervals of three months. If the Brethren and Sisters believed the person's sincerity, he or she was readmitted, but the apostate had to endure a year of surveillance. Only then was the penitent fully reinstated.

Beissel designated two special rooms in the *Saron* for writing and drawing. There, the Sisters copied his sermons into notebooks and embellished each page with sketches and *Frakturschriften*. John J. Stoudt, a student of colonial Pennsylvania arts and crafts, found that "each piece of a *Fraktur* tells its story. . . . A point is being made," he continues, "and it is a mistake to separate the point from the designs."[16] Many of these *Frakturschriften* were decorated with beautiful calligraphy and inscribed with Scriptural texts and poetry. For example, one poem reads as follows:

> Thus lives the innocent flock,
> In the inner sanctuary here together,
> Snatched away from all worldly danger,
> In burning amorous flames of love,
> And lives on them in the hope,
> Of that blessed freedom there above,
> Where they in loving memory,
> Him without time and end will praise.

In 1750, Sisters Anastasia and Etigena produced one of the most elaborate Ephrata manuscripts, *The Christian A B C Is Suffering, Patience, Hope*. It was a stylebook in which they drew letters of the alphabet in various sizes up to 12 inches high and decorated them with elegant ornamentation. They sketched the unique large capitals to create a series of "voluptuous curves, all interstices of the letter filled with additional scrollings and floral forms."[17] They filled in the letters with small stipples and dots to produce an effect similar to that of an engraving. At other places in the book they used the human form to convey a complex symbolism. In the inside top half of the letter *A* they drew a representation of a Sister and in the bottom half the body of Father Abraham. In the letter *O* Anastasia sketched Beissel crowned by a dove, a token of the Holy Ghost. Yet, in some letters such as *Z* there was no human representation; they were just filled with dense swirling lines surrounded by a brilliant border of sun wheels, stars, and rosettes.

In 1743, Beissel purchased a printing press, the second German press in America. The Brethren were soon publishing an extensive array of books and pamphlets, many of them skillfully illuminated by the Sisters in the drawing room. For a while, they printed only Beissel's works or manuscripts submitted by members of the cloister. Soon, however, their reputation for quality work brought in manuscripts from outside the commune, such as a ghostwritten account of a supernatural experience of a local farm wife. They printed a 434-page book of confessional poems called *Theosophischen Lectionen*. They published a German translation of John Bunyan's masterpiece *Pilgrim's Progress* under the title of *Eoimnes Cristen Reise Nach der Seeligen Ewigkeit* and of Anthony Benezet's antislavery polemic, *Observations on the Enslaving, Importing, and Purchasing of Negroes*. In 1748, they translated from the Dutch and printed *Martyrer-Spiegel* (A Memorial of a Holy Martyr), their most ambitious project that took 15 Brethren over three years to complete. When it appeared, the folio edition had 1,512 pages, measured 10 by 15 inches, and sold for 20 shillings, the largest single printing made before the American Revolution. And, in Alderfer's judgment, "it is properly regarded as the greatest product of the colonial bookmaker's art."[18]

Much of the work in the print shop involved the creation of choir hymnals. Like everything else at the cloister, the music was inspired by Beissel's mystical imagination. Eugene Doll writes that although "quite unschooled in the musical arts" beyond the violin, Beissel "was able in middle age to develop his own unique, even magical, system of harmony and composition, to perform wonders in training the Ephrata singers, and to compose hundreds, perhaps a thousand, poems and pieces of music for them."[19] Beissel believed that God had shown him a system of harmony that made humans sound like "the angels themselves, when they sang at the birth of Christ."[20] The harmony, which he composed, was always in four, six, and seven parts, and the Sisters sang all of them except the bass. He avoided a meter signature altogether and insisted upon a cappella singing. Instrumental accompaniment, he said, only detracted from the beauty of the human voice. Beissel not only composed the music of these sacred pieces, he wrote the lyrics, usually words from Scripture.

In a music room located next to the writing rooms, the Brethren and Sisters engaged in a frenzy of activity in transcribing hundreds of volumes of music. Initially, Beissel had turned responsibility for running the singing school over to a trained musician, a *Meistersinger* named Ludwig Blum. But Blum's personality was so obnoxious, even for the devoted who tolerated Beissel's antics, that they asked the *Vorsteher* to take his place. By the time Beissel took over the choir it had 35 Brethren and the same number of Sisters out of a total cloister population of 200 celibates. Beissel taught composition and directed a daily four-hour choir practice. He prescribed a special diet for the singers because certain foods, he thought, impaired the human voice, particularly meat, beans, eggs, and dairy products (milk, butter, and cheese). On the other hand, honey, wheat, potatoes, and turnips all cleared the throat and helped create a purity of timbre. Above all, he believed that sexual intercourse destroyed the human voice, especially in females, by causing it to become rough and harsh. Beissel's successor after his death in 1768, Peter Miller (Brother Agrippa), also elaborated on the harmful connection between sex and singing and the salutary effect of abstinence for men. Brethren who abstained, he wrote, would have their voices restored to their youthful purity. He testified in 1786 that he knew of one man who renounced sexual intercourse at the age of 60 and "had his juvenile voice return" to him.[21]

Beissel conducted his concerts in his peculiar spastic manner. Israel Acrelius, a Swedish Lutheran visitor, described the *Vorsteher's* performance: Beissel began by holding his hands at his sides. Then he "threw his head up and down, his eyes hither and thither, pulled at his mouth, his nose, his neck and finally sang in a low, firm tone." At that point the Brethren and Sisters "united in a delightful hymn, which lasted for about a quarter of an hour."[22] Beissel trained his pupils in a special falsetto and had them sing through half-closed lips to create a sound with an ethereal quality. Another visitor remarked that he heard at Ephrata "music for the soul—music that affords more than natural gratification."[23] And the Reverend Jacob Duché, rector of Christ Church and St. Peter's in Philadelphia, described female singers whose half-lipped music "throws the voice up to the ceiling . . . and the tones, which seem to be more than human . . . appear to be entering from above, and hovering over the heads of the assembly."[24] The music, Duché recalled, "had little melody, but consisted of simple, long notes, combined in the richest harmony." The women, he went on, "had sweet, shrill and small voices, but with a truth and exactness in time and intonation that was admirable."[25] The singers held two books, one in each hand, a tune book and a psalm book. So situated, they sang by looking constantly back and forth at the books, a practice Acrelius observed that "would be more difficult if the singing were not performed so regularly every day."[26]

Inspired by devotion, diet, and abstinence, in 1747 the cloister published the first collection of 277 hymn lyrics in the *Turtletaube*, or *Song of the Lonely and Forsaken Turtle-Dove, Namely the Christian Church*. Beissel composed about two-thirds of the pieces, while the celibates wrote the others. Seven years later they printed the music to 770 hymns along with the words of 200 of these sacred songs to express their joyous expectation for salvation and their conviction that Ephrata was but a taste of eternal life. The press issued two supplements to the *Turtel-Taube*, a 112-page *Nachkland*, and a 32-page *Neur Nachklang* for a total of 89 new hymns. In 1754, the first part of their most treasured hymnal appeared, the *Paradisisches Wunder-spiel* (Wonders of Paradise). Its 49 songs, some of which were the most sublime of all their compositions, were hand-lettered by the Sisters, who drew complex scroll and floral designs in blue, green, orange, and brown inks. Other books focused on life's pilgrimage. The *Unser Hoffnung* (Our Hope) reads: "Our hope must crown us there in that new world, for we are counted among those whom God has chosen." In *Die Welt ist mir ein bitter Tod* (The World Is for Me a Bitter Death) says: "Yet, while I suffer I know I will find a better home . . . life eternal, a destiny of great value for me." *Auf, du Keunches Jungfrau Heer* (Up, Thou Chaste Virgin Host) glorified celibacy: "Deck thyself with jewels. . . . Go forth in pomp and splendor to meet our Lamb. . . . The bridegroom is at hand."

For the children's education Beissel introduced a curriculum in Scripture, German, penmanship, and arithmetic and placed Ludwig Hocker (Brother Obed) in charge. In 1738, the Brother opened a Sabbath Bible school for nearby poor farm children who were not members of the community. Then he started a boarding school that stressed Latin and mathematics for both Ephrata adolescents and outsiders. Known as the Academy of Classical Studies, it enrolled students from as far away as Philadelphia and Baltimore.[27]

Ephrata children were largely neglected by their parents and were totally undisciplined. In the words of one historian, they were allowed "a risky latitude in the matter of their daily deportment" and became insolent.[28] They started to dress in gaudy clothes that mocked the plain garb of their elders. When Beissel ignored their antics, they became increasingly defiant. They organized their own youth church service and started to build a separate chapel. They baptized themselves and held their own love feasts and communion. By 1749, things had gone too far. Parents complained to the *Vorsteher* that the children were so unruly that they refused to do their work assignments. A crackdown was necessary. So, Beissel proclaimed May 15 as a fast day of recommitment and he incinerated their outlandish clothes in a community bonfire. Afterward, he rebaptized six of the children and ordered all the others to attend regular communion and to wash the feet of their elders. Then he abolished the youth service.

The children were not the only disciplinary problem Beissel faced. A growing dispute over economic policy severely tested his leadership because he paid little attention to making money and wanted Ephrata to produce only the essentials of life for itself. For instance, he never considered selling surplus grain for profit and instead gave it away free to whomever came to the cloister to pick it up. He was so oblivious to economic matters that he rejected out of hand a gift of 5,000 acres offered by the governor of Pennsylvania. Trouble began when Michael Wohlfahrt (Brother Agunius), who managed the daily work schedule, died and was replaced by Israel Eckerling (Brother Onesimus). Onesimus wanted to make the colony a profitable enterprise and initially received the endorsement of the Brethren. And, after convincing Prioress Maria, head of the Sisters, to support his reforms, they all fell in line. Although he treated Beissel with deference, Onesimus virtually took control of the community. Beissel, on his part, did nothing to stop him.[29]

First off, Onesimus purchased a sawmill and hauled lumber for sale in Germantown and Lancaster. He expanded the orchard and acquired draft horses to pull the plows. He constructed a paper mill and a shop for bookbinding. He opened a tannery and workshops for cobbling shoes, crafting leather products, weaving flax, and spinning pottery. Sisters worked away from the *Saron* in buildings where they embroidered, coupled lace, and weaved baskets. He appointed confectioners to travel to farms at harvest time to purchase surplus produce cheaply, to bring it to Ephrata to be stored and later sold for a profit. He built a communal burial vault. He constructed bridges and reinforced the foundations of the buildings. He contracted newly arrived immigrants as indentured servants to augment the workforce.

Onesimus did more than replace Beissel as director of Ephrata's economy, he eclipsed him as its spiritual leader. He called himself the "Prior," dressed in colorful liturgical vestments, and presided over the Sabbath service with interminably long sermons that two Brethren copied verbatim. He planned to start a new order for Householders who had chosen celibacy and had left their spouses and farms. He even commandeered Beissel's living quarters for himself and forced the *Vorsteher* to move to five different rooms in six months' time, hoping that such harassment would drive him out of the community.[30]

Beissel detected festering resentment over Onesimus's high-handed leadership and realized that some of the celibate felt sympathy if not compassion for him because of the Prior's shabby treatment. Beissel fought back and organized a coterie of loyal followers. The Prior became frantic and cursed anyone who had the audacity to support Beissel. He then tried to bribe Prioress Maria with money to stay with him, a foolish move that backfired. By the summer of 1745, he had become paranoid, convinced that Beissel was plotting to murder him. Beissel summoned the celibates together for a showdown meeting. They voted to banish Onesimus to the cloth-weaving shop, but would allow him to return to the cloister if he repented his actions. The Prior flatly rejected such humiliation and, with a few Brethren, left Ephrata forever.[31]

The *Vorsteher* then reassumed his role as patriarch. He ordered a drastic cutback in the new enterprises, canceled all contracts arranged by the confectioners, and abandoned the orchard. Everyone returned to grim austerity. Hoping to increase the number of celibates, he recruited new members in the Palatine by sending them money to pay for their passage to Philadelphia. In 1749, the first group arrived. Unfortunately, they all were married with families, and Beissel relegated them to the status of Householders.

By that time the 100 Brethren and Sisters had settled into a routine of prayer, singing, printing, copying, and running a modest, self-sufficient farmcraft community. Dressed in monastic garb, they puttered about the large, unadorned buildings whose narrow halls and low doorways reinforced humility and discipline. They slept in their tiny cells on benches with pine blocks for pillows. They ate with plain wooden utensils, bowls, and plates. Their diet was as meager as ever, mostly vegetables, cheese, bread, and water. Sisters busied themselves with quilting, basket weaving, sewing, and canning. The Brethren cooked, washed clothes, repaired the buildings, and mended shoes. Copy work continued without interruption in the *Saron*. And the press ran continually, putting out hymnals and psalm books. Beissel held daily choir practice. Some visitors noted, with surprise, an increased interest in Jewish practices. The cloisterites displayed the six-pointed seal of David over the doors of most buildings and some of the men were circumcised.[32]

The Ephrata Cloister became a society of complacent harmony with Beissel its only disruption. Instead of mellowing in old age he became quarrelsome and suspicious. He experienced a series of bizarre supernatural revelations, the first of which, in 1761, involved the specter of a farm wife who claimed to have hidden a large sum of her husband's money in a colony building. Worse still, according to Ezechiel Sangmeister's diary, the *Vorsteher* became an alcoholic. Although it is impossible to verify Sangmeister's account, modern historians generally agree with him. Conrad Klein conceded, reluctantly, that "in his last feeble years [Beissel] gave way before the allurements of drink."[33] His speech was incoherent and frequently slurred. He vomited a good deal. He stumbled around the colony. Sangmeister described Beissel as an evil, lecherous old man who flirted, or worse, with the Sisters. By the spring of 1768, the community could barely tolerate him. After a lingering bout with tuberculosis, Beissel made an open confession of his mistakes and admitted that he alone was responsible for Ephrata's problems. On July 5 the Brethren gave him a final kiss of peace, gathered around as he lay stretched out on a wooden bench, and watched him die.[34]

Fifty-eight-year-old Peter Miller (Brother Agrippa) took his place. A loyal disciple who remained at the *Vorsteher*'s side during those last embarrassing years, Miller was a theologian and a widely respected scientist, a member of the American Philosophical Society, and friends with Benjamin Franklin, David Rittenhouse, and Francis Hopkinson. Unfortunately, Agrippa had no leadership qualities and was content just to run the print shop and continue his theological studies and scientific research. Even so, by the time of Beissel's death, cloister life had already started to deteriorate. Only 50 elderly Brethren and Sisters still lived there and just a handful of new members, mostly German Baptist Sabbatarians from western Pennsylvania, joined the community. Economic activity withered to a few small workshops.[35]

The cloister members did, however, gain a reputation for hospitality, graciously welcoming all visitors, and for extraordinary compassion for outsiders in need. During the French and Indian War, Ephrata served as a refuge for fleeing families from western Pennsylvania, who were housed in the chapel and meeting rooms and were given clothes and food at no charge. In appreciation, the governor of the colony sent a pair of large communion goblets as a gift. And during the American Revolution, Ephrata was the hospital for George Washington's troops after his defeat at the Battle of Brandywine. Five hundred soldiers, many sick and wounded, made their way in wagons to the cloister from the battlefield located some 40 miles to the east. One American officer among the wounded later recalled that "where we expected to meet with a cold reservedness, we [were] surprised by exhibitions of the most charming affability and disinterested benevolence. . . . They all acted the part of the Good Samaritan to me," he wrote, "for which I hope to be ever grateful."[36] But the cloisterites' charity brought on a disaster. Without physicians and adequate medicine to tend the wounded, typhoid swept the overcrowded buildings and one-third of the Brethren and Sisters died of the disease. Fearing that the epidemic would spread to nearby farms, Agrippa burned all buildings used by the soldiers. Afterward, the faithful evacuated Mount Zion, converted the site into a cemetery, and moved to the banks of Cocalico Creek.

Ephrata never recovered. In 1786, the cloisterites partially dissolved the community by allowing ownership of personal property. However, they still held the land and buildings in common. Agrippa died in 1796, leader of only a dozen or so disciples. In 1814, when just four members of the order remained at the site, they incorporated as the Seventh Day German Baptist Church with the stipulation that they could live at Ephrata the rest of their lives. Thirty years later a visitor described it as a ruins of "weather beaten walls; upon which the tooth of time has been gnawing for nearly one-and-a-half century." The buildings were like "dilapidated castles, which are apparently falling to the ground, deserted and given to rooks and owls." A few Sisters, one who had been there for 55 years, subsisted by cultivating private gardens and running a flour mill. These women, one scholar writes, "led retired and mortified lives, and they may have kept up some semblance of the old conventional observances; but they were no longer nuns."[37]

Some members left Ephrata to start other communities, such as the one known as the German Seventh Day Baptists. In 1798, Peter Lehman, acting on instructions from Agrippa, led a group west to Franklin County to land donated by the Schneeberger family to build "Snow Hill." Eventually, it developed into a commune of about 40 men and women that survived until 1889.[38] Another colony was formed at "The Cove" near New Enterprise, in Bedford County. A third small congregation appeared at Stony Creek in the mountains of Somerset County. By 1900, at Cocalico Creek, Alice Felt Tyler writes, only "seventeen members, all elderly people, were the heirs to the traditions of Ephrata and to its greatly diminished property. . . . The little village was a shadow of its past," she concludes. "The vitality of its religious faith and of its communal life belonged to an era long since forgotten."[39] But Ephrata had an influence on subsequent religious utopias. For example, the Shakers, founded by English immigrants in the 1780s, and Harmony, the German society founded by Wittenberg immigrants in the 1820s, looked to the Ephrata model. Both groups sought to reconstruct the life of the disciplined, devout celibates who carved their earthly Zion out of the Pennsylvania wilderness under the erratic direction of the mystical baker from the Palatine.

In 1941, the Pennsylvania Historical and Museum Commission took over the site and started a restoration and research project. By 2002, Ephrata had a visitor's center and 19 restored buildings. They are open year-round, except for a few holidays, and special events are held in March (Charter Day) and at Christmastime.

NOTES

1. The first short-lived experiment in American communalism was at Jamestown, Virginia, in 1607 when the settlers signed an agreement with the London Company to have communal ownership of tools and supplies and to work and eat communally. See Ernest Sutherland Bates, *American Faith: Its Religious, Political and Economic Foundations* (New York: W. W. Norton, 1940) and Sigmund Diamond, "From Organization to Society: Virginia in the Seventeenth Century," *American Journal of Sociology* 53, no. 5 (March 1968). Arthur Bestor Jr., *Backwoods Utopias: The Sectarian Origins and the Owenite Phase of Communitarian Socialism in America, 1663–1829*, 2nd ed. (Philadelphia: University of Pennsylvania Press, 1970) briefly touches on the early religious communities. The most recent treatment of Ephrata is Donald F. Durnbaugh's chapter, "Communitarian Societies in Colonial America," in *America's Communal Utopias*, ed. Donald E. Pitzer (Chapel Hill: University of North Carolina Press, 1997), pp. 14–36; and Ann K. U. Tussing, "The Hungry Orphan, Conrad Beissel," *Communal Societies* 10 (1990): 87–101. Yaacov Oved, *Two Hundred Years of American Communes* (New Brunswick, N.J.: Transaction, 1988) also has a chapter on the Ephrata Cloister. Other studies of Ephrata are contained in Delburn Carpenter, *The Radical Pietists: Celibate Communal Societies Established in the United States before 1820* (New York: AMS Press, 1975); David S. Lovejoy, *Religious Enthusiasm in the New World: Heresy to Revolution* (Cambridge, Mass.: Harvard University Press, 1985); Clarke Garrett, *Spirit Possession and Popular Religion: From the Camisards to the Shakers* (Baltimore: Johns Hopkins University Press, 1987). Robert S. Fogarty, *Dictionary of American Communal and Utopian History* (Westport, Conn.: Greenwood Press, 1987) and Richard C. S. Trahair, *Utopias and Utopias: A Historical Dictionary* (Westport, Conn.: Greenwood Press, 1999) have entries on Ephrata and its leaders. Bibliographies on Ephrata are Eugene E. Funke and Aneliese M. Funke, eds., *Ephrata Cloisters: An Annotated Bibliography* (Philadelphia: Carl Shurz Memorial Foundation, 1944); Philip N. Dare, ed., *American Communes to 1860: A Bibliography* (New York: Garland Publishing, 1990); Emil Meyned, ed., *Bibliography on the Colonial Germans of North America*, revised edition (Baltimore: Genealogical Publishing Co., 1982). On the European background of Ephrata, see Donald F. Durnbaugh, *The Believers' Church: The History and Character of Radical Protestantism* (New York: Macmillan, 1968).

On the Plockhoy community, consult Leland Harder and Marvin Harder, *Plockhoy from Zurik-zee: The Study of a Dutch Reform in Puritan England and Colonial America* (Newton, Kans.: [Mennonite] Board of Education and Publication, 1951); W. H. G. Armytage, *Heavens Below: Utopian Experiments in England, 1660–1960* (London: Routledge and Kegan Paul, 1961), pp. 9, 29; Irwin B. Horst, "Pieter Cornelisz Plockhoy: An Apostle of the Collegiants," *Mennonite Quarterly Review* 23 (1949): 161–85; Leland Harder, "Plockhoy and His Settlement at Zwaanendael, 1663," *Delaware History* 3 (1949): 41–45. On the Bohemian Manor, see Bartlett B. James, *The Labadist Colony in*

Maryland, Johns Hopkins University Studies in Historical and Political Science, 17. no. 6 (Baltimore: Johns Hopkins University Press, 1899) and Ernest J. Green, "The Labadists of Colonial Maryland, 1683–1722," *Communal Societies* 8 (1988): 104–21. On the Society of the Woman in the Wilderness, see Willard M. Martin, "Johnes Kelpius and Gohann Gottfried Seelig: Mystics and Hymnists on the Wissahickon" (Ph.D. diss., Pennsylvania State University, University Park, 1973).

2. E. Gordon Alderfer, *The Ephrata Commune: An Early American Counterculture* (Pittsburgh, Pa.: University of Pittsburgh Press, 1985), x.

3. Ibid., p. 16.

4. Oved, *American Communes,* pp. 22–24. See also Walter C. Klein, *Johann Conrad Beissel, Mystic and Martinet* (Philadelphia: University of Pennsylvania Press, 1941; reprint, Philadelphia: Porcupine Press, 1972); Christopher E. Schweitzer, "The Present Status of Conrad Beissel/Ephrata Research," *Monatshefte* (1976): 171–78. An older but still valuable work is Julius Friedrich Sachse, *The German Sectarians of Pennsylvania, 1742–1880: A Critical and Legendary History of the Ephrata Cloister and the Dunkers,* 2 vols. (Philadelphia: Julius Friedrich Sachse, 1899–1900; reprint, New York: AMS Press, 1971), 1:57–59, 63–65.

5. Durnbaugh, "Communitarian Societies," p. 23. Robert S. Fogarty, *American Utopianism* (Itasca, Ill.: Peacock, 1972), p. 2.

6. See Oved, *American Communes,* p. 35, n. 14 on the development of Beissel's ideas on the "holy Sabbath."

7. Durnbaugh, ed., *The Brethren in Colonial America* (Elgin, Ill.: Brethren Press, 1967), pp. 64–89, deals with Beissel's relationship with the Dunkers (the Brethren) Church. See also Klein, *Beissel,* pp. 60–65; and Eugene E. Doll, *The Ephrata Cloister: An Introduction* (Ephrata, Pa.: Ephrata Cloister Associates, 1978), pp. 9–10.

8. Durnbaugh, "Communitarian Societies," p. 24; Jeanette C. Lauer and Robert H. Lauer, "Sex Roles in Nineteenth-Century American Communal Societies," *Communal Societies* 3 (1983): 21. A collection of descriptions of the colony is in Felix Reichmann and Eugene E. Doll, eds., *Ephrata as Seen by Contemporaries,* Pennsylvania German Folklore Society, vol. 17 (Allentown: Pennsylvania German Folklore Society, 1953). Also consult Peter C. Erb, ed., *Johann Conrad Beissel and the Ephrata Community: Mystical and Historical Texts* (Lewistown, N.Y.: Edwin Mellen, 1985).

9. Eugene E. Doll, "Social and Economic Organization in Two Pennsylvania German Religious Communities," *American Journal of Sociology* 57 (September 1951): 169; Janet R. White, "The Ephrata Cloister: Intersections of Architecture and Culture in an Eighteenth-Century Utopia," *Utopian Studies* 11, no. 2 (2000): 57–76.

10. Klein, *Beissel,* p. 94.

11. Oved, *American Communes,* pp. 25–28.

12. Sachse, *German Sectarians,* 1:134–35, 228–47.

13. Durnbaugh, "Communitarian Societies," pp. 24–26, has the most recent account of life at the cloister. An older source on the commune is Alice Felt Tyler, *Freedom's Ferment, Phases of American Social History from the Colonial Period to the Civil War* (New York: Harper Torchbook, 1962), pp. 111–15.

14. A. Monroe Aurand Jr., *Historical Account of the Ephrata Cloister and the Seventh Day Baptists Society* (Harrisburg, Pa.: Aurand Press, 1940), p. 29.

15. John J. Stoudt, *Early Pennsylvania Arts and Crafts* (New York: A. S. Barns and Company, 1964), pp. 11, 28, 29, 52, 61, 63, 133, 177, 270, 278, 282, 283.

16. Quoted in Alderfer, *Ephrata Commune,* p. 126.

17. Ibid., p. 128. Jacob John Sessler, *Communal Pietism among Early American Moravians* (New York: Holt, 1933; reprint, New York: AMS Press, 1971), p. 42.

18. Russell P. Getz, "Music in the Ephrata Cloister," *Communal Societies* 2 (Autumn 1982): 27–38; Doll, *Ephrata Cloister*, p. 11; Klein, *Beissel*, pp. 144–48; Alderfer, *Ephrata Commune*, p. 116.

19. Doll, *Ephrata Cloister*, p. 11.

20. Getz, "Music," p. 34.

21. Ibid., pp. 33–35.

22. Doll, *Ephrata Cloister*, p. 12.

23. Klein, *Beissel*, p. 147.

24. Getz, "Music," p. 34.

25. Ibid., p. 32.

26. William Alfred Hinds, *American Communities and Cooperative Colonies* (1878; reprint, Philadelphia: Porcupine Press, 1975), pp. 22–23; Carpenter, *Radical Pietists*, p. 98; Sachse, *German Sectarians*, 2:261–65.

27. Klein, *Beissel*, p. 119.

28. Doll, "Social and Economic Organization," pp. 174–75; Carpenter, *Radical Pietists*, pp. 99–100.

29. Durnbaugh, "Communitarian Societies," pp. 26–27.

30. Klein, *Beissel*, pp. 154–56, 165–66; Carpenter, *Radical Pietists*, pp. 100–110; Sachse, *German Sectarians*, 2:115–18, 214–21.

31. Doll, *Ephrata Cloister*, pp. 7–8; Fogarty, *Utopianism*, pp. 3–6.

32. Klein, *Beissel*, p. 179.

33. Ibid., pp. 180–81; Carpenter, *Radical Pietists*, p. 111.

34. Sachse, *German Sectarians*, 2:386–87, 401–3, 426–32.

35. Doll, *Ephrata Cloister*, p. 31.

36. Carpenter, *Radical Pietists*, pp. 104–5, 111.

37. Klein, *Beissel*, p. 183.

38. Charles W. Treher, *Snow Hill Cloister*, Publications of the Pennsylvania-German Society 2 (Allentown: Pennsylvania-German Society, 1968); Denise Seachrist, "Musical Treasures of the Snow Hill Cloister: Manuscripts, Monographs, and Monastical Mysteries," *Communal Societies* 18 (1998): 53–61.

39. Tyler, *Freedom's Ferment*, p. 115.

CHAPTER 2

Shaker Communities

In 1736, just as the German Solitaires were gathering at Mount Zion, the wife of John Lee, a poor blacksmith living in the gritty factory town of Manchester, England, gave birth to a daughter, the second of eight children. They called her Ann and christened her in the Anglican Church. Historians know little about young Ann, but most likely she remained illiterate since "the workplace—probably textile shops—was her school."[1] At the age of 14 years she heard about George Whitfield's gospel that if one were "born again," one could be assured of salvation, and she became preoccupied with religion. Ann also became deeply disturbed about the terrible living conditions in the Manchester slums and began to doubt whether her Anglican Church would ever deal with the social and moral problems of the factory poor.[2]

In 1758, she joined James and Jane Wardley's band of "Shaking Quakers," a radical sect of religious fanatics that had melded Quaker ideas with those of the French Prophets. From the Society of Friends they borrowed pacifism, a "meeting" instead of a religious service, and the paramount importance of the "inner light," or God's direct revelations. From the small number of French Prophets, who had emigrated to Manchester when the French authorities cracked down on Protestants after the revocation of the Edict of Nantes in 1689, the Shaking Quakers adopted the "operation of the spirit" with its violent physical gesticulations and incoherent garbles called "speaking in tongues."[3] The Shaking Quakers were also millennial. James told Ann that the "new heaven and new earth prophesied of old is about to come." When Christ appeared, he said, all "anti-Christian denominations . . . will be swept away."[4] They also condemned all carnal pleasures, even sex in marriage. And, to the chagrin of their neighbors, they were a public nuisance. They broke into Anglican services, shouting that the worship was a blasphemy and that the priest a hypocrite.

In January 1762, this short, stout young woman with blue eyes and chestnut brown hair married Abraham Stanley, another blacksmith. Despite the Shaking Quakers' proscription of sex, Ann bore four children, all of whom died in infancy. She interpreted their deaths as a message from God that she must abide by the teachings of the Shaking Quakers and admit that sex was evil, a sin of lust. She went through an agonizing internal conflict. The details of this experience are obscure and the only account of what happened appeared later in the *Testimonies of the Life of . . . Our Blessed Mother Ann Lee*, a work based on recollections of Ann and others. In any event, she apparently sank into a deep psychological depression, suffered "bloody sweats," and moaned and cried out night after night in anguish. Her bed, she later recalled, was a "couch of embers." She lost weight and became emaciated.[5]

In the spring of 1770, the local constable arrested Ann and five other Shaking Quakers for "disturbing the Congregation in the old Church."[6] Two months later the same thing happened. At one point during these incarcerations Ann had an epiphany: she saw Adam and Eve in coitus. This act, she knew at once, was *the* Original Sin. In another vision Christ told her that she would "hunger for nothing but God" and would lead his mission to the world.[7] She felt "born again." She entered a strange new world of vibrant colors and objects. She stopped sexual relations with Abraham and began a holy war against the Devil's temptations.

Shortly afterward, Ann had another vision, one of a tree with shining leaves that commanded her to emigrate to the colonies to found the "Church of Christ's Second Appearance." So, in the spring of 1774, Ann, her husband, a brother, a niece, and five relatives, calling themselves "Believers," left Liverpool for America. When they arrived in New York City, Abraham Stanley, apparently still in love with Ann but exasperated, ended the marriage. For a year the Believers, as they called themselves, earned a living by finding part-time work. Fortunately, one of them, John Hocknell, was wealthy, and in 1775, they purchased land eight miles north of Albany, New York, at a place called Niskeyuna. The following year they moved there, built a log cabin, struggled to raise enough food to survive, and adopted communal ownership of all property.[8]

Three years later a revival swept through the region. One of its leaders, a New Light Baptist minister from New Lebanon, New York, named Joseph Meacham Jr., heard about the Believers' settlement. He sent an associate, Calvin Harlow, to investigate their beliefs. Harlow met with Ann and reported back to Meacham, who was deeply impressed with their communal Christianity. He then journeyed to Niskeyuna, where Ann convinced him that Christ had revealed to her that God was both male and female and that the Messiah would appear as a woman at an imminent Second Coming. In the meantime, he must live without sin by rejecting carnal temptations and all enjoyments of the material world. Ann required Meacham, and other new members, to give an initial open confession to the community, and every Shaker had to give ongoing confessions to elders of the same sex. She justified their communal ownership of property in 1 Corinthians 10:17: "We who are many are one body, for we all partake of one bread." She advocated sharing and invited any person interested in a perfect life to visit Niskeyuna to witness first hand Christ's spiritual family. Finally, she believed that physical paroxysms—trances, trembling, rolling on the floor, shouting, and so forth—were manifestations of God's spirit in their lives.[9] By this time the Believers were known locally as the Shakers.

In the fall of 1781, Ann, her brother William, and James Whittaker, one of the original immigrants from Manchester, left Niskeyuna to proselytize. In an arduous two-year journey they traveled through eastern New York, northern Massachusetts, and southeastern Connecticut, staying in private homes and preaching to the host family. In the towns they held public gatherings at which, singing in ensemble improvisation, they denounced all things carnal. Ann began to play an increasingly maternal role, inquiring after her group's physical and spiritual needs and often hugging and touching them in loving ways. They, in turn, called her "Mother Ann," the female counterpart of Christ.

Public response to these traveling Shakers ranged from curious hospitality to outright hostility. At Harvard, Massachusetts, the Shakers discovered a millennial sect founded by Shadrach Ireland, a Baptist preacher from Charleston. Members of the sect quickly identified with Mother Ann's message about the Second Coming and offered the missionaries the use of Ireland's home, located just off Harvard Square, as their headquarters. Large crowds of the local poor began coming to their meetings, no doubt as much for free meals as for spiritual nourishment. The number of these transients became so large that alarmed town magistrates ordered the Shakers to leave. When Ann refused, the local militia arrived and escorted them away. In other places, after a similar brief period of local support, mobs attacked them, sometimes charging that Ann was a witch. In fact, the threat of physical injury by beating and stoning brought the mission to a close in September 1783.[10] Mother Ann died at Niskeyuna the next year, and James Whittaker, one of the original English Shakers who had followed Ann to Niskeyuna, took over as leader of the community.

The mission was an important stage in the development of Shakerism for three reasons. First, it "laid the groundwork for the subsequent numerical and geographical expansion of the sect."[11] Second, the body of oral history that grew out of the mission pictured Mother Ann as a Messiah who had brought the true gospel to the New World. Finally, the small groups who hosted the missionaries, and the converts who accepted the Shaker way, eventually formed the nucleus of the larger United Society of True Believers.

In 1787, Joseph Meacham replaced James Whittaker, who had moved the community to New Lebanon, New York, during the previous three years and had constructed the first Shaker meetinghouse there, organizing these scattered communities. "Father" Meacham developed a chain of command and rules of conduct. Drawing upon Mother Ann's bisexual vision of the deity, Meacham said that the Shakers, the "visible spiritual family of Christ," must be ruled by a "parental order." He designated 25-year-old Lucy Wright, a close companion of Ann Lee, as his equal and assigned her the responsibility of creating a women's order. He appointed women to two new offices of elderesses and deaconesses.[12]

Meacham's reforms caused immediate opposition from Shakers who venerated Mother Ann and refused to accept any substitutes. Undaunted, Meacham insisted that his ideas also came from divine revelation, and he worked for over a decade to get his "Shaker Order" adopted. According to Lawrence Foster, its "overall structure would remain largely unchanged throughout the history of the group."[13] The order was hierarchal, with final authority resting in Meacham and Wright, then called the "beloved Parents in Church relation." Under them were four elders, two men and two women, who lived at New Lebanon. There, Meacham constructed the "Great House" that, according to Stephen Stein, "gave the site a certain public prominence." Next, he put up "Brick House," which was occupied in December 1790. He built a bake house, a "spinning house," a building for the children and teenagers, and a retail store with an office to receive outsiders. In 1795, they added a kitchen and a workshop for the sisters.[14]

From New Lebanon Meacham and Wright appointed and removed all of the elders and elderesses for 10 Shaker villages in New York, Connecticut, Massachusetts, Maine, and New Hampshire that had been established by 1796.[15] Each village constituted a "Family" of between 30 and 100 adults, led by two deacons and two deaconesses. Although the Family was to be economically self-sufficient, Meacham and Wright permitted some of them to join together to run mutual businesses or industries. The elders assigned every adult a specific job to be done at a certain time of day. A strict sexual division of labor prevailed. Men did the physical tasks—blacksmithing, tanning, carpentry work, farm labor. Women did the house chores—washing, cleaning, cooking, and weaving of cloth—except during planting and harvesting, when they helped in the fields. Shakers prohibited all physical contact between the sexes, so there was little chance of someone learning or performing the job of the opposite sex. Or, as elder Frederick Evans told visiting Charles Nordhoff when he asked whether a woman could ever become a blacksmith: "No, because this would bring men and women into relations which we do not think wise."[16]

To visitors this labor organization seemed discriminatory against women, but no Shaker saw these assignments as gender biased. To them, all labor was the same in God's eyes. They believed that they worked together in a Christian community where everything was done for the glory of God and the good of the Family. Or, in Foster's words, "by removing all but the most basic private property and by removing the competing demands inherent in separate nuclear family arrangements, the Shakers were able to devote their entire lives to establishing their ideal of the kingdom of heaven on earth."[17] In so doing they insisted on simplicity, order, and functionalism. They were extraordinarily ingenuous and either invented or used the circular saw, screw propeller, flat broom, brimstone match, and clothespin.[18]

Shakers were sexually segregated not just at work. Every building had two sections, for men and women, each with its own stairway. Some dwellings had separate doorways and had hallways wide enough to prevent any accidental touching. Men and women ate in the same dining room but at different tables. Their only gender interaction came at the three or four weekly "Union Meetings," when a dozen men and women sat a few feet opposite each other on benches and discussed matters of community interest.

However, celibacy created a fundamental problem: what to do with the children born of Shaker couples before they joined the society and orphans and young indentures whom outside parents sent to the village for training? The elders decided that they would live in special houses, be separated by sex, and be supervised by adults. They would be instructed in Shaker beliefs and practices and admitted to religious services in the hope that they would choose to remain in the village as adults. They would be trained in the various crafts and skills and taught reading, writing, and arithmetic, boys in winter and girls in summer.[19]

By the 1790s, the Shakers, as Meacham saw it, needed not just an administrative hierarchy and an economic order but more clearly defined conditions of membership. Consequently, he published the *Gospel Orders* that all Shakers, now called the "United Society of Believers in Christ's Second Appearance," had to follow. The *Orders* mandated three classes of believers: the Novitiate Order, the Junior Order, and the Church Order. The Novitiate included individuals who kept their property but accepted the prophecies of Mother Ann and the authority of the ministry. In the Junior Order were Shakers who owned their property but who conveyed the use of it to the Family. The Church Order consisted of persons who surrendered all possessions to the Family, accepted celibacy, and promised full commitment to the society. In addition, they agreed to assume "joint interest" in the community and never sue it for their assets if they left, but just depart with a small severance grant. Only Church-Order Shakers were eligible to become elders and deacons. Most members, it turned out, qualified for the third order, and the other two classes, always a small minority, eventually disappeared.[20]

Meacham formulated detailed rules of daily life. He allowed six hours of sleep. Breakfast was at six and supper was before the "meeting at night." There were uniform standards for products made in the villages. Wool hats, for example, had to comply with regulations on style, quality, and pricing. He issued guidelines for the treatment of animals, decorations on the exterior of the buildings, and how to live a healthy life. He developed the "solemn songs," a "mixture of words & unknown sounds of words" that united everyone with their "solemn & melodious Tone." He ritualized dancing at the meetings and insisted upon the "Square Order Shuffle" to cut down on the paroxysms of the early years and to promote a more civilized, collective worship.[21]

Most important, in 1790 he published the *Concise Statement of the Principles of the Only True Church*, a tract that explained Shaker beliefs as based on the "gospel of the present appearance of Christ." This document, Stein concludes, "provided a theological framework for understanding the events that had transformed the handful of Shaking Quakers at Niskeyuna into a substantial society by 1790."[22] Its major premise was that their religious community was divinely planned. The founders of the church, Meacham claimed, had received from God the "first light of salvation" in the form of four dispensations. Circumcision, the first dispensation, was a symbol of obedience and future redemption. In the second tenant, called the covenant, God had promised Israel that if they obeyed the Ten Commandments a "future manifestation," a Messiah, would appear. The third dispensation was the actual appearance of the Messiah and the gospel that foretold the obliteration of sin and the establishment of the Kingdom of God. But this event had not happened because Christianity had been taken over by the anti-Christ and a false religion had appeared instead. The fourth dispensation began with Ann Lee's visions and revelations in which God made known that a final war against the anti-Christ had begun.

At Meacham's death in August 1796, the task of completion and consolidation fell to Lucy Wright, his successor as "the Elder or first born." Meacham had hoped that this female succession would guarantee that "the man & the woman have Equal Rights in order & Lots & Lead & Government of the Church." He was wrong. Resentment against "petticoat government" surfaced immediately. Angell Matthewson, for instance, was evicted in 1799 for saying that "wimmin are fools & that men that are willin to have a woman to rule over them are fools also."[23]

Nevertheless, Mother Lucy's ministry lasted 25 years, during which time she presided over the most creative period of Shaker history. She inaugurated the "Gathering Order" revivals at New Lebanon to attract new converts. She sent a "second mission" to the Northeast and started another successful mission to the Ohio Valley frontier. Finally, she saw to the publication of books that clarified Shaker beliefs and practices.

One of the first challenges facing Mother Lucy was the devastating attacks of young people who "forsook the Church and went into the world." By 1800, 20 young Shakers had departed New Lebanon alone, and similar defections had occurred in other villages. More embarrassing than the exodus, however, were the young people's accusations. They said that they had been virtual prisoners held in "obscene and barbarizing bondage." They charged the adults with intimidation and with psychological "terror" if they tried to make friends on the outside. They claimed that they had been threatened with beatings and held in forced confinement. They pictured the elders as hypocrites in matters of sexual conduct. To compound the embarrassment, a number of adult "apostates" endorsed these allegations. Reuben Rathbun, an elder of the Hancock, Massachusetts, village, left in 1799 after a long ordeal of doubt and frustration and wrote *Reasons Offered for Leaving the Shakers*. He confessed that when he joined in 1780 he was a true believer. Eventually, however, he saw alarming violations of the "principles of morality." He described couples going naked into the water together. He told about men who, in their celibacy, had lost control and had "involuntary evacuations" of the "seed of copulation." Whittaker, he said, was guilty of "whoredom." He gave details of drunken fights between Mother Ann and her brother, William. The founders, he wrote, had used language so obscene that "there was never a sailor that stepped on board a ship that exceeded them."[24]

Mother Lucy knew that these charges raised serious questions about the integrity of Shaker life, and so, in 1800 at New Lebanon, she convened the first Gathering Order. Essentially a recruiting revival led by Ebenezer Cooley, an evangelist turned Shaker, it became the "chief agency for the religious nurture of new Believers."[25] He designated the North House and some nearby buildings as the place where potential members would be invited to visit and where the Family would "labor" to initiate them "to receive the Gospel." Shakers were to meet the recruits with kindness, peace, and love and convince them to denounce physical pleasure, give up all former friends, and submit to the will of the elders.

As similar Gathering Order revivals took place in the other villages, the conduct of the Shakers often was bizarre. Young teenage girls in Watervliet (the new name for Niskeyuna) went into trances, spoke with God, and told about journeys to heavenly places. New Believers at South Union "were carried away in a trance to the world of Spirits." At North Union a "Polly C." was "exercised" and spoke in tongues. The Gathering Order, however, was extremely effective in forging what Rosabeth Moss Kanter has called the "commitment mechanisms" so important in molding a community: sacrifice and investment, renunciation and communion, mortification and transcendence.[26]

Mother Lucy organized a "second mission" in the Northeast under the direction of Benjamin Seth Youngs and Issachar Bates. As before, they, along with one or two companions, used family networking, first residing in private homes and then reaching out to others in public meetings. They visited congregations of Baptists, Methodists, and Presbyterians as guest preachers where they received a mixed reception but nevertheless added new converts. In January 1805, encouraged by the second mission, Mother Lucy sent out Youngs, Bates, and John Meacham on foot for Kentucky where they discovered a social matrix similar to that which Mother Lee had encountered in the New England frontier. In the trans-Appalachian foothills they met poor farmers and trappers separated from friends and families, plagued by poverty (few had title to their land), insecurity, fragmentation, and the ever present violence. There, they found a deep resentment against the intellectualism and exclusive redemption of Calvinism and an intense emotional need to find a new guarantee of salvation.

The three men faced repeated, often brutal, belligerence. Settlers mutilated their horses and night raiders burned their preaching stands. Yet they persevered. Traveling to Cincinnati, they converted two New Light Presbyterian congregations in that river town. They started Shaker villages at Gasper, near Dayton, and in Indiana at Busro along the Wabash River. Over the next 10 years the western missionaries gathered hundreds of converts into communal villages modeled after those in the Northeast. Mother Lucy used the good news from the West to reawaken enthusiasm in the older settlements. In 1807, she sent letters to all these villages urging them to purify themselves, to denounce "obscene & filthy communication," and to stop illicit conversations between the sexes.[27]

Meanwhile, at New Lebanon she supervised the publication of more books on Shaker beliefs. In 1808, Benjamin Seth Youngs completed *Testimony of Christ's Second Appearing*, a work which Steven Stein claims "gained the reputation of being the 'Shaker Bible'"[28] Youngs traced Shaker doctrines from the creation to Mother Ann. He explained their theology, communal life, hostility to other religious denominations, and millennialism. "Jesus and the woman who is called MOTHER [Ann Lee]," he wrote, "are the two first foundation pillars of the Church of Christ—the two anointed ones—the two first heirs of promise." The idea of Christ being divine and human was, he said, absurd. Christ was only "anointed" by God, the same Divine Energy that later anointed Ann Lee. Christ and Ann made "complete the order in the foundation of the new creation." Together they represented the dual nature of the Divinity, the "mystery of God," and as Father and Mother they were the Supreme Being called Almighty God and Wisdom.[29]

In 1816, the Shakers printed the *Testimonies of the Life . . . of Our Blessed Mother Ann Lee*, a reference work from which all Shakers could find answers to questions they might have about their religion. Half of the book traced the lives of the Shaker founders up to Ann Lee's death. The other half summarized her visions and teachings. Like Youngs's *Testimony*, it maintained that the spirit of Christ had reappeared in Ann Lee and, therefore, she was the "first spiritual Mother of all the children of the resurrection." It portrayed her as a young woman who, by God's grace, threw off all temptations of the flesh. As an adult she performed miracles, received visions, and issued prophecies. Ann's words "were like flames of fire and her voice like peals of thunder." God had saved her countless times from violence and injury. She willingly died in peace and went to heaven "without a struggle or a groan."

In 1821, just before her death, Mother Lucy directed the compiling of a rulebook entitled the *Millennial Laws*. Edited by Freegift Wells of Watervliet (the name given Niskeyuna in 1787), it summarized basic Shaker etiquette and the duties each believer owed to church officers. It prohibited tattling, backbiting, and holding grievances. It demanded purity and the complete separation of the sexes. It insisted on regular confession before attending a meeting. For the first time, it restricted alcohol during the week and prohibited all "distilled spirits" on the Sabbath, except when doing heavy labor. It banned any offender from religious services until he or she repented the transgression.[30]

Under Mother Lucy the Shakers clarified their rules for religious services. Group rituals called "leaps," or rhythmic dancing when both men and women moved side by side without touching, replaced spontaneous physical manifestations. In 1811, they introduced the "quick dance" in which everyone skipped around in a circle to show their spiritual zeal. Religious songs and airs sung by a chorus accompanied the leaps and quick dance. They used physical gestures, called "motionings," while singing. Like the Ephrata choir, the Shakers sang a cappella since they also believed that instrumentation detracted from the simplicity of the music. In 1813, the *Millennial Praises* appeared, a work that contained the lyrics of 140 hymns that Shakers had composed. They called the book a "gift of songs" that reflected their basic beliefs in love, thankfulness, trust, union, and order. The lyrics celebrated the relationship of Jesus and Ann Lee as "the blessed Son and Daughter, Completely join'd in one." Some tunes denounced the anti-Christ and false gospel. One song condemned all non-Shakers as "illegitimate offspring" of carnal sex whose parents "wax wanton . . . as all carnal creatures will do."[31]

Just after Mother Lucy's death in 1821 the officers placed Seth Wells in charge of Shaker education. Until then, the ministry had given it no priority, except to establish separate day schools for the instruction of boys and girls in reading, writing, arithmetic, and village crafts. The teachers stressed character building and self-discipline as more important than academic training and higher education, which, they said, filled "the brain with sawdust." But Wells was an experienced teacher before he became a Shaker, and in *The Summary View of the Millennial Church* (1823) he argued that education must combine the older values of cleanliness, honesty, order, and discipline with the knowledge of mathematics, chemistry, geography, and music. He argued that talent was a gift from God that must be developed. More significant, he allowed non-Shakers to enroll in the schools and, by so doing, made them into public institutions under the control of state inspectors.[32]

After 1821, leadership passed to church elders and elderesses who further consolidated Shaker principles and practices. In 1828, they authorized John Donlevy of Pleasant Hill, Kentucky, to publish *The Manifesto*. Going beyond *Testimony* and *Testimonies*, it explained Shaker ideas on confession, joint interest, and withdraw from the world—all of which marked them apart from everybody else. But, Donlevy declared, Shaker beliefs by themselves were inadequate and true followers must accompany their faith with right conduct.

By the late 1820s, the Shakers were uplifted by a sense of unity and security for having overcome almost all internal dissension. They had developed a common theology and code of conduct. They were "confident that the expansion and consolidation they had experienced were both fulfillment of prophecy and the foretaste of greater things to come."[33] Membership had increased by 67 percent since 1800 to 4,000 adherents and, despite the earlier defection of the young people, 20 percent were under the age of 16. Compared to the Ephrata Cloister, the growth of the United Society of True Believers in Christ's Second Appearing was impressive.

The Shaker population was representative of American society, despite its initial missionary success in the West among the more downtrodden elements of the class structure. The villages mirrored the diverse social and economic levels of Jacksonian America and counted among their members workers, artisans, merchants, farmers, teachers, and clergy. They were spread over half of the United States: the village at Alfred, Maine, was a thousand miles away from the one at South Union, Kentucky. They organized efficient lines of communication through a chain of command from the central ministry at New Lebanon and its western hub at Union Village, Ohio.

The villages were essentially religious agricultural communes, an attempt to turn the wilderness into efficient, well-ordered gardens; in other words, to create a heaven on earth. This terrestrial Kingdom of God had to be purged of the usual sights and smells of the farm, and so, they made a fetish of order and spotlessness. Cleanliness was their cardinal rule. "Clean your room properly," they insisted, "after all good souls don't dwell in filth, there is none in heaven." They filled their villages with austere buildings constructed without frills according to the axiom that "simple is beautiful." Their fields produced crops for the glory of God, not for profit. Their workshops made the essentials of village life, nothing more: brooms, clothing, and furniture. The women canned jams, jellies, and vegetables and preserved medicinal herbs. Elders labored side by side with the newest converts.[34]

Shakers had regular contacts with other utopian communities. For example, the Busro Creek Family had close ties with the Rappites at Harmony, some 50 miles away. Two Harmonists joined this Shaker village, and the two communities learned each other's ways and language. Historian John A. Bole found that in 1856 Shakers from New Lebanon came to the relocated Rappite Colony at Economy, Pennsylvania, and proposed integrating the two societies. For over two years, Shakers sent the Rappites music, hymns, and theological tracts, but nothing developed on the merger.[35] After Robert Owen purchased New Harmony in 1825 the Busro Creek Shakers invited him to visit them, and two Shakers from South Union joined New Harmony. When New Harmony collapsed, a number of Owenites went to live at South Union, Kentucky, and some of them, such as Daniel Fraser, became elders. Shakers from North Union, Ohio, stayed with the Separatists at Zoar. When Elder Issacher Bates broke his arm during his western mission, the Zoarites nursed him back to health. Shakers communicated with the Amana colony and discussed a possible federation with it. Benjamin Seth Youngs, in *Testimony*, published a formal proposal that the two communities unite because such a combination would "please God." However, since the Amanites allowed marriage, the merger never occurred. The frequent contacts between the Massachusetts Shakers and the Oneida Perfectionists were well documented in the writings of Elder Evans, John Humphrey Noyes, and his son Pierrepont.

After 1831, Shakers were increasingly attracted to spiritualism and telepathy. That winter, at New Lebanon, one man saw "tongues, visions etc." and another had visions of "the heavenly host" and Ann Lee. In 1834, the Hancock village recorded an appearance of "departed friends." In October 1836, New Lebanon reported the power of God as seen in "tongues & diverse operations" at meetings. The following January, James Smith, at Watervliet, wrote that brothers and sisters "in this society have been waking up to life, zeal & power for some weeks past. . . . Even the public meetings," he went on, "are full of . . . diverse operations & gifts of the Spirit." In August, Gideon Kibbee at the same village saw Ann Lee at the head of "a company of heavenly host" floating three feet off the ground.[36]

In 1837, a spiritual revival at New Lebanon inaugurated the "era of Manifestations" when teenage girls fell into a trance with spasms and leaps, "appeared withdrawn from the scenes of the time," spoke with angels, and saw visions of "heavenly places." The elders pronounced the event a visitation from God and decided that the girls were mediums with the Divine. Shortly afterward, 14-year-old Ann Goff said that she saw and touched an angel covered by "white feathers" having the body of a man "very beautiful but difficult to describe" who walked and flew through the air. That fall, at Watervliet, visitors saw Shakers leaping and turning and talking to deceased friends and angels. Other villages recorded similar exotic manifestations, almost all of them involving visions of Mother Ann Lee. In June 1838, at South Union, two sisters fell into a deep spiritual trance. At Pleasant Hill the "power of God moved like electricity" through a meeting. At North Union a little girl spoke in "unknown tongues" and 18 young men fell to the floor paralyzed by seizures and visions. Some of the spiritual episodes bordered on the bizarre. Believers saw an "invisible hand" push Sarah Simons like a mop across a dirty floor to clean up debris. Others started eating food off the floor and acted "drunk with new wine," beset with "giddy, hysterical laughter."[37]

Spiritualism reached its peak in April 1841 with the visitation of "Holy Mother Wisdom," the female person of God, who spoke at New Lebanon through Sister Miranda Barber. Mother Wisdom bestowed gifts on the elders—gold breastplates for the men, "robes of needlework, covered with flowers" for the women. Shakers saw Mother Wisdom move through the assembly and make each person repeat a vow: "I am bound for the Kingdom of Heaven." She gave each Believer a gold headband with the words "Touch not mine Anointed." During the rest of the year, Mother Wisdom appeared at other villages and asked Shakers to repent their sins and walk the Narrow Path.[38]

After these visits the villages closed their meetings to the public. Now, more than ever, the Shakers secluded themselves from the rest of the world and suspended all regular outside contacts. They christened their villages with new spiritual names. They called Watervliet "Wisdom's Valley" with a sacred "Center Square." New Lebanon was "Holy Mount" with its "Mount of Olives." Harvard was "Lovely Vineyard" with its "Holy Hill of Zion." Union Village was "Wisdom's Paradise" with its "Jehovah's Chosen Square." South Union was "Jasper Valley" with its "Holy Ground." Only Pleasant Hill kept its name, but it, too, had a sacred "Holy Sinai's Plain." Shakers became oblivious to the great political and moral questions emerging over the future of slavery in America. And they were unresponsive to the coming of a war that decided the question, a war that imposed new difficulties for them. But they grew and prospered. At mid-century on the eve of the "irreversible conflict" there were 3,842 True Believers living in 21 Families scattered from Maine through western Kentucky.[39]

During the Civil War, because of their pacifism, they refused to support the conflict. The central ministry at New Lebanon wrote: "Believers, who are obeyers, cannot, under any circumstances engage in military servitude of any name or nature." The elders sent instructions on how to resist the draft by stating their "nonresistant principles, and conscientious scruples" against violence. When 70 young men defiantly enlisted in the Union army, the elders petitioned President Abraham Lincoln to discharge them and promised to pay a huge deferment fee for the exemption. The 70 recruits, however, remained in uniform. But in 1863, Secretary of War Edwin Stanton ordered the release of all Shakers from active duty. Kentucky Shakers had a special problem during the war. Their neutrality caused both the Union and Confederate forces to pilfer their villages for food and supplies and to confiscate their animals and wagons for military use. One observer in Pleasant Hill wrote that in the fall of 1862 "ragged, greasy and dirty troops . . . marched into our yards & surrounded our wells like the locusts of Egypt."[40]

By war's end all the villages had experienced a steady decline of membership and a growing division among those who remained on the Narrow Path. The restrictions they had adopted were frustrating to the new generation of Believers who wanted to relax the strict rules on owning personal belongings. They felt that they should be able to receive outside gifts of French cologne, to install carpets and mirrors in their homes, and to wear jewelry.

Older members condemned these worldly temptations and insisted on the traditional values of order and simplicity. They still embraced spiritualism and continued to see angels and departed friends. But the younger generation argued that small material pleasures only enhanced the spiritual way, and, to prove their point, they appeared always cheerful and optimistic. But some of them ridiculed their elders, calling them fussy, somber, dullards. They even joked about celibacy. The generations split over music. The younger group wanted to use instrumental accompaniment and to sing in four-part harmony. The older Shakers insisted upon keeping the a cappella format and predicted disaster if they surrendered to these temptations.

In the 1870s, Frederick Evans assumed leadership of the United Society, and under his rule the generational divisions worsened, only then over new issues. Evans, born in England in 1808, was an Owenite and active social reformer who rose rapidly to the rank of elder at Mount Lebanon. In his influential publication, *The Shaker*, a periodical appearing between 1871 and 1899, he continually urged them not to remain aloof from national politics. Specifically, he urged them to support socialism, a position they could take without sacrificing celibacy, pacifism, communal property, and temperance. Harvey L. Eads became his nemesis. A conservative South Union elder, the personification of the rigid Shaker, Eads abhorred Evans's activism and insisted that Believers remain separate from the divisive forces of the Industrial Revolution. He said that America, more than before, was alien to the pastoral ideals of the founder's heavenly garden village.

Evans went on the offensive and organized a mission to gain new converts among the laboring classes of the eastern cities. Unfortunately, his rural spiritualism seemed irrelevant to the needs of these American workers. He then traveled to England, but there, in the factories, he converted only a few souls. He next tried to increase membership by inviting Americans to visit Shaker villages to enjoy their congenial, comfortable life. This effort also failed. He reached out to other communal societies in hopes of getting them to join. For example, he contacted Cyrus Teed at Estero, Florida, and invited him, unsuccessfully, to link his Koreshan Unity community with a nearby Shaker village.[41]

Between the Civil War and the end of the century Shaker membership declined catastrophically. Admissions fell off sharply, most of the elderly died, and young people left the villages. Backsliding became rampant. Many True Believers began to retail Shaker-made products for lucrative profits. There were constant complaints to the elders of brothers and sisters meeting together—laughing, talking, and singing in their rooms. One outraged New Lebanon man reported that the room next to his "was more like a noisy Bar Room than like a decent retiring Room. . . . Sisters were there the whole of the time," he complained, "and a constant laugh and gabble by both [men and women]" continued till eleven o'clock at night.[42]

With their numbers shrinking, many villages hired outsiders to serve in the workshops and cultivate the fields. They eliminated many crafts and concentrated on making furniture, baskets, brooms, and clothing. Although agriculture remained their main source of income, they had to compete with mechanized American farmers who were able to underprice Shaker produce in the marketplace. As the financial base of the society declined, they started to sell off farms, houses and lots, and timber tracts. The Hancock Village realized $550 in the sale of two houses and small lots. The Shirley, Massachusetts, village made $2,500 by selling a farm of one of its members. In 1908, it sold the entire village to the state for $43,000. Peter F. Sering, in 1910, bought 780 acres from Whitewater, Ohio, for $40,000. A parcel of land at Watervliet the same year went for $15,500, and Fiske Warren purchased the Harvard compound in 1918 for $60,000. By 1920, only 12 economically viable villages remained.[43]

Another striking aspect of what was called the "Time of Transformation" was the feminization of the society. It became "a women's sect." Records show that after 1860 the villages always took in more women than men as new members and, by 1890, 75 percent of the Shakers were women. So, women took over jobs and leadership positions. One historian observed that this phenomenon brought women more equality than was ever theoretically feasible under the Millennial Laws. "Not since Lucy Wright," Stein concludes, "had women exercised so much power."[44]

Evans's *The Shaker* reflected this feminization when, in 1873, he changed its title to *Shaker and Shakeress* and appointed Antoinette Doolittle as coeditor. She, in her first editorial entitled "Appeal," urged her sisters to submit poetry and essays. "Scribbling" Shaker women such as Ruth Webster of Union Village submitted articles that criticized the theological justification of female subordination. She said that women were not responsible for Adam's fall and should not be blamed for human sinfulness. Another writer exalted Mother Ann as the harbinger of female emancipation. Martha J. Anderson, a Mount Lebanon sister, wrote that Ann Lee had uplifted and released women "from the thralldom of sin and set her in her proper place as the helpmeet [*sic*] and co-worker with man in all the duties and services of life."[45] Evans printed letters that praised the "sense of sisterhood" that the journal conveyed. A sister from Hancock, Massachusetts, was delighted because the magazine presented a "full manifestation of the Christ Spirit in both male and female." Another admitted that she now possessed a "lively interest in what I consider a *living cause*, of vital importance."[46]

Although a new editor of the journal, George Lomas, in 1876 changed the title back to *The Shaker* and later to *The Shaker Manifesto*, sisters continued to support it as a "blessing." They urged women to broaden their horizons beyond their narrow, traditional concerns with the village. Led by Antoinette Doolittle and Anna White, both at New Lebanon, and Aurelia Mace at Sabbathday Lake, they went on public lecture tours to crusade for women's rights and to fight against sex discrimination in the workplace and professions. They supported, and joined, the American chapter of the World Peace Movement. In 1904, Anna White, in her essay "Shakerism, Its Meaning and Message," wrote that because of this new role the Shaker sister was "the freest woman in the world." Still, most sisters stayed anchored in domestic chores in the villages. They continued to make pies, bake bread, churn butter, can fruits, care for the sick, clean the buildings, and wash the clothes. They sold comestibles such as pickles, jams, baked beans, horseradish, and applesauce. They knitted sweaters, shawls, and mittens and worked in the craft shops.[47]

Shakers in the twentieth century adapted somewhat to the outside world. They pushed for cleanliness, order, peace, and stability, just as before; but they discarded dancing in their worship and kept only the singing. They left the villages regularly for medical treatment or to attend sports events. They purchased automobiles and used tractors on the farms. They brought electricity to their kitchens and washrooms. A new interest in Shaker history appeared. In 1920, they built their first museum at Prospect Hill as part of the Fruitlands Museum. Afterward, other museums opened at Shaker villages to display furniture, tools, clothing, and crafts.

In 1992, the last resident of Canterbury, New Hampshire, Sister Ethel Hudson, died. Today Sabbathday Lake, Maine, is the sole surviving Shaker village. Located just off Route 26 about 30 miles north of Portland, it welcomes visitors, at $5 a ticket. It has a dozen white-painted, frame buildings that stand stark and austere around a 48-room Dwelling House. In this brick structure a dozen Shakers, segregated by sex, sleep, work, and dine. A guide escorts people through the various craft shops, and one can tour their Shaker Museum and Shaker Library. The True Believers largely ignore the outsiders and go about undisturbed in a daily routine of working in the Dwelling House and shops, cultivating their 1,900 acres to raise culinary herbs, and gathering three times for meals and prayer. Despite its tiny membership, Sabbathday Lake has deep symbolic significance to Shakers.[48] "As long as there is a Shaker settlement and a group of Shakers, even though small," a young member told historian Yaacov Oved in 1981, "Ann Lee's light will enlighten the world and there is hope for her message to encompass all."[49] Most visitors get a sense of dignified permanence when they come to Sabbathday Lake. Gustav Niebur, who went there in the summer of 1998, wrote in the July 31 issues of the *New York Times* that he left "with thoughts of the creativity and durability of this community."

NOTES

1. Stephen J. Stein, *The Shaker Experience in America: A History of the United Society of Believers* (New Haven, Conn.: Yale University Press, 1992), p. 3. He has a discussion of the primary sources on Shakerism under "Suggestions for Further Readings," pp. 521–23.

2. Edward Dunning Andrews, *The People Called Shakers* (New York: Dover, 1963), pp. 3–7; Oved, *American Communes*, pp. 39–40; Priscilla J. Brewer, "The Shakers of Mother Ann Lee," in *America's Communal Utopias*, ed., Donald E. Pitzer (Chapel Hill: University of North Carolina Press, 1997), pp. 37–38; M. Fellows Melcher, *The Shaker Adventure* (New York: Shaker Museum, 1975), pp. 8–9.

3. A discussion of this group of Quakers, called Camisards or the French Prophets who left France for England, specifically Manchester, after the revocation of the Edict of Nantes in 1685 is in Stein, *Shaker Experience*, pp. 5–6 and Oved, *American Communes*,

pp. 39–40. However, Diane Sasson, in *The Shaker Spiritual Narrative* (Lexington: University Press of Kentucky, 1983), p. 3n, thinks that there was no historical connection between the radical Quakers and the French Prophets. Rather, the Wesleys and George Whitefield influenced their radical evangelical beliefs. See also Pricilla J. Brewer, "Shakers," pp. 38–39.

4. Priscilla J. Brewer, *Shaker Communities, Shaker Lives* (Hanover, N.H.: University Press of New England, 1986), p. 39.

5. Andrews, *Shakers*, pp. 7–8; Brewer, "Shakers," p. 40; Oved, *American Communes*, p. 48.

6. Stein, *Shaker Experience*, p. 4.

7. Andrews, *Shakers*, p. 8.

8. Stephen A. Marini, *Radical Sects of Revolutionary New England* (Cambridge, Mass.: Harvard University Press, 1982), p. 76; Stein, *Shaker Experience*, pp. 10–12.

9. Brewer, "Shakers," p. 41. For a discussion of the millennial fever that spread through the Baptists and Methodists living in the New England frontier, see Nathan O. Hatch, *The Sacred Cause of Liberty: Republican Thought and the Millennium in Revolutionary New England* (New Haven, Conn.: Yale University Press, 1977). Oved, *American Communes*, p. 69 n. 8 also has a discussion of millennialism and revivalism at the time of the arrival of Ann Lee and her followers in America.

10. Brewer, "Shakers," p. 40.

11. Ann Lee's "public ministry" and mission are thoroughly treated, along with a map designating the locations of her travels, in Stein, *Shaker Experience*, pp. 18–20.

12. Ibid., pp. 45–46, 50, 101; Brewer, "Shakers," pp. 42–43. Lucy Wright, the former wife of a merchant from Richmond, Massachusetts, had become the dominant female personality at Niskeyuna by the time of Ann Lee's death.

13. Lawrence Foster, *Women, Family, and Utopia: Communal Experiments of the Shakers, the Oneida Community, and the Mormons* (Syracuse, N.Y.: Syracuse University Press, 1991), p. 30.

14. Stein, *Shaker Experience*, pp. 32–49; Stephen Paterwic, "From Individual to Community: Becoming a Shaker at New Lebanon," *Communal Societies* 11 (1991): 18–33.

15. These villages for the gathering "into gospel order" were Watervliet (Niskeyuna), New York (1787); Hancock, Massachusetts (1790); Enfield, Connecticut (1790); Harvard, Massachusetts (1791); Tyringham, Massachusetts (1792); Canterbury, New Hampshire (1792); Shirley, Massachusetts (1793); Enfield, New Hampshire (1793); Alfred, Maine (1793); and Sabbathday Lake, Maine (1794).

16. Charles Nordhoff, *The Communistic Societies of the United States* (London: John Murray, 1875), p. 166; Rosemary D. Gooden, "A Preliminary Examination of Shaker Attitudes toward Work," *Communal Societies* 3 (1983): 1–15; Lauer and Lauer, "Sex Roles," pp. 19, 23–24; Edward R. Hogan, *The Shaker Holy Land: A Community Portrait* (Harvard, Mass.: Harvard Common Press, 1982), pp. 47–56; Hinds, *American Communities*, pp. 42–44; Edward D. Andrews, *The Community Industries of the Shakers* (Albany: University of the State of New York, 1932; reprint, Philadelphia: Porcupine Press, 1972); Wendy Chimielewske, Louis J. Kern, and Marlyn Klee-Harzell, eds., *Women in Spiritual and Communitarian Societies in the United States* (Syracuse, N.Y.: Syracuse University Press, 1993); Oved, *American Communes*, pp. 413–20.

17. Foster, *Women, Family and Utopia*, p. 32.

18. Oved, *American Communes*, pp. 50–53; Brian J. L. Berry, *America's Utopian Ex-*

periments Communal Havens from Long-Wave Crises (Hanover, N.H.: University Press of New England), pp. 38–39.

19. See Oved, *American Communes*, pp. 53–54 on Shaker children and education; and Brewer, "Shakers," p. 44; Oved, *American Communes*, pp. 396–405.

20. John E. Murray, "Determinants of Membership Levels and Duration in a Shaker Commune, 1780–1880," *Journal for the Scientific Study of Religion* 34, no. 1 (1995): 35–48 and "Stature among Members of a Nineteenth Century American Shaker Commune," *Annals of Human Biology* 20, no. 2 (1993): 121–29; Metin M. Cosgel, Thomas J. Miceli, and John E. Murray, "Organization and Distributional Equality in a Network of Communes: The Shakers," *American Journal of Economics and Sociology* 56, no. 2 (April 1997): 129–144.

21. Stein, *Shaker Experience*, pp. 48, 101–6; Daniel W. Patterson, "Shaker Music," *Communal Societies* 2 (1982): 53–64.

22. Stein, *Shaker Experience*, p. 47.

23. Ibid., p. 53; Jean McMahon Humez, "'Weary of Petticoat Government': The Specter of Female Rule in Early Nineteenth-Century Shaker Politics," *Communal Societies* 11 (1991): 1–17.

24. Stein, *Shaker Experience*, p. 51; Elizabeth A. Dewolfe, "'So Much They Have Got for Their Folly': Shaker Apostates and the Tale of Woe," *Communal Societies* 18 (1998): 21–35; Reuben Rathbun, *Reasons Offered for Leaving the Shakers* (Pittsfield, Mass.: Chester Smith, 1800).

25. Stein, *Shaker Experience*, p. 54.

26. Ibid., p. 172. Rosabeth Moss Kanter, *Commitment and Community: Communes and Utopias in Sociological Perspective* (Cambridge, Mass.: Harvard University Press, 1972), pp. 74–75. The other villages experiencing the Gathering Order revival were Shawnee Run, Kentucky (1807); Pleasant Hill, Kentucky (1809); Busseron Creek, Indiana (1809); Watervliet, New York (1837 and 1847); South Union, Kentucky (1838).

27. As a result of the western mission, by 1827 eight more villages had been built at Union Village, Ohio (1806); Watervliet, Ohio (1806); Pleasant Hill, Kentucky (1806); South Union, Kentucky (1807); West Union, Indiana (1810); North Union, Ohio (1822); Whitewater, Ohio (1824); and Sodus Bay, New York (1826).

28. Stein, *Shaker Experience*, p. 459.

29. Brewer, *Shaker Communities, Shaker Lives*, p. 45; Oved, *American Communes*, pp. 48–49; Andrews, *Shakers*, pp. 95–99; Julia Neal, "The American Shakers," *Communities: Journal of Cooperation* 68 (Winter 1985): 16–17; Glendyne R. Wergland, "Lust, 'A Snare of Satan to Beguile the Soul': New Light on Shaker Celibacy," *Communal Societies* 15 (1995): 1–24.

30. Stein, *Shaker Experiences*, pp. 95–98, 155–59, 198–99, 301–4. The appendix to Andrews, *Shakers*, has a reprint of the title page of the *Millennial Laws* as well as the text of the *Laws*, pp. 243–88.

31. Stein, *Shaker Experiences*, pp. 103–4.

32. Andrews, *Shakers*, pp. 180–84; Harvey Elkins, *Fifteen Years in the Senior Order of the Shakers: A Narration of Facts Concerning That Singular People* (Hanover, N.H.: Dartmouth Press, 1853; reprint, New York: AMS Press, 1973), pp. 23–31, 37, 40–44, 76–84.

33. Stein, *Shaker Experience*, p. 106.

34. Andrews, *Community Industries*, pp. 60–111, 118–21; 139–212, 229–48; Brewer, *Shaker Communities*, p. 100; Flo Morse, *The Shakers and the World's People* (New York:

Dodd, Mead, 1980), p. 133; Margaret Van Alen Frisbee Sommer, *The Shaker Garden Seed Industry* (Old Chatham, N.Y.: Shaker Museum Foundation, 1972), pp. 10–16; Nancy L. Hillenburg, "Shaker Trade Routes," *Shaker Quarterly* 18 (1990): 40–46; Edward R. Horgan, *The Shaker Holy Land: A Community Portrait* (Harvard, Mass.: Harvard Common Press, 1982); Karen K. Nickless and Pamela J. Nickless, "Trustees, Deacons, and Deaconesses: The Temporal Role of the Shaker Sisters, 1820–1890," *Communal Studies* 7 (1987): 16–24; John E. Murray and Metin M. Cosgel, "Regional Specialization in Communal Agriculture: The Shakers, 1800–1890," *Communal Societies* 19 (1989): 73–84; Oved, *American Communes*, pp. 428–39. Other specialized accounts of Shaker village economies can be found in Stein, *Shaker Experience*, pp. 471–72.

35. John A. Boyle, *The Harmony Society: A Chapter in German American Culture History* (New York: AMS Press, 1973), pp. 121–27; Jane F. Crosthwaite, "The Spirit Drawings of Hannan Cohoon: Window on the Shakers and Their Folk Art," *Communal Societies* 7 (1987): 1–15.

36. Stein, *Shaker Experience*, p. 167; Lawrence Foster, "Shaker Spiritualism and Salem Witchcraft: Perspectives on Trance and Possession Phenomena," *Communal Societies* 9 (1991): 1–17.

37. Lois J. Kern, *An Ordered Love: Sex Roles and Sexuality in Victorian Utopias—The Shakers, the Mormons, and the Oneida Community* (Chapel Hill: University of North Carolina Press, 1981), p. 106; Julia Neal, *By Their Fruits: The Story of Shakerism in South Union, Kentucky* (Chapel Hill: University of North Carolina Press, 1947; reprint, Philadelphia: Porcupine Press, 1975), ch. 2; Morse, *Shakers*, pp. 171–84; Tyler, *Freedom's Ferment*, pp. 72–76; Andrews, *Shakers*, pp. 113–16, 152–74, 204–12; Hinds, *American Communities*, p. 49; Henri Desroche, *The American Shakers: From Neo-Christianity to Presocialism*, trans. John K. Savacool (Amherst: University of Massachusetts Press, 1971), pp. 84–87; Diane Sasson, "Individual Experience, Community Control, and Gender: The Harvard Shaker Community during the Era of Manifestations," *Communal Societies* 13 (1993): 45–70.

38. See Stein, *Shaker Experience*, pp. 174–75 on the visit of Holy Mother Wisdom. See also Brewer, *Shaker Communities*, pp. 125–26; Andrews, *Shakers*, p. 162; Edward Deming Andrews and Faith Andrews, *Fruits of the Shaker Tree: Memoirs of Fifty Years of Collecting and Research* (Stockbridge, Mass.: Berkshire Traveler Press, 1975), pp. 45–50; Diane Sasson, *The Shaker Spiritual Narrative* (Knoxville: University of Tennessee Press, 1983), pp. 103–21.

39. Oved, *American Communes*, pp. 56–57.

40. Quoted in Stein, *Shaker Experience*, p. 202. See also Neal, *By Their Fruits*, pp. 177–97 and Thomas D. Clark and F. Gerald Hann, *Pleasant Hill and Its Shakers* (Pleasant Hill, Ky.: Shakertown Press, 1968), pp. 63–70; Oved, *American Communes*, pp. 56–57.

41. Frederick William Evans, *Autobiography of a Shaker and Revelation of the Apocalypse* (1888; reprint, New York: AMS Press, 1973), pp. 1–30; Andrews, *Shakers*, pp. 232–36; Morse, *Shakers*, pp. 215–27; Brewer, "Shakers," p. 48; Ovid, *American Communes*, pp. 57–58.

42. Brewer, *Shaker Communities*, pp. 179–80 and "'Numbers Are Not the Thing for Us to Glory In': Demographic Perspectives on the Decline of the Shakers," *Communal Societies* 7 (1987): 25–35; Bradley B. Andrew and Metin Cosgel, "Regional Differences

in the Size and Composition of Communal Membership: The Shakers, 1850–1870," *Communal Societies* 20 (2000): 45–58.

43. Brewer, "Shakers," p. 49. A table in Berry, *Utopian Experiments*, p. 29 shows the date of the founding and closing of all Shaker villages, as does Andrews, *Shakers*, pp. 290–92; William Sims Bainbridge, "The Decline of the Shakers: Evidence from the United States Census," *Communal Societies* 4 (1984): 19–34. See also Oved, *American Communes*, pp. 59–60.

44. Stein, *Shaker Experience*, p. 357.

45. Ibid., p. 261.

46. Ibid., p. 261.

47. Ibid., pp. 204–7, 263, 266–68, 310–11, 316–17, 320–21, 338–39.

48. Morse, *Shakers*, pp. 231–36, 243–47, 278–83; Andrews, *Shakers*, pp. 224–40; Oved, *American Communes*, pp. 62–64.

49. Oved, *American Communes*, p. 64.

CHAPTER 3

Separatist Colonies: Harmonists, Bethel/Aurora, Zoar, Amana, Bishop Hill

Not long after the Shakers had started to fashion their heavenly garden villages the first group of religious refugees called Separatists (because they wished to be separate from the established Lutheran state church in Germany and Sweden) immigrated to the United States. Altogether they formed 17 communal utopias in Pennsylvania, New York, and the Midwest. The most significant of these were the Harmonist colonies, Bethel/Aurora, Zoar, Amana, and Bishop Hill. Despite their different locations, they shared a number of characteristics. They were millennial and anticipated the imminent coming of Christ, believed in celibacy at least some of the time, were pacifists, and practiced communal ownership of property.

THE HARMONISTS

Johann Georg Rapp, the founder and charismatic leader of the Harmonists, was born on November 1, 1757, in the village of Iptingen, near Stuttgart, Germany, the second of five children of Adam Rapp, a farmer and vineyard owner. Educated in what was called a common school, Johann acquired a rudimentary knowledge of reading, arithmetic, and geometry. As a young adult he helped out on the farm and learned how to operate a hand loom. He became a weaver, married, and in 1783 settled down at his birthplace. He had two children, a son and a daughter.

In the meantime, the writings of Michael Hahn and other Pietist teachers caused Rapp to question the structure, rituals, and formal dogma of the Lutheran Church. He became convinced that the clergy were hypocrites and church sacraments were a form of idolatry. He concluded that to support the state church in any way, even to pay church taxes, was an abomination to the Lord. At the age of 30 he started to preach these dangerous ideas to neighbors in his home. By 1791, in the words of Karl J. R. Arndt, "this mere peasant from Iptingen had become the outspoken leader of several thousand Separatists in the southern German duchy of Württemberg."[1]

At that point the civil authorities, prodded by Lutheran pastors, cracked down. Local constables compiled a list of Rapp's followers, and the police arrested them. They were fined for not paying taxes and for holding private religious services. In addition, the courts served them a writ of banishment that, fortunately, the king of Württemberg refused to enforce. Undaunted, Rapp continued to condemn the worldliness and corruption of the clergy and to prepare the Separatists for Christ's Second Coming.

In 1798, he published *Articles of Faith*, a work that summarized his beliefs. All Separatists, he stated, must live a life of honesty, toleration, and compassion. They must form a church as it had been under the Apostles, without infant baptism and confirmation. They must take oaths only to God, avoid violence, and oppose all military service. Although the *Articles* did not mention celibacy, Rapp had already made clear his views on sexual intercourse. After 1785, when he and his wife became celibate, he maintained that sexual abstinence should be an integral part of the quest for spiritual perfection. He believed that Adam had been a "biune" creature with no sex organs but, nevertheless, had male and female components. In the Fall the female element separated, and this event caused "alienation from God and a loss of universal harmony."[2] However, it was not until 1807, in America, that the Separatists, in anticipation of an imminent Second Coming of Christ, adopted celibacy as a communal requirement.

By 1802, the Separatists had grown in number to about 12,000 and the Württemberg government decided that they were a dangerous threat to social order, perhaps a precursor to a repetition of the Peasant War of 1525. Rapp was summoned to Maulbronn for an interrogation and the government confiscated Separatist books, the most controversial of which was the *Gülden Rose* (The Golden Rose). When released in the summer of 1803, Rapp told the Separatists to pool their assets and follow him on a journey for safety to the "land of Israel" in the United States.[3]

That autumn, Rapp and two other men sailed for Philadelphia. There, with community funds, he purchased 5,000 acres of land on the Connoquenessing Creek in Butler County, 30 miles from Pittsburgh. The next year 300 Separatists emigrated and two other groups of 269 and 270 followed them to Philadelphia. Soon, over 800 Harmonists were living in the United States. In September 1804, Rapp led a contingent of 80 men to Butler County, where they started to erect log houses. There, on February 15, 1805, after everyone had joined the advance guard, they signed the Articles of Association. This document formally created the "Harmony Society" and required everyone to deed their possessions to Rapp and a group of officers called associates. The officers would supply everyone with the necessities of life, medical treatment and would raise any orphans. They would provide instruction for the children in a church school. They designated the day of the adoption of the articles, February 15, as "Harmonie Fest," the anniversary of the society.[4]

Under Rapp's stern but benevolent direction the industrious Germans got down to work. The men wore dark trousers, blue jackets, and broad-rimmed hats. They planted grape vines, constructed workshops, put up a flour and saw mill. In 1807, they adopted celibacy, dissolved all existing marriages, and forbade any future unions. Unlike the Ephrata Cloister and the Shaker villages, there was no separate housing for the sexes; men and women continued to live together but only as brothers and sisters. By 1814, the Harmony Society was a prosperous farm community with 700 people living and working in 130 brick, frame, and log buildings. They had over 2,000 acres under cultivation and operated a mill, tannery, woolen factory, and distillery.[5]

However, Harmony faced some serious problems. The Americans living in the area became suspicious of the Germans and resented their economic competition. To reach retail markets in Pittsburgh involved an expensive and time-consuming hauling of their produce and goods overland to the Monongahela River. Besides, Rapp had always thought of the place as only a temporary location where he would organize for a permanent move farther west to await the millennium.[6] Consequently, in 1814 he investigated opportunities in the Indiana Territory and found newly opened federal land on the Wabash River selling at $2 an acre. The location seemed idyllic: plenty of water, level fields, and forests with lumber for homes and furniture. He eventually purchased 30,000 acres with $100,000 that he realized from the sale of Harmony Society property. That spring some 800 Rappites moved on flatboats down the Ohio River and then up Wabash to "New Harmony."[7]

But life was not easy on the frontier. The area was swampy and malaria swept through the colony: during the first two years, 120 Harmonists died. Every spring worms infested the grass and in the summer mosquitoes became intolerable. In winter, wolves attacked their livestock. But Rapp was optimistic. He wrote to a friend in December 1815 that he expected to make a great deal of money "raising wine." He told him that they now had "more opportunity here than we had in Pennsylvania, to make of a wild country, fertile fields and gardens of pleasure."[8] They forged bricks and with them built a church and four large rooming houses, mills, workshops, a school, a tavern, and a 60-foot-square mansion for Rapp. They erected an elaborate labyrinth of shrubs, vines, and trees and placed a shrine in its center as a place for meditation and prayer.[9]

Each Sunday Rapp preached about humility, self-sacrifice, brotherly love, the efficacy of prayer, and the need for self-examination. To minimize friction and squabbles he insisted that everyone who had "sinned" during the day confess to him, as "Father Rapp," before retiring at night. "Let not the sun go down on thy wrath," he warned. Weekdays began at five in the morning and ended at a nine o'clock bedtime. The men continued to wear the same blue clothing and broad-rimmed hats. The women donned somber-colored skirts, light blouses, and Normandy caps. Marching to and from work to the music of a band, they worked side by side in the vineyards, fields, and shops. From a central kitchen the women distributed five meals throughout the day that included a wholesome diet of vegetables and meat, but no pork. They marketed their products as far north as Pittsburgh and as far down the Mississippi River as New Orleans. Money also came in from local sales because "New Harmony was the only place around where they could purchase supplies, have their grain ground, or tend to their banking needs."[10] By the early 1820s, New Harmony was one of the largest towns in Indiana, and Father Rapp skillfully exploited its political clout both in Indianapolis and in Posey County. With the promise, or threat, of the community's block-vote support at election time he persuaded the legislature to charter a bank at the colony. And he convinced the county commissioners to locate the new county seat on 100 acres of land owned by the community.

In 1824, Rapp published his ideas on education in *Thoughts on the Destiny of Man*. He insisted that children be trained for community life and be instilled with a Christian conscience enlightened by an understanding of Scripture. As adults, he wrote, they must be able "to live up to the laws of God contained in his Word given for the life and happiness of mankind thereby attaining the best preparedness for the world to Come."[11] Everyone had to be able to read the Bible so that individuals could see for themselves the divine justification for their communal life. They could see that Saint Paul had advocated celibacy in his letter to the Corinthians when he admonished: "It is good for a man not to touch a woman."

At the colony school the teachers, led by headmaster Christopher Mueller, instructed some 100 children up to the age of 14 in English, German, French, music, reading, mathematics, physics, chemistry, geography, and history. The students included those born before the adoption of celibacy, children of new members, and orphans. Classes began at eight o'clock and ended at noon. Teachers used question-and-answer sessions, memorization and recitations, spelling bees, craftwork, and physical activities. They had students compose essays on various moral issues and Rapp published the best of them in a book, *Fiery Coals of Ascending Love Flame*. Vocational training began at the age of 14. Every boy chose a craft from a list of trades practiced in New Harmony. He could become a hatter, saddler, shoemaker, blacksmith, breaches maker, tinnier, mason, dyer, nail maker, tailor, cooper, potter, wagon maker, weaver. He could choose to learn "agricultural skills." A girl's options, though, were limited to "the art and mystery of housekeeping." Both at school and in vocational training Rapp stressed the importance of music. "Music to the Harmonists," wrote Melvin Miller in his 1973 doctoral dissertation, "was truly their melody of life."[12] As adults, they continued their education and received instruction in reading and writing, artwork, and music using a 340-volume library located in the community store. They participated in symposiums at which they discussed religious issues. They submitted essays and poetry in literary competitions.[13]

Although the Harmonists left little documentation of those early years, visitors have left accounts of the bucolic life on the banks of the Wabash. An Englishman, John Woods, described their terraced vineyards, fine horses, and fat milk cows. Richard Flower, an English traveler, commended their sturdy spirit of hard work, a striking contrast he thought to the shiftless American frontiersman. Morris Birkbeck, of nearby Prairie Albion in Illinois, wrote in his diary that New Harmony's success was based on the "association of numbers in application of good capital," but he was critical of their "disgusting superstition." Another Englishman identified as "Mr. Courtney" described their school as "well conducted by a respectable tutor . . . all clean, neat and orderly . . . a most pleasing, peaceful and active scene."[14] And he praised the tavern, calling it one of "the most comfortable I have met in the western country." It was, he commented, "remarkable for its cleanliness, neatness, and good order; and the manager, while civil to all his guests, effectually prevents excessive drinking."[15] Historian Alice Felt Tyler claims that New Harmony was unique in that even the famous Lord Byron in Canto the Fifteenth of *Don Juan* penned lines of romantic admiration on it. He wrote,

When Rapp the Harmonist embargo'd marriage
    In his harmonious settlement (which flourishes
Strangely enough as yet without miscarriage,
    Because it breeds no more mouths than it nourishes,
Without those sad expenses which disparage
    What Nature naturally most encourages)—
Why call'd he "Harmony" a state *sans* wedlock?
Now here I've got the preacher at a dead lock,
Because he either meant to sneer at harmony
    Or marriage, by divorcing them thus oddly.
But whether reverend Rapp learn'd this in Germany
    Or no, 'tis said his sect is rich and godly,
Pious and pure, beyond what I can term any
    Of ours, although they propagate more broadly.[16]

However, by 1824 Rapp again grew restless and talked about returning to Pennsylvania. He realized by then that the Indiana soil was not as suited to growing grapes as he had first expected. Retail markets were just too distant and shipping costs too high. Their wool cloth found few buyers among a western population that did their own spinning. The Panic of 1819 further depressed markets for New Harmony products. Frustrations mounted. These Germans never acclimated to, or liked, the hot, humid summers of the lower Wabash valley. Their American neighbors became just as hostile and envious as those back in Pennsylvania. And there was Rapp's growing concern that life had become *too* comfortable, *too* easy. He thought that building a new society about every 10 years was essential in order to reinforce communal bonds and promote discipline and morale. Besides, he "was keenly aware" that any weakening of these bonds "could seriously undermine his leadership."[17]

For a combination of reasons, therefore, Rapp hired Richard Flower on commission to sell New Harmony for the best price to any buyer he could find. Flower returned to England, went to New Lanark, Scotland, and talked with Robert Owen, whom Flower learned was looking for an American location for his own utopia. The two men agreed on a total price of $135,000 for New Harmony's lands, buildings, and equipment. Meanwhile, Rapp dispatched his adopted son, Frederick, to Pennsylvania to find another location. There, Frederick found 1,000 acres at a spot 10 miles north of Pittsburgh on the Ohio River and purchased the entire tract for about $10,000.[18]

On May 24, 1824, the first contingent of Harmonists was ready for the journey to a third home which they called *Oekonomie*, or Economy, a name that meant to them "Divine Economy," another term for the new order to come after the millennium. As before, Father Rapp predicted that he would build "a city in which God would dwell among men, a city in which perfection in all things was to be obtained."[19] Rapp told Frederick in a November 1824 letter: "And thus the true and divine human form will again appear and has really appeared. . . . Thus under a beautiful and clear sky," he wrote, "it will develop to that beautiful form of new and loftier plains."[20] By June 1825, all the Harmonists had arrived at Economy. They immediately purchased 2,186 more acres of land for $33,445, occupied the three houses that already were there, and started putting up new buildings of both log and brick. Within a year they were operating a cotton and woolen mill and a steam-powered flour mill.

In May 1826, the Duke of Saxe-Weimar visited Economy and wrote a vignette of the community. He described Father Rapp as "a large man of seventy years" whose "hair is gray but his blue eyes overshadowed by heavy eyebrows . . . full of fire and life," who spoke "in the Swabian dialect with some English mixed in."[21] Frederick was "a large good looking man" who directed the society's business activities. Residents warmed the workshops throughout the cold months by steam heat. Young girls sang in shops and mills and decorated each machine with fresh flowers. The duke commented on how "the neatness which universally reigns in Economy is in every respect worthy of praise."[22] Their order and discipline impressed another visitor, the German economist Frederick List. He noted how they were adding new industries of wine making, whiskey distilling, silk weaving, and hat making and were hiring outside laborers from Pittsburgh. They had a large warehouse where they stored manufactured articles for sale to outsiders and for community use. The building also stocked clothing and food. He described the 45-room Great House where Rapp presided over a colony that now had added a visitor's hotel, a brick music hall, schoolhouse, museum, post office, apothecary, 82 brick and frame houses, and a brick church with a towering steeple. In 1830, the sale of their products brought in $160,000, much of it from wine and whiskey. They took special pride in the manufacturing of silk. Based upon experiments in sericulture, or the making of silk from silkworms, they developed a cloth that was recognized in America and Europe for its superior quality. They had an orchestra of 18 musicians that played regular concerts in a community museum that housed a library with a collection of newspapers. That year Economy had 700 residents.[23]

But troubles started when the editor of a Pittsburgh newspaper claimed that the community had such an influence over local manufacturers and businesspersons that it was soon going to destroy all American competition. Political tensions also surfaced. In 1828, Economy men voted in a block for the Democratic presidential candidate Andrew Jackson, which the Pittsburgh Whigs condemned as subversive of American democracy for which every man was supposed to vote his conscience.[24] Inside the colony discontent against Rapp started to develop. Some people muttered that he and Frederick were cheating the society. Celibacy became another controversial issue. It had been adopted in 1807 as a preparation for the millennium and Rapp had always banished those who would not remain chaste. But in 1826 he began a sexual relationship with young Hildegard Mutschler, and even the most loyal members of the community could not ignore this unfairness, inconsistency, and hypocrisy.[25] Then there was the problem of the millennium. Rapp had predicted the precise time of the Second Coming to be on September 24, 1829. The day came and nothing happened. Many were demoralized. Rapp postponed doomsday until 1836.

A serious crisis hit in 1832 when Bernard Mueller, calling himself the Count de Leon, and 50 of his friends joined Economy. The count claimed to be the "anointed of the Lord" who would prepare the people for the year of divine manifestation four years ahead. Rapp believed him and warmly welcomed the group. Mueller, unfortunately, was a troublemaker. He said that Rapp had violated the terms of the Articles of Association and that "his teachings and his behavior contradict fully the word and law of God."[26] He proclaimed Rapp unworthy to continue as supreme director of the society. More alarming, he stated that celibacy, the "crucifixion of the flesh" he called it, would end in the new order after the millennium. By the early winter of 1832, over 250 members of Economy supported the count, including Christopher Mueller.

At that point, Rapp decided to get rid of the count, to buy him out. In an agreement reached in March he promised to pay the count $105,000 in three installments if Mueller and his followers would leave within three months and renounce all claims against the society. The count and 176 dissidents, about one-third of the community, agreed and relocated 10 miles away to start the "New Philadelphia Society." Soon afterward, the count tried unsuccessfully to sue Rapp for additional money. Failing that, he left New Philadelphia with a handful of followers to plan another community in Natchitoches Parish,

Louisiana, where, in 1836, he died. Some of the dissidents returned to Economy, but most of them reorganized under another leader, William Keil, and returned to the Midwest to try to build a communal utopia at Bethel, Missouri.[27]

Historians believe that the schism had a mixed impact on Economy. On one hand, Christiana F. Knoedler finds that the "insurrection proved a blessing in disguise, because it served to separate the dissatisfied members from the faithful. . . . Those who remained," she writes, "were henceforth devoted followers of Father Rapp, heart and soul."[28] On the other hand, Yaacov Oved thinks that it "was traumatic and left its members with a profound suspicion of every newcomer," especially of the Shakers who tried to initiate closer religious and cultural relations.[29] And Karl Arndt states flatly that although the "Harmony Society officially endured for seventy-four years after the 1832 schism, the Count de Leon affair marked the beginning of the end."[30]

Most likely it caused Economy to turn inward and reemphasize a life of humility, self-denial, and "each in honor preferring the other." More than ever the Harmonists made music the center of life, an expression of spiritual strength and ties of amity and love. Their choir and orchestra, without solo or virtuoso, performed anonymous works written by community members. They gave concerts on Saturdays and on festivals of the Anniversary (in February), the Harvest House (in August), and the Love Festival (in October). Led by Dr. Johann Christoff Mueller and William Peters, the orchestra soon gained a national reputation. By the late 1830s, it performed not only religious works but operas, symphonies, and choral pieces by composers such as Handel, Haydn, Mozart, Rossini, and Sterkel. Peters himself composed a symphony, "the earliest composition west of the Alleghenies."[31]

Music was the solace for loss of Frederick Rapp who, at the age of 59 and after a long illness, died on June 24, 1843. For the next 13 years Romelius L. Baker and Jacob Henrici took over his responsibilities as director of Economy's businesses. But Frederick was irreplaceable and the community went into economic and physical decline. When Father Rapp died on August 7, 1847, at the age of 89, there were only 288 residents of Economy. At that time they reorganized. Henceforth, a council of nine elders and two trustees (Baker and Henrici) controlled both economic and religious matters. But it was no substitute for Father Rapp's charisma. There was no replacing a man who had for so long been "the supreme arbiter in all questions that arose."[32]

The silk factory closed in 1852, and six years later the cotton factories shut down. An increase in the federal whiskey tax in 1862 meant the end of the profitable distillery. The trustees sold the factories and the distillery and used the money to invest in railroad and canal stock, and Economy rebounded somewhat. They drilled oil wells and refined kerosene that was the best in the nation: in 1868 alone they sold over 100,000 barrels of it. During the next five years, they drilled 73 more wells, some of which daily yielded 250 barrels of crude petroleum. They invested in coal mines in the villages of Connelton and Darbington. In 1869, they acquired 900 acres of land 30 miles from Pittsburgh and plotted a satellite village. They built factories to make cutlery, glass, steel, railroad cars, and bicycles with most of the work done by hired laborers.

But this increasing emphasis on economic expansion and profit changed Economy from a religious commune into a business enterprise. Original members died and the community admitted few newcomers because most applicants seemed to be interested only in getting a larger share of the community's wealth. When Charles Nordhoff visited Economy in 1874, he found only 110 adults (all over 40 years of age) and 20 adopted children. Hired men did most of the work.

In 1890, the colony elected 22-year-old John Duss as a junior trustee alongside Henrici. Duss had been born in Cincinnati and, after his father was killed in the Civil War, went with his mother to Economy when she joined as a war widow. Duss was educated in the community and then for 11 years he worked in the West at odd jobs as a laborer. In 1892, at Henrici's death, Duss became the sole trustee. Unfortunately, in that capacity he squandered much of the community's remaining capital on his own grandiose musical career. He employed outside musicians to expand the orchestra and named himself its conductor. He combined the colony orchestra with the one at Pittsburgh and then "spent a fortune on advertising [a] concert tour and presented himself as a 'musical wonder.'"[33] In the summer of 1903, using $20,000 of community funds without approval of the council, he arranged to have himself appear as a guest conductor of the New York Metropolitan Opera orchestra. Without approval of the colony, he spent $100,000 to make Madison Square Garden into a replica of Venice as the place for the performance. Afterward, he took the orchestra on a yearlong, coast-to-coast tour with all expenses paid by Economy. Then Duss left to become permanent leader of the "Duss Symphony Orchestra."

In his absence his wife, Susie, took his place as trustee. She immediately awarded her husband $50,000 as compensation for his tenure as head of the community for the previous 13 years. She persuaded the second trustee, Franz Gillman, to sign a document that gave her title to all of Economy's nonpersonal property, pending dissolution of the commune. In 1906, Duss returned and resumed, with his wife, the position of co-trustee. The couple immediately began the dissolution of the society. By then, however, they faced growing opposition.

Outsiders with claims against Economy went to court to prevent the conversion. A judge ruled that it was a religious charity and that the Commonwealth of Pennsylvania, not the Dusses, was legally its only heir. Eventually, in 1916, a compromise determined that Economy's assets would be divided evenly between the Dusses and the state. The couple lived the rest of their lives alternately in the Great House at Economy or in Florida, where John Duss composed religious music that he published in the Volkwein's Press of

Pittsburgh. Susie died in Florida and was cremated; her husband passed away at the age of 91 in 1935. "He was buried, according to Harmonist tradition," one student of Harmony music wrote, "in an unmarked grave in the Harmonist cemetery in Ambridge, Pennsylvania, with the ashes of his wife in an urn at his feet."[34]

The state used the money from the 1916 settlement to invest the Pennsylvania Historical and Museum Commission with funds to operate it as a historical site. So, as Oved observes, "it was the state of Pennsylvania that erected a monument for Harmony, not its members or their descendants."[35] "Thanks to organized preservation, restoration, and public interpretation efforts at historic Harmony, New Harmony, and Economy," Arndt writes, "the Harmonists' legacy may still be witnessed in their church buildings, cemeteries, private dwellings, communal dormitories, wine cellars, granaries, workshops, and re-created gardens."[36] In 2003, "Old Economy Village" included 17 restored buildings dating from the 1824 to 1832 period and the George Rapp Garden. It advertises itself as a reflection of the Harmonists' piety and economic discipline that enabled them to build one of America's longest-lived religious utopias.

BETHEL/AURORA

William Keil, a Prussian tailor, was born in 1812 and emigrated to New York City in 1836 with his wife. In 1838, they, with a year-old son, moved to Pittsburgh. There, he practiced medicine without a license, calling himself "Doctor Keil." After attending a revivalist meeting, he converted to the Methodist Church and abandoned medicine. Soon he became an evangelist preacher who claimed "miraculous powers from a book written in blood."[37] He said that salvation came from relying upon the literal interpretation of Scripture to prepare for the imminent Second Coming of Christ. He gathered a small following from the Rappites at New Philadelphia and converted German immigrants scattered throughout Pennsylvania, Ohio, and Kentucky. At that time the following had no formal rules of communal ownership but was simply a "voluntary association" that used the Bible as the sole guide to life. In 1844, they moved to 2,560 acres of newly opened federal land in Shelby County, Missouri, located on a wagon road 45 miles west of Hannibal. By the spring of 1845, all of Keil's followers arrived there from Pennsylvania and Keil laid down the guidelines of his communal society.

Bethel, meaning "the House of God," would remain a voluntary association without formal rules or regulations, only obedience to Keil's instructions. The association would seek no formal charter from the state of Missouri. Keil held title to all the land in his name. He kept no books or accounting records and there was no money exchanged inside the community; individuals just came to Keil and received food and clothing from a common storehouse. His rules on admission were open and casual. He would even admit individuals who had no religious convictions whatsoever, although in fact these recruits never stayed long in the community. Under the direction of Conrad Finck, followers formed a fine 30-piece cornet band that performed at Bethel and in towns in the area. Keil invited his American neighbors to join Bethel in its spring and fall festivals and to come to the colony to hear the choir.

The Bethelites quickly developed supporting industries such as a sawmill and gristmill, distillery, tannery, and sewing shop. Skilled cordwainers made gloves and shoes that were sold in national markets. They made wagons and sold them for a considerable profit to the thousands of Americans passing through the county heading for Kansas City and the start of the Oregon Trail. In a large brick and stone church with three bells Keil preached energetic sermons in German every Sunday, commenting on the Bible and emphasizing righteous living and self-discipline.[38] Their most profitable industry was distillation of corn and rye whiskey that they sold in Hannibal, Missouri, and Quincy, Illinois, for $.25 a gallon. Under the direction of Conrad Finck, they promoted German musical traditions with a cornet band and folk singing. By 1855, the community of about 650 sturdy Germans prospered, their assets were estimated to be worth $200,000, and their land holdings amounted to 4,000 acres.[39]

But Keil, like Rapp before him at New Harmony, became restless and apprehensive. He felt that if he wished to keep their community truly separate, they had to leave this increasingly crowded part of Missouri. As Keil later complained in a letter dated October 1855, because of the frequent contacts with outsiders their children were growing up "in a blasphemous and unspiritual life."[40] Therefore, he sent nine men to Oregon to survey an alternative place for his utopia. They found one near the mouth of the Willapa River, where they built some cabins and then returned to Bethel.

In the summer of 1855, Keil and a party of 150 colonists set out in covered wagons for a 2,000-mile trek to the Pacific. Keil's son, Wilhelm, had just died of malaria, and they carried him along, embalmed in alcohol, in a tin-lined coffin. When they reached the Willapa River in November, they buried the boy in a nearby forest.[41] The following spring Keil purchased 320 acres near the Pudding River on the road between Oregon City and Salem, within easy reach of markets in the two towns. He called it Aurora, after one of his daughters. Eventually, 252 Bethelites, about half of the community, went to Aurora, most of them in wagon trains but some by steamship around Cape Horn. Bethel remained under the control of deputies appointed by Keil. Unfortunately, most of its young people left soon afterward and it dwindled to about 150 members by the time Nordhoff visited it in 1871. He described it as made up of "simple Germans of the lower class" who "live comfortably after their fashion."[42]

Keil and his family lived at Portland while the colonists at Aurora cut trees, built more cabins, and started constructing his permanent home there, appropriately called *Das Grosse Haus* (the Big House). The men put up frame houses for people who wanted to live at Aurora, called "Dutchtown" by the Americans, although a number of families bought their own farmsteads. The colony had a small band that played in Butteville and Oregon City. At the Aurora school a university graduate named Karl Ruge taught the children in German and English. Keil held Sunday services at his home, where he preached, forceful as always, on brotherly love, self-sacrifice, and simplicity. By 1870, Aurora had a church with a 114-foot-high steeple, two mills, a hotel where the band gave concerts from a rooftop platform, a storehouse, and a community house for dances, concerts, and celebrations. More wagon trains arrived with immigrants from Swabia, Bavaria, and other parts of southern Germany. By 1872, the colony had over 1,000 members and owned 23,000 acres of land.[43]

Keil held all the property in his name, although he governed with a board of trustees under an 1868 written constitution. The men worked as hatters, tailors, cobblers, weavers, blacksmiths, millers, carpenters, cabinetmakers, and farmers. The women spun wool cloth, made candles, and wove straw baskets. Each family placed whatever it made or grew into a storehouse either to sell to Americans or to be used as a stockpile from which members could withdraw whatever was essential. As at Bethel, no money was exchanged. Life was pleasant. "They were living well," Eugene Snyder writes, "not working very hard, enjoying many small pleasures, and the leader was doing whatever worrying needed to be done."[44]

Keil, advancing in age, realized that Aurora was a community held together only by his presence and that it would not likely survive his death. So, in 1872, he divided the communal property, by giving deeds to each male family head, hoping that it would endure as a collective community if not a communal one. By then only three of his nine children, all sons, were alive, but none of them had any interest in Aurora. By then, too, most of the younger generation had left the colony, apparently more attracted to the diversions of American life than to Aurora's monotony and collective dependence.

In 1877, a year after Keil's death, the trustees, supported by a majority of the 250 adult members of the community, voted to dissolve the society. At the same time, Bethel sent out two representatives to discuss distribution of its assets. By June 1879, the two groups decided that Bethel and Aurora, still listed in Keil's name and valued at a total of $109,000, would be sold together. Everything was finalized by 1883. Aurora continued as a village of about 250 inhabitants, and Bethel incorporated as a Missouri town of 100 citizens who ran the store, mills, and shops.[45]

ZOAR

The same religious and political dissent in Germany that caused the Harmonists to immigrate to America brought members of the Separatist Society of Zoar to eastern Ohio. Their leader, Joseph Bäumeler, a charismatic, crippled hunchback, was, like Rapp, a farmer from Württemberg. Like the Harmonists, these Separatists endured government harassment because of their beliefs. They refused to send their children to Lutheran schools and, instead, taught them at home. They were pacifists and refused to perform the required military service. Some would not pay taxes. They were chiliasts and expected the millennium to occur in 1836. They denounced baptism and all the Lutheran sacraments. They saw marriage as just an agreement done orally before other church members. A few were vegetarians and some adopted celibacy.[46]

In 1817, 300 of them met at Hamburg to find a way to migrate to America, but only a few had money to pay for passage. Fortunately, a group of English Quakers heard of their plight and sympathized with a sect whose pacifistic views so closely approximated their own. These Friends told Quakers in and around Philadelphia about the Separatists and these American Quakers guaranteed reimbursement of the cost of passage, about $18 per person, when they arrived.

Soon after they landed in the city in August 1817 Bäumeler met Godfrey Haga, a merchant and land agent, who arranged for them to buy 5,500 acres of land in Tuscarawas County in northeastern Ohio for $25,000 paid in 15-year installments. The Quakers loaned them the money for the down payment and advanced them another $5,000 to cover costs of moving to the location. Bäumeler and a few men went to the site, erected some log cabins, and arranged to work as field hands for local farmers. They called it Zoar after the city to which Lot had fled from Sodom. To them the name indicated that their community was an oasis of purity in a world of sin.

Initially, Bäumeler had no intention of creating a communal society. But within a year he recognized that if they remained dispersed, working on farms in the region, they could not worship as a group to prepare for the millennium. Economic considerations also intervened. Some of the men, because of advanced age or sickness, were not able to earn enough money to support their families. So, on April 15, 1819, 53 men and 104 women signed a communal agreement. In creating the Society of Separatists of Zoar they abolished all private property and placed it under the control of trustees.[47] Women had equal voting rights with men. They adopted celibacy as a practical way to limit the size of the community in the face of their dire economic circumstances. It was seen as a means to limit growth and keep down expenses in order to pay the mortgage installments. So, at Zoar, unlike at the Harmonist colonies and Bethel/Aurora, communalism and celibacy were practical, not religious, matters. Consequently, 10 years later they abandoned it without much fuss when Bäumeler announced that he intended to marry his pretty, young housekeeper. Most Zoarites recognized by that time that however admirable celibacy might be, to forbid marriage meant a steady decline in their population and the eventual end of the community.[48] Still, everyone had to marry within the society, and those who found other mates had to leave.

In 1833, they received a charter from the state that replaced the 1819 agreement. Now three trustees, elected by men and women for three-year terms, governed Zoar. Under the charter, women could be elected to community offices. In making decisions the trustees had to consult with a standing committee of five men, chosen for five-year terms, that also functioned as a court of law. Zoar had an "agent general," Bäumeler, the only business contact with the outside and the colony treasurer who controlled all finances. The new charter created two kinds of members: one-year probationers and children in one class, and full members in the other. The probationers kept their property during the first year but had to turn over their cash to the trustees. They could, though, vote and hold office.

In church on Sunday morning everyone sang hymns and listened to Bäumeler's "discourses," not sermons. Published three years after his death in 1853 as *The Discourses*, the book summarized Zoar's essential beliefs. Bäumeler condemned all established religions and told his followers to maintain an inner morality. True Christians, he said, must prepare for the millennium by subduing passion and selfishness and must subordinate themselves to God. Ceremonies such as baptism and communion were "useless and injurious." He preferred "complete virginity" to marriage. One should never take oaths or send children "into the schools of Babylon, where other principles contrary to these are taught." Zoarites must refuse to "serve the state as soldiers, because a Christian cannot murder his enemy, much less his friend."[49] Like the Quakers, Bäumeler taught that all men were equal before God and, therefore, Zoarites should never bow or tip their hat in deference to any human.

Zoarites rose at daybreak, had breakfast at seven, lunch at noon, and dinner at six. After dinner they returned to their jobs until eight in the evening. In 1833, they helped construct the Ohio-Erie Canal across their lands with a contract from the state for $20,000. This money enabled them to liquidate their mortgage and to build a foundry, a water-powered milling factory, a stove factory, a dye house, distillery and cider press, and a tannery. They operated two blast furnaces located on the canal above and below the village. They made pig iron and castings that were shipped as far away as New York City. At the heart of the community was the general store and, across the street from it, a hotel. The latter could accommodate up to 80 guests and was regularly filled by crews and passengers on the canal boats. By 1835, Zoar had become a popular tourist attraction.[50]

By then it was a self-sufficient community. All of its food, except for tea, coffee, and rice, was produced there. It made all the clothing, except for some cotton women's dresses and men's hats. It fabricated the stoves that heated the buildings. Its cabinet shop crafted all the furniture. The tin shop made the kitchen utensils. The blacksmith shop produced the farm machinery. They made pottery and ceramics from local clay deposits. Hinds describes "immense fields of corn, wheat, oats and other crops." Over 1,000 sheep and 77 cattle were housed in a huge barn containing 104 stalls. Zoar had a large community garden with a central circle "surrounded by a thrifty well kept cedar hedge; from which radiate twelve triangular beds, in which one may notice the familiar petunias, balsams, verbenas, amaranths, dahlias, geraniums, etc."[51] Bäumeler's residence was a two-story brick structure with a balcony and cupola. Most of the other homes, however, were "common in style and material." Zoar's population increased to 500 when 170 new colonists arrived in mid-decade. In 1838, they had an estimated wealth of $2 million and owned 12,000 acres.[52]

Zoarites lived together in 27 multifamily homes. There was no communal kitchen or dining room, however, and the homes had eating facilities in a centrally located room. Each home sent a representative, as needed, to the communal storehouse, dairy, and bakery to pick up supplies in a "distribution room" where they were identified by house number. Children over the age of 5 lived away from their parents in dormitories, girls and boys separated. Until the age of 15 they attended a day school in a two-story brick building that was a part of the county school system. It was in session year-round and teachers, Zoar members, instructed the pupils in religion, reading, writing, mathematics, German, and English. Parents, though, had to provide the boys training in a trade and the girls experience in household duties.

Zoar had a 30-man brass band that played secular music, mostly Viennese waltzes and Wagner, both in the community and in surrounding towns. Two of the homes had pianos, and Peter Bimeler, Bäumeler's grandson, had a pipe organ in the flour mill where he was the supervisor. Music was their only real cultural activity, for they had little use for literature and had no library. In fact, they condemned fiction as carnal and frowned upon periodicals and newspapers. Zoar men drank an excellent strong beer that was made in the communal brewery on the northwest edge of the village. They were also served a pint of beer at four o'clock each day and it was always available during the heavy work such as log cutting, butchering, or harvesting. At the noon lunch the women, joined by the men, drank wine made from currants and grapes.[53]

When Bäumeler died in 1853, he was succeeded by Jacob Sylman, and then by Christian Weebel and Jacob Ackerman. Like the leaders who followed Rapp and Keil, none of these men measured up to the charismatic founder. And without Bäumeler's guidance many young people left. Some of them, such as Levi, another of Bäumeler's grandsons, turned on their parents and saw them as religious fools and bigots. Machine-made American goods steadily underpriced Zoar's handcrafted products. By the mid-seventies Zoar had just 300 members and had closed the dye house and iron stove factory.[54]

In 1898, the remaining members dissolved the society and a three-man commission divided its assets. Each person received $250 in cash and a share of the property worth $2,000. Most of them sold their inheritance and departed. Some older men and women stayed on and created an incorporated village.[55] Today, the Ohio Historical Society operates the Historic Zoar Village. It has restored 18 buildings and is in the process of renovating the hotel.

On weekends during April, May, September, and October its 10 museums are open to the public.

AMANA

Amana, or the Community of True Inspiration, was the fourth German Separatist communal utopia created in America. Although it started in the same place as the others, in Württemberg, its origins ran deeper, to the early eighteenth century when a group of peasants and simple craftspeople gathered under the inspirational preaching of Eberhard Ludwig Gruber and Johann Friedrich Rock, both of whom were, interestingly, from Lutheran clergy families. In 1714, they formed the Community of True Inspiration and emphasized the essential differences between true inspiration from God and evil inspiration, or temptation, from the devil. They believed that God through his *Werkzeuge*, or Instruments, would reveal this true inspiration. Although Gruber wrote some of the doctrines of Inspirationism, Rock was the one who claimed close contact with God. Together, until Gruber died in 1728 and Rock in 1749, they traveled in Germany, Austria, Switzerland, and eastern France preaching their revelations.[56]

The Inspirationists shared many of the beliefs of the other Separatists. They condemned the Lutheran Church as not based on true inspiration; but corrupted by state financial support and elaborate, useless rituals. They were pacifists. They relied on direct revelations from God and on a literal interpretation of the Bible. When membership in the Community of True Inspiration expanded, the authorities began to investigate it and serious harassment followed. This persecution, accompanied by the deaths of Gruber and Rock, caused the sect to decline. It did not revive until 1817 when other *Werkzeuges* appeared: Michael Krausert, a tailor from Strasbourg; Christian Metz, a carpenter; and Barbara Heinemann, a 22-year-old factory worker.[57]

With renewed activity under the leadership of these new Instruments, police surveillance resumed. Metz, in response, called his scattered congregations together at the town of Armenberg, where the men found work in the city's factories. But because they refused to send their children to the clergy-run schools and would not sign up for military service, the police threatened to arrest them. They left Armenberg and went to estates that Metz had leased near Ronnanburg, in Hesse, where their artisans and merchants made a living on the estates by selling their wares to other Germans. A few men found jobs on the farms. However, they were still a religious sect and not a communal society. "Property was not held in common at this time," Jonathan Andelson writes, "but a greater cooperation and a fuller sense of shared destiny began to develop."[58]

In the 1840s, magistrates hounded them for unpaid church taxes. Rents for the leased properties increased. To escape this situation Metz, in 1842, announced that they would immigrate to America. This decision was crucial to the formation of the Amana Community. Until then the Inspirationists had lived private lives and came to Ronnanburg from congregations scattered all over Germany and Switzerland. They might have elected to leave in small family groups. But immigration imposed a common bond. Since they spoke only German, they felt tied together for practical purposes in order to make a living in an English-speaking land. In addition, their recent, mutual experiences of persecution "coupled with the sense of mission that accompanied the prospect of immigration to America, created in the Inspirationists a high level of religious enthusiasm."[59] Finally, the German sense of *Gemeinde*, or community, made them feel like brothers and sisters, separate from the profane world.

In September 1842, Metz and four men sailed to New York City and then made their way to Buffalo. They purchased nearby vacant Iroquois land for $10 an acre and named it "Eben Ezer" after the Old Testament site mentioned in the first book of Samuel. The next spring the first contingent of 320 Inspirationists arrived, and soon another group of 217 immigrants followed. They purchased 4,000 more acres of land and subdivided Ebenezer into four villages: Middle, Upper, Lower, and New. At first Metz allowed members to keep their property. But when disagreements broke out between the prosperous members and the poor ones, he proposed a mutual sharing of all assets. He drafted a charter that created a communal society in which they shared all assets, except clothing and household goods. All land titles were turned over to 16 Trustees. Everyone worked without pay. The Trustees provided each member, through village officers, food and housing and a small allowance to buy personal items at the local store. Each village had its own government and ran its own school, store, and workshops. When some individuals opposed communal property, Metz cursed them as violators of God's inspiration (in other words, Metz's ideas) and expelled them. In the end, Andelson believes, by "adopting communalism the Inspirationists simply reconciled practical necessity with Christian tradition."[60]

Although Ebenezer made money from the sale of farm produce and woolen goods, Metz felt uncomfortable with the rapid increase of American settlers living near the colony. In 1854, when the city of Buffalo expanded its municipal boundaries to the edge of Ebenezer, Metz decided to sell out. He sent agents to the Mississippi Valley to see what land might be available. Some of the agents went to Kansas. But this was the time of the bloody "Kansas Civil War" over the expansion of slavery, and they decided that they could never find a safe place to live there. A second search party located 7,000 acres in central Iowa for sale by a group of German Brethren in St. Louis and 19,000 acres of contingent property. They contracted to buy the two parcels, pending the sale of their property in New York. Metz called the place Amana after the mountaintop vista mentioned in the Song of Solomon: "Come with me from Lebanon, my spouse . . . look from the top of Amana." By 1865, over 1,300 people, including new immigrants from Germany, had moved from Ebenezer and were living together under a charter from the state of Iowa that incorporated them as a communal society.

Duplicating Ebenezer, they laid out seven villages, each about a mile and a half apart: at Amana, East Amana, Middle Amana, High Amana, West Amana, South Amana, and Homestead. As before, each village was a separate unit, and, under Metz and Barbara Heinemann, who succeeded him in 1861, the villages prospered. Each village looked pretty much the same. It had four-apartment family homes, community kitchens, a church, a school, general store, meat plant, and farm buildings. Amana, the central and largest village, had a woolen and soap factory, a textile mill, a tannery, and flour and sawmills. When Nordhoff came there in 1874, he found a prosperous utopia of 1,480 people living in the villages, each with workshops for shoemakers, tailors, and blacksmiths. The woolen mill turned out high-quality blankets, flannels, socks, and gloves. The textile mill produced a high-quality calico cloth died in indigo patterns. They sold all sorts of items to local markets: soap, lumber, shingles, and laths. Their farms produced cereals, vegetables, fruit trees, and they raised herds of sheep, cattle, pigs, and horses and flocks of chickens.[61]

They ate in communal dining halls: Amana, for example, had 15 such halls for its 450 inhabitants. A bell summoned everyone to meals—breakfast at six-thirty, lunch at eleven-thirty, dinner at six o'clock—where they sat at separate locations for men, women, and children. Under the direction of a woman "kitchen boss," teams of young girls cooked and served the food. The older women tended the kitchen garden, while others looked after the sewing. "There is but little conversation at table," Nordhoff writes. "The meal is eaten rapidly but with decorum; and at its close, all stand up again, someone gives thanks, and thereupon they file out with quiet order and precision."[62]

They educated the children, separated by sex, from the ages of 6 to 13 at a village school. From seven until eleven-thirty in the morning, male teachers instructed them in arithmetic, reading in English, and writing. They taught them crafts and musical notation, but forbade playing an instrument. A certain anti-intellectualism permeated the colony. One man told Nordhoff: "Why should we let our youth study? We need no lawyers or preachers. . . . What they need is to live holy lives, to learn God's commandments out of the Bible, to learn submission to his will, and to love him." They did, however, send a few young men outside the colony to be trained in medicine, pharmacy, and dentistry. The Amana Society had no libraries and subscribed to only a few newspapers. Like the Zoarites, they were simple German peasants and crafts-people who attended church services 11 times a week and who were "quite, a little stolid, and very well satisfied with their life."[63] If this way of life was not satisfactory to any member, that person was free to leave. Amana was in this sense an open community. As Metz had said: "A doorway to the world is always open for those who do not wish to obey."[64]

After Heinemann died in 1883, the community reorganized. Thirteen Trustees, elected annually by the men, chose a president, and together, meeting annually, they ran the community. Women could not vote or hold office. In every village elders and an elected foreman supervised the work and kept accounts that they submitted each year to the Trustees. At each village the elders gave adult men an annual stipend of between $40 and $100, depending on need. Each woman received $25 to $30, and a child was worth $5 to $10. With these funds the head of the household purchased the necessities of life in the village store.

The men had a patriarchal, if not condescending view, of women. One of Amana's rules warned: "Fly from the society of women-kind as much as possible, as a very highly dangerous magnet and magical fire." The community condemned dancing because "at the best there is sin."[65] Women could have no jewelry, had to wear drab clothing, and had to keep their hair tied back and covered in a black cap. The sexes were separated both at village meetings and church services, where they came and left the room separately. Amana made special efforts to discourage teenage contact between the sexes and tried strenuously "to hide the charms of the young women, to make them, as far as dress can do so, look old and ugly, and to keep the young men away from them."[66] The colony discouraged marriage as containing "a certain large degree of worldliness." No man could marry until he was 24 years of age. Even so, most of the young people, unlike the other Separatist communities, remained at Amana; or if they left the community, most soon returned. Apparently, they were satisfied with its security, regularity, peacefulness, and austere morality.[67] Amana's population declined slightly over the years from a peak of 1,813 in 1881 to 1,365 in 1932, and some of those who stayed in the community strayed. Teenage boys played baseball or, worse, cards; and young women fixed their hair and wore bright-colored clothing. More disturbing, "young couples manage to arrange for trysts away from the eyes of their parents or their elders." Still, many Amanites "followed most of the rules most of the time."[68]

Other pressures added to the internal tensions. As the American population around Amana increased and roads and railroads reached the colony, the "circle around the community designed to keep the world out" started to weaken.[69] It became something of a tourist attraction that annually drew thousands of visitors. One sign of trouble was the disappearance of the traditional German dress. Men began to wear the clothes of midwestern farmers, and conventional skirts and blouses and long hair replaced the women's drab attire and hairstyle. Young people acquired cars, radios, and other worldly items. Without the inspirational leadership of a Metz or a Heinemann, religious enthusiasm waned. Some members purchased farms outside of Amana and others worked full-time away from the community. During World War I, their pacifism went against the intense patriotism of the conflict, and many Americans became resentful and hostile toward the colony.

When the Great Depression seriously curtailed production of Amana products, the community faced bankruptcy. Its unpaid debts by 1931 amounted to over $500,000. The Trustees created a Committee of Forty-seven to recommend a solution to the crisis. It came up with two choices. They could recommit to the communal way of life, oust all dissenters, and try to get by on an austere budget. Or they could reorganize as a joint stock company, guarantee salaried work for shareholders, and continue just as a religious sect. Seventy-five percent of the adults, men and women, voted to reorganize in what they called the "Great Change." Between July 1931 and May 1932, they put the plan into effect. They abolished the communal eating houses. They divided the society's assets of about $2 million into shares with each share worth $50. They distributed a parcel of 1,200 nonnegotiable voting shares to every adult. They divided another batch of shares "according to different criteria and the majority (32,400 shares) were distributed according to seniority." They became "the foundation of member's property, providing them with the means to acquire homes and cattle."[70] From then on Amanites worked for wages and lived as ordinary Americans, but the religious life in the seven villages continued as "The Amana Church Society."[71]

BISHOP HILL

The last Separatist community that emerged from discontent with the Lutheran Church in Europe took shape in the 1850s in Henry County, Illinois. Called Bishop's Hill (after the founder's birthplace in Sweden) and later just Bishop Hill, it was led by Eric Jansson, a self-proclaimed preacher who interpreted Scripture to the poor peasants of Uppland and Hälsingland. Alice Felt Tyler portrays him as a strikingly ugly individual "of middle height, pale with sunken cheeks, long prominent teeth, and a scarred forehead, hypnotic blue eyes, and twitching facial muscles."[72] In 1830, at the age of 22, this emaciated, rheumatoid young man fell from a horse and heard God ordain him as the "vicar of Christ" who would found a New Jerusalem. Afterward, he said that he could perform miracles such as exorcising the Devil and curing disease. He foretold the imminent end of the world. He preached perfectionism, that anyone who was truly saved would lead a sinless life. He denounced the Lutheran clergy as "pillars of hell." He led marches of hymn-singing peasants along public roads and gathered them together in front of parsonages to pray aloud for the occupants, the "arch purveyors of the devil." At the towns of Alta and Forsa they burned religious books in a "glorious jubilee."[73]

Such radicalism caused the clergy to have Jansson arrested twice in 1846, and they convinced the government to confiscate farms owned by his followers. This persecution, plus some growing opposition to Jansson's eccentricities within the sect, made him decide to leave Sweden. He sent Olof Olsson, a trusted friend, to America to find a place for his New Jerusalem. Olsson contacted a Swedish Methodist clergyman in Victoria, Illinois, and arranged to buy land on the open prairie some 12 miles north of the town. He wrote to Jansson that the place was "like the Kingdom of Heaven. . . . It contains all that is good and free," he continued, "a land where the laborer, as well as the regent, may eat his loaf of white bread."[74]

In the spring of 1846 a migration of what eventually amounted to about 1,400 Janssonists began, 1,000 of whom left Sweden during the first year. Arriving at New York City, they traveled to Albany, moved across the Erie Canal, and then took lake steamers to Chicago. From there they walked 100 miles south to "Bishop's Hill." Only about 400 colonists completed the journey, however. Many died from disease in the crossing. Others just stayed in New York after they discovered that they could not suddenly speak in English as Jansson had promised.

In Illinois they endured the first deplorable winter living in 25-by-18-foot dugout caves where often 40 people huddled, freezing against the bitter cold. Each morning at dawn, Jansson called everyone out for a sermon and admonished them to have faith in him. He predicted wealth and riches and promised a rapid growth of their church into the thousands before the end of the world arrived. Cholera, which had struck down many during the immigration, ravished the settlement, killing 150 Janssonists including Mrs. Jansson and two of her children. Conditions were so awful that the next year over 300 members left the colony.[75]

But those who remained survived, and by the end of 1849 they had constructed brick living quarters and a large, three-story frame church. They planted crops on 700 acres of land. But the food was insufficient to feed the colony and Jansson required periods of fasting and temporary celibacy to keep the numbers down. In 1850, in an abrupt change of mind, he arbitrarily reinstated marriage, paired off couples "regardless of personal likes or dislikes," and married all of them in group ceremonies.[76] Only "100 men, 250 women & girls, and 200 children" were there in the summer when lawyer Britton A. Hill sent these figures to the state government. Later that year, though, the U.S. census marshal recorded only 406 inhabitants. Still, new immigrants, encouraged if not misled by letters the colonists sent to friends and relatives, continued to arrive. By 1856, one estimate had about 800 people living at Bishop Hill.

The community's most important activity was weaving flax into linen and carpets, an important source of income until cotton cloth manufactured in New England became available. Then the Janssonists grew Indian corn and broomcorn, crops suited to Illinois's soil and climate. They purchased from the Pleasant Hill Shakers a herd of several hundred Durham cattle, a breed that grazed well on prairie pastures. They constructed a four-mile railroad spur to Galva to connect with the Rock Island and Peoria Railroad so that they could directly ship their products by rail to these cities. They used a highly organized communal labor force of men and women who, in teams, planted the crops, operated the brickyard, and built bridges and ponds.

In 1936, Minnie C. Norlin, in a biography of her mother, a colonist named Catherine, depicted the role women played in the spring planting. They took positions at the end of 24 rows of long markers, held at the other end by a man. "Toeing this marker," each woman "had folded up one corner of her apron and tied it securely, making a little bag. This held the seed corn. With a hoe, in rhythmic time she made a hole and dropped in the seed. The marker was then moved ahead for the next hole and thus this human check-row planter moved steadily on."[77] One visitor, John Swainson, watched the operation firsthand. "In one place," he wrote, "we noticed fifty young men with the same number of horses and plows cultivating a cornfield where every furrow was two miles in length. . . . They moved with the regularity of soldiers," he marveled.[78] Other young men in groups of 30 to 40 milked the cows and drove the oxen.

From the sale of broomcorn alone they received a yearly income of $50,000. With the money they purchased more land, and by 1859 they owned over 11,000 acres valued at $400,000. They constructed additional brick buildings. In quick succession appeared the 96-room dormitory called Big Brick, a hotel, a wagon shop, bakery, blacksmith shop, meat storage house, a brewery, an apartment house called the Steeple Building, and an administrative building. Another visitor, Baron Axel Adelsward, in 1856 observed: "They seem to live contented and happy. . . . They are capable and hard-working, and to join together, as they have done, is a sure way to amass wealth in America, although it seems to me they can have precious little joy for their riches."[79]

He was right. Life in Bishop Hill was rigorous and regimented. Families lived in apartments but ate food prepared in communal kitchens and dining rooms. Big Brick, the largest building, had 72 family rooms and several dining rooms. Members rose each day for a two-hour religious service before going to breakfast in Big Brick. They had lunch there at noon, a "supper" at four o'clock, and the evening meal at six. The dining rooms, a visitor from the Icarian colony at Nauvoo in 1859 wrote, were "clean; the tables are covered with white table-cloths; the plates and dishes are of porcelain, the glasses shining, etc."[80] The men and women sat at separate tables and the children ate in a different room. The men said the grace in unison and then the women sang a hymn. Their attire, made by the women, was simple. Women wore blue drilling on workdays and calico on Sunday. Men wore woolen or denim pants and shirts all the time. Every member of the colony annually received two suits of clothing and one pair of boots and shoes.

Unlike the German Separatist communities, they hired an American to teach the children English and made the youngsters memorize the names of American presidents and the counties of Illinois. Young women of the colony, such as Jansson's 14-year-old daughter, instructed them in basic arithmetic and writing skills with both sexes together, at first in the church and later in the steeple building. The colony did not have its own school, though, until 1862, after the dissolution of the community. At the age of 14 the children joined one of the work units.[81]

Sunday religious services were held at ten in the morning and at seven in the evening and opened with hymn singing and a prayer. Then Jansson preached on the meaning of Scripture and reviled anyone caught not paying rapt attention. Jansson at times even subjected God to abusive language. During one sermon, delivered when extensive rains threatened to delay construction of a dam, he yelled: "If You, O God, do not give good weather so that we can finish the work we have at hand, I shall depose You from your seat of omnipotence, and You shall not reign in heaven or on earth, for You cannot reign without me!"[82]

Bishop Hill suffered an irreversible setback in Jansson's unexpected death. In 1849, he tried to break up a marriage between his cousin and an American named John Root after the man left the colony and took his wife along with him. Jansson formed a posse that pursued the pair and brought her back to Bishop Hill. Root organized his own posse, surrounded the colony, and threatened to burn it down if Jansson did not surrender his wife. Jansson refused. Root backed off. Later, both Jansson and Root went to the Henry County courthouse on separate business. While the court was in session, Root, during a recess, went outside and, through an open window, shot Jansson in the head. The colonists placed Jansson's body on the altar of the church and for three days kept a vigil, fully expecting that he would, as promised, rise from the dead. But the effect of the summer heat on the corpse soon proved otherwise, and they interred him in the colony cemetery. Jansson's wife tried to get her 12-year-old son named as his successor, but the colony chose Jonas Olsson and a group of trustees instead.[83]

Olsson, it turned out, was just as arbitrary and domineering as Jansson. In 1854, he imposed celibacy by fiat, prohibiting new marriages and commanding married couples to abstain from sexual intercourse. He expelled individuals who would not, or could not, obey him. Olsson, on his own, had the colony incorporated with himself, as chief trustee, and his close friend Olof Johnson in control of community finances. For a while Bishop Hill seemed to prosper. But when the Panic of 1857 severely reduced its income, the members discovered that they were on the verge of bankruptcy. They also discovered that Olsson and Johnson, without approval, had spent $98,000 speculating in railroad and bank stock and other investments, most of which were now almost worthless. The adult males voted to dissolve the charter.[84]

Between 1860 and 1862, they made a detailed inventory of land, buildings, Galva real estate, livestock, implements, and tools, and they listed total community assets of $846,278. Legal matters of dissolution delayed the final division of the assets until 1869. By then most Janssonists had left Bishop Hill to live as American citizens throughout the Midwest. Some joined the Pleasant Hill Shakers, others joined a nearby congregation of Adventists, and still others became strong supporters of Robert Ingersoll, the noted agnostic from Peoria. Only about 200 Janssonists remained at the colony. In the 1870s, Nordhoff described it "slowly falling into decay" and its inhabitants strangely reticent about their history.[85] By 2003, much of the colony was reconstructed under the auspices of the Bishop Hill Heritage Association and the Old Settlers Association, with financial support of the state of Illinois and private benefactors.

NOTES

1. Karl J. R. Arndt, "George Rapp's Harmony Society," in *America's Communal Utopias*, ed. Donald E. Pitzer (Chapel Hill: University of North Carolina, 1997), p. 57. Arndt was the foremost authority on the Harmonists both in Europe and America. His works include 10 published monographs, which are, in alphabetical order: *Economy on the Ohio, 1826–1834: George Rapp's Third American Harmony* (Worcester, Mass.: Harmonie Society Press, 1984); *George Rapp's Disciples, Pioneers, and Heirs: A Register of the Harmonists in America*, ed. Donald E. Pitzer and Leigh Ann Chamness (Evansville: University of Southern Indiana Press, 1994); *George Rapp's Harmony Society, 1785–1847* (Rutherford, N.J.: Farleigh Dickinson University Press, 1972); *George Rapp's Re-established Harmony Society: Letters and Documents of the Baker-Henrici Trusteeship, 1848–1868* (New York: Peter Lang, 1993); *George Rapp's Separatists, 1700–1803: The German Prelude to Rapp's American Harmony Society* (Worcester, Mass.: Harmonie Society Press, 1980); *George Rapp's Successors and Material Heirs, 1847–1916* (Rutherford, N.J.: Farleigh Dickinson University Press, 1971); *George Rapp's Years of Glory: Economy on the Ohio, 1834–1826* (New York: Peter Lang, 1987); *Harmonie on the Connoquenessing, 1803–1815: George Rapp's First American Harmony* (Worcester, Mass.: Harmonie Society Press, 1980); *Harmony on the Wabash in Transition to Rapp's Divine Economy on the Ohio and Owen's New Moral World at New Harmony on the Wabash, 1824–1826* (Worcester, Mass.: Harmonie Society Press, 1982). His articles on the communities include "Luther's Golden Rose at New Harmony, Indiana," *Concordia Historical Institute Quarterly* 49 (Fall 1976): 111–22; "George Rapp's Harmony Society," *Communities: Journal of Cooperation*, no. 68 (Winter 1985); and with Richard D. Wetzel, "Harmonist Music and Pittsburgh Musicians in Early Economy," *Western Pennsylvania Historical Magazine* 54 (1971): 2–4. His most recent contribution, "George Rapp's Harmony Society," pp. 37–87, was published posthumously in 1997.

Other sources on the Harmonists are John Archibold Bole, *The Harmony Society: A Chapter in German American Culture History* (Philadelphia: Americana Germanica, 1904); Aaron Williams, *Harmony Society at Economy, Pennsylvania, Founded by George Rapp, A.D. 1805* (Pittsburgh: W. S. Haven, 1866; reprint, New York: AMS Press, 1971); Hilda A. Kring, *The Harmonists: A Folk-Culture Approach*, ATLA Monograph Series, no. 3 (Metuchen, N.J.: Scarecrow Press and American Theological Library Association, 1973); Christiana F. Knoedler, *The Harmony Society: A 19th Century American Utopia* (New York: Vantage Press, 1954); Lucy Jayne Kamau, "The Anthropology of Space in Harmonist and Owenite New Harmony," *Communal Societies* 12 (1992): 68–89; Tonya K. Flesher and Dale L. Flesher, "The Contributions of Accounting to the Early Success of the Harmonists," *Communal Societies* 4 (1984): 109–20; Richard D. Wetzel, "Harmonist Music between 1727 and 1832: A Reappraisal," *Communal Societies* 3 (Autumn 1982): 65–84.

2. Arndt, "George Rapp's Harmony Society," p. 60.

3. Ibid. p. 61.

4. Ibid., pp. 72–90; Knoedler, *Harmony Society*, pp. 6–8; Donald E. Pitzer and

Josephine M. Elliott, "New Harmony's First Utopians," *Indiana Magazine of History* 75, no. 3 (September 1979): 228–30; John C. Andresshon, trans. and ed., "The Arrival of the Rappites at New Harmony," *Indiana Magazine of History* 42 (1948): 83–89.

5. Arndt, *Harmony Society*, pp. 62–66; Knoedler, *Harmony Society*, pp. 8–18; Oved, *American Communes*, pp. 70–71; Williams, *Harmony Society*, pp. 48–59.

6. Williams, *Harmony Society*, pp. 60–61; Arndt, "George Rapp's Harmony Society," p. 66.

7. See Arndt, *Harmony Society*, pp. 133–40, on the purchase of the town of Harmony.

8. Knoedler, *Harmony Society*, p. 16; Pitzer and Elliott, "First Utopians," p. 227; John W. Larner, Jr., "Nails and Sundrie Medicines: Town Planning and Public Health in the Harmony Society, 1805–1840," *Western Pennsylvania Historical Magazine* 45 (1962): 225.

9. The mansion is described in Elias P. Fordham, *Personal Narrative of Travels in Virginia, Maryland, Pennsylvania, Ohio, Indiana, Kentucky; and of a Residence in the Illinois Territory, 1817–1818*, ed. F. A. Ogg (Cleveland: Arthur H. Clark, 1906), p. 207.

10. Arndt, "George Rapp's Harmony Society," p. 68 and *Harmony Society*, pp. 172–79; Oved, *American Communes*, pp. 436–38.

11. Melvin R. Miller, "Education in the Harmony Society, 1805–1905" (Ph.D. diss., University of Pittsburgh, 1972), p. 203. Rapp's *Thoughts on the Destiny of Man* is found in Williams, *Harmony Society*, app. G.; Lauer and Lauer, "Sex Roles," p. 20.

12. Miller, "Education," p. 200; Richard D. Wetzel, *Frontier Musicians on Connoquenessing, Wabash, and Ohio: A History of Music and Musicians of George Rapp's Harmony Society, 1805–1906* (Athens: Ohio University Press, 1976); Arndt, "George Rapp's Harmony Society," pp. 70–72; Oved, *American Communes*, pp. 393–97, 414–20; Stephen A. Marini, "Hymnody in Religious Communal Societies of Early America," *Communal Studies* 2 (1982): 12–13.

13. For a full discussion of education in Harmony, see Arndt, *Harmony Society*, pp. 290, 335, 337, 359–60; Arndt, "George Rapp's Harmony Society," pp. 70–71; Donald E. Pitzer, "Education in Utopia: The New Harmony Experience," in *Indiana Historical Society Lectures 1976–1977: The History of Education in the Middle West*, ed. Donald E. Pitzer and Timothy L. Smith (Indianapolis: Indiana Historical Society, 1978), pp. 77–78, 82–90.

14. Arndt, *Harmony Society*, p. 205; Oved, *American Communes*, pp. 449–58.

15. Arndt, *Harmony Society*, p. 205; Oved, *American Communes*, pp. 70–71.

16. Tyler, *Freedom's Ferment*, p. 123.

17. Arndt, "George Rapp's Harmony Society," p. 74; Lucy Jane Kamau, "Neighbors: Harmony and Conflict on the Indiana Frontier," *Journal of the Early Republic* 11 (Winter 1991): 507–29.

18. On the sale to Robert Owen, see Arndt, *Harmony Society*, pp. 287–301 and "George Rapp's Harmony Society," p. 74. See also Donald E. Pitzer, "The Original Boatload of Knowledge down the Ohio River: William Maclure's and Robert Owen's Transfer of Science and Education to the Midwest, 1825–1826," *Ohio Journal of Science* 89 (December 1989): 134.

19. Arndt, *Harmony Society*, p. 308.

20. Ibid., p. 309.

21. Knoedler, *Harmony Society*, p. 24.

22. Ibid., p. 25.

23. Arndt and Wetzel, "Harmonist Music," pp. 2–4.

24. Arndt, *Harmony Society*, pp. 400–415.

25. Ibid., 425–32, 475.

26. Ibid., p. 475.

27. Ibid., pp. 499–546, and Arndt, "George Rapp's New Harmony," pp. 76–78; Oved, *American Communes*, pp. 73–74.

28. Knoedler, *Harmony Society*, pp. 30–31.

29. Oved, *American Communes*, p. 78.

30. Arndt, "George Rapp's Harmony Society," p. 78.

31. Oved, *American Communes*, p. 75.

32. Williams, *Harmony Society*, p. 40. Rapp's death is described in Arndt, *Harmony Society*, pp. 596–601.

33. Oved, *American Communes*, p. 80.

34. Wetzel, *Frontier Musicians*, p. 134.

35. Oved, *American Communes*, p. 81.

36. Arndt, "George Rapp's Harmony Society," p. 82.

37. On William Keil's background, see Eugene Edmund Snyder, *Aurora, Their Last Utopia* (Portland, Ore.: Binford & Mort Publishing, 1993), pp. 7–13. See also Adolf E. Schroeder, *Bethel German Colony 1844–1883* (Bethel, Mo.: nd).

38. H. Roger Grant, "Missouri's Utopian Communities," *Missouri Historical Review* 65 (October 1971): 23–24; William G. Beck, "A German Communistic Society in Missouri," *Missouri Historical Review* (October 1908–January 1909): 58–61; Lauer and Lauer, "Sex Roles," p. 25.

39. Beck, "German Communistic Society," p. 64; Snyder, *Aurora*, pp. 29–46; Oved, *American Communes*, pp. 95–97; David Nelson Duke, "The Evolution of Religion in Wilhelm Keil's Community: A New Reading of Old Testimony," *Communal Societies* 13 (1993): 45–70; Julie Youmans, *The Musical Life of Bethel German Colony 1844–1879* (Bethel, Mo.: Historic Bethel German Colony, 1990).

40. Snyder, *Aurora*, p. 50.

41. The touching journey to Oregon with the coffin of young "Willie" is described in Tyler, *Freedom's Ferment*, pp. 127–28. See also Snyder, *Aurora*, pp. 47–62.

42. Nordhoff, *Communistic Societies*, p. 329; Robert J. Hendricks, *Bethel and Aurora: An Experiment in Communism as Practical Christianity* (New York: Press of Pioneers, 1933), pp. 51–57; Grant, "Utopian Communities," p. 29.

43. Snyder, *Aurora*, pp. 63–73.

44. Ibid., p. 81; Grant, "Utopian Communities," pp. 29–31; Nordhoff, *Communistic Societies*, pp. 319–23, 328; Oved, *American Communes*, p. 98.

45. Snyder, *Aurora*, pp. 97–106; William Alfred Hinds, *American Communities and Cooperative Colonies* (Philadelphia: Porcupine Press, 1975), pp. 334–39; Nordhoff, *Communistic Societies*, p. 328. Alice Felt Tyler claims that in 1883 there were 300 inhabitants of Bethel and 250 inhabitants of Aurora. See Tyler, *Freedom's Ferment*, p. 126.

46. The most recent scholarly treatments of the Separatists of Zoar is Kathleen Fernandez, "The Separatists Society of Zoar," *Communities: Journal of Cooperation*, no. 68 (Winter 1985); and Hilda Deschinger Morhart, *The Zoar Story* (Dover, Ohio: Seibert, 1967) and *Zoar: An Ohio Experiment in Communalism* (Columbus: Ohio Historical Society, 1997). Earlier but useful studies of the community are E. J. Bognar, "Blast-furnaces Operated by the Separatist Society of Zoar, Ohio," *Ohio State Archaeological and Historical Quarterly* 39 (1930): 503–13; Catherine R. Dobbs, *Freedom's Will: The Society of the Separatists of Zoar—An Historical Adventure of Religious Communism in Early*

Ohio (New York: William-Frederick Press, 1947); George B. Landis, "The Separatists of Zoar," *American Historical Association, Annual Report* (1898): 165–220; Wilfred Free McArtor, "Arts and Industries of the Zoarites, 1817–1898" (Master's thesis, Ohio State University, 1939); Edgar B. Nixon, "The Zoar Society: Applicants for Membership," *Ohio State Archaeological and Historical Quarterly* 45 (1936): 341–50 and "The Society of Separatists of Zoar" (Ph.D. diss., Ohio State University, 1933); Emilius O. Randall, *History of the Zoar Society* (Columbus, Ohio: Press of Fred J. Heer, 1904).

47. Morhart, *Zoar Story*, pp. 16–28; *Zoar: An Ohio Experiment*, pp. 17–20; Randall, *History*, pp. 97–98; Oved, *American Communes*, pp. 82–83; Nordhoff, *Communistic Societies*, pp. 99–108.

48. Nordhoff, *Communistic Societies*, p. 108.

49. Ibid., pp. 103–4.

50. Morhart, *Zoar: An Ohio Experiment*, pp. 21–25; Oved, *American Communes*, pp. 438–39.

51. Hinds, *American Communities*, p. 25.

52. Morhart, *Zoar: An Ohio Experiment*, pp. 27–37; Oved, *American Communes*, pp. 449–53.

53. Morhart, *Zoar: An Ohio Experiment*, pp. 37–51; Nordhoff, *Communistic Societies*, pp. 103–13; Arndt, *Harmony Society*, p. 69; Randall, *History*, pp. 27–30; Morhart, *Zoar Story*, pp. 16–28; Oved, *American Communes*, p. 418.

54. Morhart, *Zoar: An Ohio Experiment*, pp. 57–62.

55. Hinds, *American Communities*, pp. 129–31; Morhart, *Zoar: An Ohio Experiment*, pp. 63–73; Oved, *American Communes*, pp. 84–87.

56. Walter Grossmann, "The European Origins of the True Inspired of Amana," *Communal Societies* 4 (1984): 133–49; Donald F. Durnbaugh, "Ebehard Ludwig Gruber and Johann Adam Gruber: A Father and Son as Early Inspirationists Leaders," *Communal Societies* 4 (1984): 150–60. Jonathan G. Andelson is the foremost authority on Amana communalism. His publications include "The Community of True Inspiration from Germany to the Amana Colonies," in *America's Communal Utopias*, ed. Donald E. Pitzer (Chapel Hill: University of North Carolina Press, 1997), pp. 181–203; "Introduction: Boundaries in Communal Amana," *Communal Societies* 14 (1994): 1–6; "What the Amana Inspirationists Were Reading," *Communal Societies* 14 (1994): 7–19; "Postcharismatic Authority in the Amana Colonies: The Legacy of Christian Metz," in *When Prophets Die: The Fate of New Religious Movements*, ed. Timothy Miller (Albany: SUNY Press, 1991), pp. 29–45; "Tradition, Innovation, and Assimilation in Iowa's Amana Colonies," *Palimpsest* 69 (Spring 1988): 2–5; "Living the Mean: The Ethos, Practice, and Genius of Amana," *Communities: Journal of Cooperation* 68 (Winter 1985): 32–38; "The Gift to Be Single: Celibacy and Religious Enthusiasm in the Community of True Inspiration," *Communal Societies* 5 (1985): 1–32; "The Double-Bind and Social Change in Communal Amana," *Human Relations* 34 (1980): 111–25; "Routinization of Behavior in a Charismatic Leader," *American Ethnologist* 7 (1980): 716–33.

Other recent articles on Amana include Lanny Haldy, "In All Papers: Newspaper Accounts of Communal Amana, 1867–1924," *Communal Societies* 14 (1994): 20–35; Metin M. Cosgel, "Market Integration and Agricultural Efficiency of Communal Amana," *Communal Societies* 14 (1994): 36–48; Peter Hoehnle, "With Malice toward None: The Inspirationists Response to the Civil War, 1860–65," *Communal Societies* 18 (1998): 62–80; Barnett Richling, "The Amana Society: A History of Change," *Palimpsest* 58 (1977): 34–47; Gary D. Carman, "The Amana Colonies: Change from Communalism to Capitalism in 1932," *Social Science Journal* 24 (1987): 157–67. Standard monographs are Diane L Barthel, *Amana: From Pietist Sect to American Community* (Lincoln: University of Nebraska Press, 1984); Lawrence L. Rettig, *Amana Today: A History of the Amana Colonies from 1932 to the Present* (Amana, Iowa: Amana Society, 1975); Bertha M. Shambough, *Amana That Was and Amana That Is* (New York: Benjamin Blom, 1932); Philip E. Webber, *Kolonie-Deutsch: Life and Language in Amana* (Ames: Iowa State University Press, 1993).

57. Oved, *American Communes*, pp. 87–88; Barthel, *Amana*, pp. 8–16.

58. Andelson, "Community of True Inspiration," pp. 181–86; Nordhoff, *Communistic Societies*, pp. 25–28.

59. Andelson, "Community of True Inspiration," p. 187; Nordhoff, *Communistic Societies*, pp. 29–30.

60. Andelson, "Community of True Inspiration," p. 189, and "Living the Mean," pp. 176–77; Frank J. Lankes, *The Ebenezer Society* (West Seneca, N.Y.: West Seneca Historical Society, 1963).

61. See Andelson's Ph.D. dissertation for a detailed analysis of Amana's economic organization: "Communalism and Change in the Amana Society, 1855–1932" (Ann Arbor, Mich.: University Microfilms, 1974). See also Cosgel, "Market Integration," pp. 37–48; Robert Edwin Clark, "A Cultural and Historical Geography of the Amana Colony" (Ph.D. diss., University of Nebraska, 1974), pp. 121–33; Nordhoff, *Communistic Societies*, p. 32.

62. Nordhoff, *Communistic Societies*, p. 33.

63. Ibid., p. 34.

64. Andelson, "Community of True Inspiration," p. 193.

65. Nordhoff, *Communistic Societies*, p. 52.

66. Ibid., p. 35.

67. Andelson, "Gift to Be Single," pp. 20–23, 27–32.

68. Andelson, "Community of True Inspiration," pp. 195–96.

69. Shambough, *Amana*, p. 362.

70. Oved, *American Communes*, p. 94.

71. Carman, "Amana Colonies," pp. 160–67; Henry Schiff, "Before and After 1932: A Memoir," *Communal Societies* 4 (1984): 161–64; Shambough, *Amana*, pp. 377–481; Rettig, *Amana Today*.

72. Tyler, *Freedom's Ferment*, pp. 133–34.

73. Ibid., p. 134.

74. Jon Wagner, "Eric Jansson and the Bishop Hill Colony," in *America's Communal Utopias*, ed. Donald E. Pitzer (Chapel Hill: University of North Carolina Press, 1997), pp. 297–300; Oved, *American Communes*, p. 106 n. 95 discusses the Swedish Pietists; Hinds, *American Communities*, pp. 340–42; Nordhoff, *Communistic Societies*, pp. 343–44; M. A. Mikkelsen, *The Bishop Hill Colony: A Religious Communistic Settlement in Henry County, Illinois* (Baltimore: Johns Hopkins University Press, 1892), pp. 1–30; see also Silvert Erdahl, *Eric Jansson and the Bishop Hill Colony* (Philadelphia: Porcupine Press, 1972); George M. Stephenson, *The Religious Aspects of the Swedish Immigration* (Minneapolis: University of Minnesota Press, 1932); Paul Elmen, *Wheat Flour Messiah: Eric Jansson of Bishop Hill* (Carbondale: Southern Illinois University Press, 1976); Olov Isaksson, *Bishop Hill: A Utopia on the Prairie* (Stockholm: L. T. Publishing House, 1969); John S. Lindberg, *The Background of the Swedish Immigration* (Chicago: University of Chicago Press, 1930); Charles H. Nelson, "The Erik Janssonist Movement

of Pre-Industrial Sweden," *Sociological Analysis* 38, no. 3 (1977): 209–25; Wayne Wheeler, "Eric Janssonism and Freedom in Nineteenth-Century Sweden and America," *Western Illinois Regional Studies* 12 (Fall 1989): 7–15. For a listing of extant published works on the colony in 1989, see Robert P. Sutton, ed., "Bibliography of English Language Publications on Bishop Hill," *Western Illinois Regional Studies* 12 (Fall 1989): 105–8.

75. Wagner, "Bishop Hill Colony," pp. 300–302; Nordhoff, *Communistic Societies*, pp. 344–45; Mikkelsen, *Bishop Hill*, p. 30; H. Arnold Barton, "The Eric-Janssonists and the Shifting Contours of Community," *Western Illinois Regional Studies* 12 (Fall 1989): 16–19.

76. Wagner, "Living in Community: Daily Life in the Bishop Hill Colony," *Western Illinois Regional Studies* 12 (Fall 1989): 71.

77. Quoted in Wagner, "Living in Community," p. 67.

78. Ronald E. Nelson, "Bishop Hill: Swedish Development of the Western Illinois Frontier," *Western Illinois Regional Studies* 1 (Fall 1978): 116; Wagner, "Bishop Hill Colony," pp. 305–6.

79. Nelson, "Swedish Development," p. 118; Nordhoff, *Communistic Societies*, pp. 344–45; Ronald E. Nelson, "The Bishop Hill Colony: What They Found," *Western Illinois Regional Studies* 12 (Fall 1989): 36–45.

80. Elise Schebler Dawson, "The Folk Genre Paintings of Olof Krans as Historical Documents," *Western Illinois Regional Studies* 12 (Fall 1989): 82–104; Ronald E. Nelson, "The Building of Bishop Hill," *Western Illinois Regional Studies* 12 (Fall 1989): 46–60; Wagner, "Living in Community," p. 73.

81. Wagner, "Bishop Hill Colony," pp. 310–13; Oved, *American Communes*, p. 100; Lilly Setterdahl, "Emigrant Letters by Bishop Hill Colonists from Noma Parish," *Western Illinois Regional Studies* 1 (Fall 1978): 121–75.

82. Quoted in Tyler, *Freedom's Ferment*, p. 137.

83. Oved, *American Communes*, p. 100; Wagner, "Bishop Hill Colony," pp. 306–7.

84. Oved, *American Communes*, pp. 102–3; Wagner, "Bishop Hill Colony," pp. 309–10.

85. Nordhoff, *Communistic Societies*, pp. 348–49; Wagner, "Bishop Hill Colony," pp. 313–15.

CHAPTER 4

Oneida Perfectionists

The second major religious communal utopia erected by Americans was at Oneida, New York. Like the Shakers, the Oneidians were millennialists and perfectionists who believed that they could lead a sinless life by inner illumination while preparing for the Second Coming. In contrast to the celibate Shakers, though, they encouraged sexual intercourse in "complex marriage." Or, as John Humphrey Noyes, Oneida's founder and charismatic leader, explained in an 1837 letter to a friend: "In a *holy community*, there is no more reason why sexual intercourse should be restrained by law, than why eating and drinking should be, and there is little reason for shame in one case as in the other."[1]

Noyes was born in 1811 at Battleboro, Vermont, the first son of a Dartmouth College professor and U.S. congressman and a deeply religious mother. When he was 10 years old, the family, then including several of his younger brothers and sisters, moved to Putney, a small town 10 miles north of Battleboro, where the senior Noyes ran a prosperous grocery business. While a teenager, John Humphrey showed an intense uneasiness around women, a "curious combination of intimacy and distance," in Lawrence Foster's words.[2] He enrolled at Dartmouth, was elected to Phi Beta Kappa, and in 1830 gave a speech at his commencement. For a year he read law under Larkin Mead, his brother-in-law, at Chesterfield, New Hampshire. Then, in September 1831, he attended a four-day revival at Putney held by the fiery evangelist Charles Grandison Finney. The next day, sick in bed, he prayed, read the Bible, broke out in a cold sweat, and experienced the ecstasy of a conversion. He abandoned the law and enrolled at Andover Theological Seminary.

While at Andover, Noyes confided to his diary: "Oh God! Cleanse thou me from secret faults." He was tormented by dreams of fights between God and the Devil and "was ready to sink under the infirmities of flesh and spirit." He agonized about his "desperate wickedness" and condemned his classmates as worse off than he, as mired in "levity, bickering, jealousy . . . and worldliness and pride and unholy ambition."[3] In the fall of 1832, he transferred to Yale Divinity School.

At Yale he tried to avoid these torments by forcing himself to study 16 hours a day, but the old nightmares returned. This time, though, he suddenly realized that even the worst sinner could be saved by repentance and complete acceptance of Christ's promise to lift the burden, and guilt, of sin. Scripture showed him that everyone must try to live the perfect life and reach the condition of complete surrender in which "*all* the affections of the heart are given to God, and in which there is no sin." This epiphany came one afternoon when he came across a crucial passage in the New Testament: "The Holy Ghost shall come upon thee and the power of the Highest shall overshadow thee; therefore also that holy thing which shall be born of thee shall be called the Son of God." To Noyes these words meant the promise of the "baptism of the Holy Spirit and the second birth." That evening, rejuvenated, he preached to a small congregation of the New Haven Free Church about his experiences. Then, afterward, while lying in bed, "three times in quick succession a stream of eternal love gushed through my heart. . . . Joy unspeakable and full of glory filled my soul." Noyes believed that he was saved, cleansed of sin, free from all human laws, and under a covenant with God in which he could do no wrong. When the faculty of the Divinity School heard about Noyes's perfectionist theology, they first revoked his temporary license to preach and then expelled him; so did the Free Church congregation.

With no future as a minister, Noyes formed a partnership with John Boyle, another New Haven Free Church pastor who had been dismissed for similar preaching. Together they began publication of a monthly newspaper called the *Perfectionist.*[4] Then for three years he wandered about New England and New York asking clergymen for permission to preach to their congregations. Most ignored him. He ended up in 1837 in a locked room of a New York City boardinghouse, where he went through three weeks of turmoil. Assaulted repeatedly by Satan, he wrote in his *Confession of a Religious Experience*, published in 1849, he was blasted by "strange thoughts" that "coursed through my brain, [that] finally settled into a strong impression that I was about to part with flesh and blood." He laid down to die. He stopped breathing. Suddenly, near the "very borders of Hades and then in the last agony" the terror turned to joy. However, intermittent seizures continued and relatives, fearing that he was going insane, brought him back to Putney. There, he gradually recovered and organized a discussion group among friends and family members called the Bible School.[5]

Foster believes that this period of Noyes's life was filled with intense sexual anxiety and that this tension was the cause of his psychic turmoil. No doubt Noyes felt torn by the conflict between his sexual urges and his conviction that he was a reborn Christian free of sinful desires. He was able to rationalize this tension by applying "the same principles to sexual relations that he had to understanding religious truths."[6] He concluded that sex, like any other of life's activities, when engaged in by Christians living together in a holy community, could be shared freely and blamelessly among all members. He condemned celibacy as a perversion. "The Shaker," he wrote, "with a prurient swollen imagination of the importance of the act, pronounces it a damnable abomination prohibited to the saints."[7] While at Putney, Noyes developed more ideas on sexual behavior, such as male continence and complex marriage, that he eventually published in 1847 as *The Berean: A Manual for the Help of Those Who Seek the Faith of the Primitive Church*. It "became the Perfectionists bible."[8]

The 74-chapter book contained the essence of his Perfectionist theology, although not the final word on it since Noyes would later write a number of other articles on the perfectionism. Frequently citing the Old and New Testaments, especially Paul, he argued Scripture as interpreted by inspired men was the key to understanding God's word. Noyes believed that the Second Coming had already happened in A.D. 70, at the time of the destruction of the Temple in Jerusalem and the great dispersal of the Jews. But after that event Christians had strayed into apostasy. Therefore, all current churches were invalid and perfection on earth had never been achieved, although Paul and a few early Christians had been perfect. A second, final, Judgment Day was now about to happen, he said, and the church at last "is now rising to meet the approaching kingdom in the heavens, and to become its duplicate and representation on earth."[9]

What should be done in 1847? Through prayer, careful reading of the Bible, and concentration on God's goodness one could have a second birth, a profound awareness of Christ in one's soul that would produce an acute sense of perfection. Even though perfect, sin was still a possibility because humans had an inner and an outer self. Fortunately, the inner self was purified by the religious experience, the "confession of Christ" he called it, that enabled a person to get control of the sinful outer self. "We are bound to wait on it [the inner self]," Noyes wrote, "to give it the benefit of our power and wisdom in providing for it good influences."[10] The result: behavior modification, the elimination of sinful conduct, and the appearance of the "ideal man." This ideal man would have contact with what Noyes called "invisible spirits" and God, and they together "would teach him more than he could ever learn from other men."[11] Most important, the ideal man would joyfully relish the experiences of life, since life itself was God's gift.

In the chapter "Love of Life" he wrote about sex and marriage. He claimed that it was natural to have "frequent congress of the sexes, not for propagative, but for social and spiritual purposes." Intercourse was "the order of nature for the gratification of ordinary amative instincts."[12] A man would have intercourse with a woman but through self-control, or "male continence," avoid a climax and ejaculation. Noyes likened it to a process in which a "skillful boatman," when approaching the rapids above the waterfalls, struggles with the current "in a way that will give his nerves a severe trial" and avoids plunging the boat over the waterfalls. It might be a difficult skill, he admitted, but if "he is willing to learn, experience will teach him the wisdom of confining his excursions to the region of easy rowing" unless, of course, he *wanted* to go over the falls.[13] He thought that such training should be provided to young men by women past menopause, while older men should instruct teenage girls in the technique. Male continence, therefore, was a form of birth control and of enjoying sexual intercourse without worrying about the consequences.

Noyes justified his concept of complex marriage by arguing that nothing in Scripture required a permanent union to only one person at a time. In fact, he thought monogamy actually went against the New Testament's emphasis upon universal love. Saint Paul, he pointed out, had argued that it was absurd to believe that Christians who "should be allowed and required to love in all directions" would be "forbidden to express love in its most natural and beautiful form, except in one direction." God had given us sexual appetites "to give love more intense expression than is possible between persons of the same sex." Open sex was practiced in heaven because, Noyes asked, how could God "abandon that design by unsexing his children, or impede it by legal restrictions on sexual intercourse in the heavenly state?" Besides, monogamy was boring and "gives to sexual appetite only a scanty and monotonous allowance." Lapsing into metaphor as he had when expressing himself on male continence, Noyes wrote that just because "a man loves peaches is no reason why he should not, on suitable occasions, eat apples or cherries." In a fellowship of perfect Christians traditional marriage was not only tedious but disruptive and incompatible with its communal purpose for existing. "Love, in the exclusive form," he wrote, "has jealousy for its complement and jealously brings on strife and division."[14]

Mutual criticism was another integral part of perfect Noyes's perfectionism. It involved daily evening meetings of the community during which a person's weaknesses would be brought into the open and acknowledged by the individual. This way, Noyes asserted, annoying personality differences could never fester and become serious irritants within the community. In these self-help encounters each person evaluated everyone else, and the one receiving criticism had to listen to all comments without responding. Any topic was appropriate for review: health, physical appearance, cooperation in the workplace, attitudes toward the community, theology, and sexual performance. Foster, in assessing the long-range importance of mutual criticism later at Oneida, saw it as "the chief means of informally establishing and sustaining community cohesion and norms."[15]

One of the early converts who came under Noyes's spell was Harriet A.

Holton. A bashful, 29-year-old well-to-do woman from nearby Westminster, Vermont, she had gone through a conversion in 1831 after attending a revival, had renounced "special attachments to persons," and had committed herself to universal love. Three years after her conversion, at the age of 23, she read one of Noyes's early essays in the *Perfectionist*, "The Second Coming of Christ," and promptly declared herself free from sin forever. She broke her engagement with a widower who lived in Mississippi, telling him that now "cleared of all special attachments to persons; she loved everybody."[16] In the spring 1835, she heard Noyes preach at Putney and was captivated by his ideas. But at this first meeting this woman with sad eyes and turned-down mouth apparently made little impression on Noyes. He later wrote that there "was no particular love of the sentimental kind between us."[17] Nevertheless, he knew that she was infatuated with him, and that she had money.

In January 1838, he sent her a business-like letter proposing "a partnership which I will not call marriage till I have defined it" properly. He thought that they were already "one with each other and with all saints." Calling her his "yoke-fellow," he predicted that she, as his wife, would "love all who love God ... as freely as if she stood in no particular connection with me."[18] He expected her to allow him the same freedom. After listing her "desirable qualities," especially her "faith, kindness, simplicity and modesty," he confessed that despite his past "irregularity" and "seeming instability" he was ready to get married. Harriet immediately wrote her "morning star in the theological heaven" to accept. She said that her only hope was to be "blessed" with his "society and instruction as long as the Lord pleases and when he pleases."[19] On June 28, 1838, Larkin Mead married them at Chesterfield, New Hampshire. The couple then moved to Putney to be close to the Bible School and members of Noyes's family.

With Harriet's property as collateral, John Humphrey secured a loan and purchased a printing press to start a fortnightly paper called the *Witness*, later renamed the *Perfectionist* (the first *Perfectionist* had gone defunct in early 1838 when Boyle closed the press and took a job in a machine factory), and then the *Perfectionist and Theocratic Watchman*. It became the vehicle for Noyes to spread his ideas to a small audience in the Northeast, some of whom came to Putney to join the Bible School, which by 1841 probably involved not more than a dozen people. That winter Noyes's father, before his death, bequeathed a total of $20,000 (including two farms) to his four children, all of whom were members of the Bible School. With these funds as capital Noyes formed the "Putney Corporation," consisting of himself, his brother, and two brothers-in-law. He invited interested persons to join the "Society of Inquiry." By 1844, it had grown to include 28 adults and 9 children.

A typical day began with a five o'clock breakfast (the only meal prepared and served by the women; the other two meals were buffets). After breakfast they read the Bible for about a half hour and then went to their jobs on the farms, in the print shop, or in a small store where they sold produce. In the afternoon they met again to discuss Scripture and other topics such as the history of the Holy Land.[20] They organized the community on what Noyes labeled "Bible Communism." Like Charles Fourier, with whose doctrines he was fully conversant, Noyes wanted to make work as pleasant as possible by frequently changing assignments. Like Fourier, he saw manual labor as equal in value to intellectual pursuits. But unlike Fourier, Noyes did not see human regeneration as coming from a new environment; it came from a religious experience after which true Christians could create a perfect society. "The sole purpose of such a community as had taken shape at Putney," Spencer Klaw writes, "was to make it easier for its members to live a true Christian life and to spread the truth about God's intentions for the world."[21]

The Putney Corporation was like a religious family in which Noyes ruled as a father to protect it from "the disorderly doings of individual members." However, Noyes was a paternal autocrat who claimed that God had selected him for the position and that his followers must accept all his decisions. "He allowed no opposition to his doctrines," Maren Carden observes, "even his sisters submitted to his choice of husbands for them . . . not even the mother escaped: he demanded that she humble herself to his will and cease trying to manage the family."[22] Noyes predicted that the Second Coming was to occur soon and that everyone must exert a special effort to prepare for it by creating a "community of hearts."

The "community of hearts," it turned out, meant implementing complex marriage, and the first example of this arrangement was Noyes's relationship with Mrs. Mary Cragin. Mary, along with her husband, George, was one of the new recruits to the Putney community. Then 35 years of age, she was a deeply religious woman who was often suicidal because of guilt over recurring "evil passion" and "sexual desire." Yet she was "a woman of great warmth and vivacity, with a huge capacity for loving."[23] In any event, one evening in May 1846 Noyes and Mary went for a walk and sat on a rock to rest. Noyes later remembered that God inspired him right then to have intercourse with her but that he hesitated, momentarily. On the way back to the village, he later wrote in his *My First Act in Sexual Freedom*, "we stopped and took some liberty of embracing, and Mrs. Cragin distinctly gave me to understand that she was ready for the full consummation." They went home and met with Mr. Cragin and Mrs. Noyes to ask their permission to proceed. George was understandably upset but soon acquiesced and approved; so did Harriet. Noyes remembered that the discussion ended amicably, "that we gave each other full liberty all around, and so entered into complex marriage in the quartette form."[24]

Soon other couples, first Noyes's two sisters and their husbands, entered into complex marriages, all with Noyes's approval. Not everyone received his sanction, however, because he insisted that since complex marriage brought couples nearer to God, it could not be practiced by anyone who would feel guilty. For example, he refused for six months to allow John Miller, one of his brothers-in-law, the dispensation. Everyone linked in the "partnership" had to share his or her reactions to it. But, Noyes warned, no one outside of the community must ever learn of what was going on.[25]

The secret held for about a year. In the fall of 1847, Noyes made a terrible mistake. Trying to recruit another brother-in-law, Daniel Hall, to the "community of hearts," he described to him the details of its sexual freedom. Hall went to the state's attorney at Battleboro and had the county sheriff arrest Noyes on the charge of adultery. Noyes posted bail, was released, and bragged that he looked forward to the chance to get his ideas about his Christian community into the open, at court. His sister Harriet, Daniel's wife, wrote to their mother that John Humphrey was "radiant" and "walking with elastic buoyancy . . . midst shout and laughter."[26]

But Noyes was in deep trouble. A local minister denounced him as a "hydra-headed monster." Other Putney citizens called for a town meeting to decide how to break up the community. Larkin Mead, when he found out what had been going on, refused to believe that anyone in his family was guilty of adultery. Nevertheless, in a letter to John Miller he advised that if the charges were true "the sooner [Noyes] is shut up in some kind of prison the better for all concerned."[27] From Battleboro, Mead sent another letter suggesting that Noyes leave the state immediately. Noyes agreed and moved to Hamden, Connecticut, to live with friends. The next morning, at two o'clock, the Cragins quietly slipped out of Putney to join him. They left behind their two-month-old baby, Victor, whom Noyes had sired with Mary the previous winter, when the current had pulled him over the waterfalls.

When the good neighbors of Putney heard of the escape, they held more "indignation meetings" and sent the community an ultimatum. They insisted that Miller and George Noyes, John Humphrey's brother, both of whom stayed behind as de facto leaders, stop publication of the *Perfectionist*, sign a confession that they had broken the law, and promise forever to abandon complex marriage. The two men refused to confess but agreed never to mention complex marriage again. Noyes, by then living with other friends in New York City, wrote to Miller to assure him that they had done the right thing to compromise. However, he stated, there could be no backing down on their conviction and that "the Kingdom of God has commenced, or acknowledging that we have done wrong."[28] Time passed and things returned to normal at Putney.

Meanwhile, from New York City Noyes searched for another location for his community, hopefully far from meddlesome neighbors where he could practice Bible Communism in peace. He found it in January 1848 in western New York on land that had been purchased by the state from the Oneida Tribe and then sold to Americans. Jonathan Burt, a born-again Christian, had bought one of these parcels near Oneida Creek and had erected a sawmill. By the fall of 1847, Burt, his wife, and three families—about a dozen adults and their children—were operating a lumber business and trying to start their own perfectionist community. When Burt read of the Putney episode in the local newspapers, he wrote to Noyes and offered his place as a refuge.

Noyes met with Burt and told him that if he moved his community there he alone would be in charge and would insist on total obedience. Burt agreed. Noyes gave him $500 as a contribution to start "a New York community" and then moved in with the Burts. "Everything comprises to bring about concentration here," he confided to George Cragin in a letter. "I have the confidence of all now" because they realized that "my 'tyranny' instead of being an annoyance is highly useful in protecting them from the wolves."[29] Noyes told him that he was going to purchase a farm of 23 acres just across the road from the Burt house.

Over the next 18 months, 31 adults and 14 children came to the site. By January 1849, 87 men, women, and children were living at the "Oneida Association," its legal name by that time. The adults were from all over the Northeast and came from a wide variety of backgrounds. Most of them, as their 1853 publication *Bible Communism* phrased it, were "sober, substantial men and women of good previous character and positions in society." Their occupations included a former Methodist minister, a printer, trap maker, architect, wagon maker, gunsmith, carpenters, cabinetmakers, shoemakers, and several farmers. Robert S. Fogarty's study of Oneida shows that most of them joined the community not because of its unorthodox sexual system but for compelling psychological reasons. They were young, in their twenties and thirties, and had undergone a conversion experience after which they were unable to live comfortably in normal society. They had been on an "emotional roller coaster," Lawrence Foster writes, of high hopes of salvation and the deep despair over sinfulness. They found Oneida's structured yet sheltering environment, and Noyes's firm leadership, a way to "overcome the disorder they experienced and to become resocialized to a more secure and satisfying way of life."[30]

The physical center of Oneida was the Mansion House. Eventually completed in 1869, it was a colossal structure designed and built by experienced architect Erastus Hamilton who, along with John Miller, managed Oneida when Noyes was away. The first floor contained kitchen and dining areas, laundry, library, and sitting and study rooms. On the second floor, just above the dining area, was the printing office where they published their periodical the *Circular.* Also on this floor, in the front, was a large auditorium, called the Family Hall, with a stage and balcony. To the north of it across a stairway and hall was a formal parlor surrounded by small chambers where sexual intercourse or "interviews" took place. At night men actually *slept* in a second-floor dormitory and women went to similar quarters on the third floor. Children lived in a separate building, until 1869, when a special wing for them was added to the Mansion House. Nordhoff, when he came there in 1872, remarked on the simplicity of the Mansion's interior. "All the rooms are plainly furnished," he wrote, "there being neither any attempt at costly or elegant furnishings, nor a striving for Shaker plainness." Directly across the road in front of the Mansion House was the nursery and school, a laundry, and a building with rooms for offices, a chemical laboratory, and lectures. Next to these structures they placed barns, stables, a silk-dye shop, and a small factory for children who, in their leisure time, made boxes for silk spools, embroidered slippers, and fashioned men's hats.[31]

The workday began with breakfast, served at eight o'clock. The only other meal was a dinner at four in the afternoon at which groups of a dozen men, women, and children sat at round tables, each with food placed on a lazy Susan. They had meat only twice a week and Noyes proscribed hard liquor and tobacco. Men had no special dress requirements, but the women cropped their hair just below the ears and wore bloomer pants with knee-length skirts. Nordhoff thought their appearance "fatally lacking in grace and beauty." Mothers cared for their children until weaned and then placed them in the nursery. At the school male and female teachers instructed the older children in the Bible and in history, grammar, French, Latin, geology, and other academic subjects.[32]

Oneida's economic success was in part caused by the huge influx of capital donated by new members that, by 1857, amounted to about $108,000. It was also based on the effective business leadership of John Miller. A "gifted farmer and economist" with the shrewd instincts of a Yankee trader, he was able to combine their radical religious convictions with conservative ideas of free enterprise capitalism. Miller diversified their agriculture and developed a profitable industry of canning corn, peas, tomatoes, jams, and jellies. They made rustic outdoor furniture of twisted cedarwood designed by Charles Ellis, one of their own. They manufactured traveling bags, designed by Noyes, and brooms.

In 1848, their blacksmith, Sewall Newhouse, crafted a steel trap. It became so popular with hunters east of the Mississippi and with mountain men in the Rockies that within a few years Oneida had orders for up to 400 traps a month. Newhouse, to fill these requests, had some men help him in the forge from time to time. But in 1854, Noyes asked William Inslee, a machinist, to find a better way of making them by machine. Inslee designed a water-driven press that stamped out the trap parts and completely eliminated hand hammering a bar of steel 120 times for each trap. He made special traps for beavers, bears, and moose. Soon Oneida was selling over 100,000 traps annually, and profits peaked in 1865 when they made 275,000 of them. That year they moved production to a factory located about a mile north of the Mansion House. Oneidians boasted of their economic success in the *Circular*, in which they claimed that "fine mechanical skills and inventive genius are [developing] curious and wonderful machines which do their work rapidly and in the most perfect manner."[33]

Their ingenuity rivaled the Shakers. They invented the first lazy Susan, a mechanized mop wringer, potato peeler, and washing machine. The women contrived the flat-soled shoe to replace the high-heeled lace boot of the day. They made the first garter belt. They installed their own steam cookers, silk-spinning machinery, and Turkish baths. Their horticulturalist, Henry Thacker, landscaped the grounds around the Mansion House according to plans that Frederick Law Olmstead used for New York's Central Park—shaded paths, hedges, formal garden, ascending elms, and trimmed lawns on which they placed their rustic chairs and tables. In 1866, they purchased raw silk and started to spin thread on water-powered machines in the same factory where they manufactured the traps. Production outran their own capacity to provide enough workers, though, and by 1862 they had to hire over 160 local men and women to run the factories and 35 field hands to help on the farm. Nordhoff found that these hired workers did most of the unpopular tasks such as jobs in the laundry and furnace room. But, he conceded, the Oneidians "pay good wages, and treat their servants kindly; looking after their physical and intellectual well-being, building houses for such of them as have families and need to be near at hand, and in many ways showing interest in their welfare."[34]

Every member of the community believed that work was an expression of an unending search for moral perfection. They thought that the order and simplicity of mechanization and landscaping reflected harmony and beauty. The *Circular* declared that "simplicity, absence of pretension, and the straight forward adaptation of means to end, will ultimately prove . . . in all things else, to be the truest standard of taste."[35] Noyes agreed with Fourier that all labor should be enjoyable, a "sport, as it would have been in the original Eden state."[36] So, he allowed each person to pick the job he or she wanted and often permitted the Oneidians to determine how many hours they would stay at that task. Jessie Kinsley later recalled her varied routine. She waited on tables, washed dishes, swept and dusted, filled lamps and helped in the dairy, laundry room, and infirmary. She canned fruit and cared for the children. "All these labors and others not remembered," she wrote, "came and went and came again as time passed by."[37] Since the assembly-line tasks were monotonous, Noyes insisted on rest periods to play games, take walks outside, or read. No one ever stayed at a single assignment for longer than a few weeks, unless by choice. Noyes enjoyed hard physical work and moved around from job to job. There were no wages until 1862, when he started giving each adult a modest allowance. Until then everyone, regardless of what he or she did, had an equal share of community food, clothing, and housing. They received whatever they needed by sending a note to the appropriate committee in charge of the item, and a coat, window curtain, chair, footstool, and so forth would be provided.[38]

Slackers were a rarity. Once in a while Noyes had to censure someone for not doing his or her fair share. For example, he reproached William Inslee for thinking he was too good to do the unskilled tasks in the trap factory. Community pressure was another powerful force for work discipline. One Oneidian confessed that because of the "strong current here which favors activity" he found it impossible not to want to work hard. Besides, he said, "if I wanted to be lazy I should choose some other place." Or, as the *Circular* put it, the "great secret of securing enthusiasm in labor . . . is contained in the proposition, 'loving companionship and labor, and especially the mingling of the sexes, makes labor attractive.'"[39]

Evening convocation in the Family Hall was a combination of a communal meeting and religious service. On stage a meeting leader, who sat next to Noyes, opened with a group song and then a fife and drum trio played martial music. The first part of the agenda usually involved business matters, such as consideration of new applications, finances, building maintenance and construction, and care of the children. The other part of the evening focused on moral and religious issues. It began with an extemporaneous speech by Noyes called "Home Talks" on topics such as patience, meditation, humility, and prayer. If he were not present, then the leader would read from one of his publications. Then, when appropriate, they engaged in mutual criticism.[40]

Mutual criticism at Oneida, unlike the earlier practice at Putney, could be a grueling experience that, as Noyes put it, would "make crooked sticks straight." Sometimes the criticism was general and they analyzed problems in the abstract. At other times they selected special individuals as examples of spiritual deficiencies such as vanity, pride, or "a softness of the heart." Small groups, usually chosen by the person to be criticized, did the evaluation. But Noyes expected every adult from time to time to stand before the entire group for a review. He punished any individual who refused to comply by restricting his or her opportunity for sexual intercourse.[41]

The *Circular* described the tone of mutual criticism as compassionate and considerate, "as soothing as a mother's touch," and always accompanied by praise of the person's redeeming qualities. Unfortunately, though, much of what was said was scathing. People were castigated for egotism, laziness, frivolity, and a preoccupation with personal appearance that they called "body tending." They told one man to improve his way of talking and not to be so arrogant and abrupt. They scolded an adolescent because he "talks for effect and walks for effect, he flourishes his handkerchief for effect; takes out his letters and watch for effect." They cautioned one woman that she was "gross in her alimentiveness." Another was condemned for her "indolence and vanity." They censured a third for not being "virgin-like" because she talked too much about her sexual partners. They criticized an old gentlemen for his "stiffness of character" and, of all things, for having "not enough vivacity."[42]

Nordhoff thought that mutual criticism was the "main instrument of government," a way to eliminate "uncongenial elements" and make those who stayed there remain in "harmony with the general system and order."[43] Some Oneidians could not take this regimen and left. Most accepted it and wrote up their responses as testimonials that were published in the *Circular*, where they all conceded that they were much better off for having gone through the ordeal. Jonathan Burt said it enabled him to be humble, the way a true Christian should be. Another confessed it made him able to control "a dreamy imagination, which made me prone to build castles in the air." A young woman said it changed her whole personality by destroying her selfishness. Another woman called "S" had "found Christ in her heart . . . [and] delights in the society of her superiors."[44] Some Oneidians claimed almost miraculous effects from the criticism. The *Circular* told of how a girl who had undergone the process had her earache cured. A woman who suffered from back problems and fever felt better afterward because, she said, it "literally separated me from the spirit of the disease that was upon me." Harriet Noyes believed that it cured her psychological depression or "the hypo" where for years the "evil eye" had "transformed good into evil." A few, although remaining loyal Oneidians, were not so sure. One women wrote that "the mental chaos" of the criticism was enough to make her "go away by myself to take thought and cry a little."[45]

Mutual criticism was based upon unwritten rules of conduct that Noyes made sure everyone understood. First of all, Christians had a duty to please God and not themselves. He admonished them not to pursue happiness "too directly." They must be cheerful and praise others. He demanded "pliancy of will" and censured one man, the *Circular* reported, because he was boring and his conversation "labored, tedious, and awkward." On the same point Noyes told a woman to lighten up, to make her conduct "more refreshing." Noyes insisted on ruthless suppression of egotism. John Sears, to overcome his own weaknesses in this regard, had to stop using the first-person pronoun. Noyes was particularly worried about "diotrephiasis," or excessive competition in trying to outdo the other person. He punished Frank Wayland-Smith, whose preoccupation with playing the violin had become an obsession, by locking the instrument in a closet. Another unwritten canon was complete obedience to Noyes, God's appointed viceroy. This rule was most keenly felt when Noyes applied it to sex. Young people naturally preferred coitus with partners their own age. But Noyes knew that the community would never survive very long if this pattern took hold. He therefore made the young Oneidians have intercourse with the older members who, Noyes maintained, were their "spiritual betters."[46]

The discipline of obedience extended to status. Though everyone could vote in the Family Hall meetings, Oneida was an undemocratic community. Noyes assigned each member a place in a hierarchical structure according to his assessment of his or her spiritual perfection. Every saint, he wrote, had to "stand below a wiser in his or her place, and love to submit to those who are above."[47] Most members complied with the rule, but a few, such as Noyes's nephew Joseph Skinner, left to find "liberty of conscience." Helen Barron later recalled that her life there had been demeaning and that her obedience to Noyes had been "man-worship." Having "to do things and think a certain way because Mr. N thinks it the only way to do and think" was submission to despotism. "In the Community," she remembered, "I never felt that I could have an opinion about anything and have it respected."[48]

Noyes proclaimed, contrary to the prevailing view that normal women did not think sex pleasurable, that it was a joyful religious act for them. Christ had said that intercourse should make men and women "love one another burningly" and "flow into each others hearts." Women should make men sexually happy, and, therefore, they must be attractive, "bewitching," and avoid any brusque or cool behavior. They ought to emulate Mary Cragin and be "the servant of love." Most liberating of all was that fact that an Oneida woman, through male continence, could enjoy sex without getting pregnant.[49]

Noyes forbade coitus interruptus and expected men never to ejaculate. If that happened, he said, that meant that the man had focused too much on his own pleasure and not on the woman's. Noyes thought that there was no adverse physical effect of such restraint and that the accepted remedy for any discomfort was cold water. He denounced masturbation and thought that retention of semen made the man healthier and more energetic. If a man was unable to control ejaculation, Noyes either assigned him to women past menopause or forbade all sexual intercourse. Most men apparently avoided the "propagative crisis," and "between 1848 and 1868 when male continence was almost the sole sanctioned method of sexual relations" Foster found that "only twelve unplanned births [occurred] in a group numbering approximately 200 adults." Still, Klaw concluded, the extant historical evidence offers "few clues as to how men at Oneida really felt about—and coped with—sex without orgasm." Of course, if a woman wanted a child, she could, with Noyes's approval, become pregnant.[50]

Oneida women were not feminists. They willingly performed the domestic chores such as making beds, cooking food, dusting furniture, and washing clothes. They were grateful to be exempted from hard physical work in the fields and from "outdoor manly industry." They agreed with Noyes that men were nobler, smarter, and wiser and that they were inferior creatures of "feeling" incapable of sound judgment. Women's intellectual capabilities were only *almost* equal to men. "I want the right of the most intimate partnership with man," one woman wrote, and "I would rather be tyrannized over by him, than to be *independent* of him."[51] Noyes quoted Saint Paul, who said that men should serve Christ as master and then command respect and subordination from women. Since Noyes was Christ's representative on earth, this sexual hierarchy placed him in total control and allowed him to establish "his personal authority over all his followers, both men and women."[52]

In 1869, Noyes began "stirpiculture," or breeding. He had toyed with the idea of eugenics as early as 1846 when he argued that perfect men and women could assist the war against the Devil by propagating the earth with their own offspring. He assumed, without question, that the children would inherit their parents' superior spiritually. Besides, it was far more efficient than the "oppressive" and "random procreation . . . unavoidable in the marriage system." In 1859, Noyes had been influenced by Charles Darwin's ideas on evolution and natural selection that, as he interpreted them, provided a scientific rationale for selective breeding of humans. And when Sir Francis Galton's *Hereditary Genius* appeared in 1869, it convinced Noyes that the time had arrived to experiment. And, so, he announced: "All who love God and mankind . . . pray that we may succeed, for our success will surely be the dawn of a better day for the world."[53]

Noyes, in consultation with a committee, selected individuals he considered as prime breeding stock. Fifty-three women and 38 men qualified and signed a document agreeing to participate. They assented that they belonged "first to *God*, and second to Mr. Noyes as God's true representative" and promised, if necessary, to "become martyrs to science." Couples applied in writing to Noyes for permission to get started. Once approved, the woman would mate with only one man, although the man could, with continence, have multiple sexual partners with women in the group. When a woman became pregnant, Noyes introduced the couple to the evening meeting and announced that the baby would be the community's child.[54]

Since Noyes thought himself the most perfect of the perfect he believed that his blood line should dominate. Nine of the 58 stirpiculture babies were his. Sometimes the task of fatherhood was, in one woman's account, forced on him. Tizah Miller remembered that when Leonora Hatch discovered that Noyes intended "to only 'try' *once* during the month," she insisted that it should be more frequent. Leonora "gave me distinctly to understand," Miller continued, "that she had pretty much taken the business into her own hands & was going to 'make him do it'—her own expression." Miller then wrote that Leonora "came back to me all aglow with the success of her interview" with Noyes.[55] Noyes insisted that all his children participate in stirpiculture regardless of apparent physical limitations. His son Theodore, a fat, indolent man who had suffered a nervous breakdown, fathered four babies. Noyes justified his decision by writing in the magazine *Modern Thinker* that blood lines would overcome any physical deficiencies and, the "blood of the noble father," himself, would be distributed.

By the time of the stirpiculture experiment, however, serious disruptions started to appear in Oneida. Some younger people who had attended college were no longer willing to obey without question a dogmatic leadership that seemed justified only by Noyes's religious arguments. Others rebelled against stirpiculture as a practice that benefited only older members or a clique of Noyes's relatives. Noyes just ignored the discontent and began a nationwide crusade to unite, perhaps under his direction, all religious communal societies. In the first issue of the *American Socialist*, his new name for the *Circular*, he claimed that societies such as the Shakers, Rappites, and Amana, totaling then about 5,200 members, had much in common as communists and Christian Perfectionists. If they remained separate, he argued, they would soon dissolve. The Shakers agreed to discuss the idea of a merger, but the others rejected unification because they saw their differences as insurmountable. Noyes refused to be discouraged and devoted most of his time to running the *American*

Socialist and crusading for unification. He declared: "I shall in a certain sense cease to be a member of this Community" and in effect passed leadership of Oneida on to his son Theodore.[56]

Theodore promised a new unity in "pursuit of truth in the great circle that embraces Spiritualism, Christianity, Communism, stirpiculture, and science of every kind."[57] But he was much less capable than his father in leading the society. He had earlier rejected Christian revelation and, so, could not claim, as did John Humphrey, the backing of the Almighty. Worse still, he created problems. During the years before John Humphrey's retirement, Oneidians had begun to ignore the requirement of getting his prior approval for sexual intercourse. Theodore announced that such negligence would have to stop and that intercourse would be restored to the preapproved mating of the younger people with their older spiritual superiors. Also, all "interviews" had to be reported to him. Then he got into difficulty over his relationship with Ann Hobart, an attractive, blue-eyed girl whom he had appointed as superintendent of the women. When John Humphrey realized that she and his son had a permanent love affair, he tried to get rid of her. He claimed that Ann was an egotist afflicted with "diotrephiasis," a "love of power and weak in conscience and veneration." A phrenologist, he pointed out that the shape of Ann's head confirmed these fatal weaknesses. He said that his son had been infatuated and then captivated by this mesmeric woman. Then, in the winter of 1878, John Humphrey renewed his control of Oneida.[58]

But it was too late. James William Towner, a Universalist minister and lawyer before he joined Oneida in 1873, had formed a permanent opposition party along with William Hinds, the business editor of the *American Socialist*. The "Townerites" wanted to stop Noyes, as "first husband" to all teenage girls, from initiating them in sexual intercourse. They also said that Noyes could no longer force women to take the sexual partners he chose for them. Actually, the challenge to Noyes's administration of complex marriage "was in reality a move to gain free access to the young and sexually most exciting women."[59] The Townerites also wanted to have an elected government accountable to the community. Such a change was impossible for Noyes to accept because to allow democracy meant that he would have to renounce his claim to divinely inspired leadership. He told a friend that God had given him his position and he was accountable only to "the men and women of the invisible world." Noyes tried to deal with these issues by having the evening meetings focus on entertainment and on discussion of trivial matters, such as gum chewing. It worked for a while, but only as a camouflage. One man admitted that, despite the apparent "homelike" atmosphere of the meetings, a "spirit of evil-thinking . . . is constantly brooding over the Community."[60]

While pressure for change mounted inside the Mansion House, events intruded from the outside: economic recession and growing public intolerance for Oneida's sexual practices. The Panic of 1873 caused five years of sustained economic contraction that resulted in a drastic cutback in demands for the community's manufactured products. Only the development of a new industry, silverware, kept Oneida afloat financially. A more serious threat, however, came in attacks on their morals. In 1874, John W. Mears, a professor at nearby Hamilton College, demanded an investigation. With the backing of some Presbyterians and Baptists, he began to look into rumors of child breeding but failed to turn up any evidence. To his surprise, he ran into local opposition to the probe because many hired factory workers were grateful to have regular work and defended the community. For example, the editor of the *Fulton Times* stated: "A foul and corrupt fountain cannot send forth a stream so clean and thrifty, respectable and peaceful." Mears would not be stopped. He gathered more support from Episcopalians and Methodists, and called a meeting of 50 clergymen at Syracuse to discuss the "corrupt concubinage" at the "Utopia of obscenity." They agreed that complex marriage and stirpiculture were abominations but were uncertain on what to do about it.[61]

In June 1879, the *Syracuse Standard* printed a feature story about Noyes's imminent arrest. "Testimony Being Taken," it headlined. At first Noyes discounted such threats because he believed that the sexual conduct of the community was a private matter. But when he found out that the Townerites were willing to cooperate with a criminal investigation, he recognized that his position was no longer tenable. Theodore later remembered that the Townerite defection "broke his hold and decided him to leave the Community."[62] Just after midnight on June 23 Noyes, in stocking feet and carrying his boots, sneaked out of his second-floor room in the Mansion House. He went outside to the porch, pulled on his boots, and walked to a carriage where two men were waiting to drive him 25 miles to a railroad depot at Holland Patent. There, he purchased a ticket for Ogdensburg, New York, with a final destination of Niagara Falls, Canada.[63]

From Canada, Noyes kept in touch with the Mansion House through intermediaries, since he wanted to keep his exile a secret to avoid extradition, and he tried to govern in absentia. But he found this impossible and placed Theodore in charge. In August 1879, he sent an open letter to the community in which he suggested that they give up complex marriage "in deference to the public sentiment which is evidently rising against it." He thought they might adopt monogamy but strongly recommended celibacy instead. He said that they should continue to "hold our property and business in common, as now."[64] The majority of adults agreed with him and abolished complex marriage. As Noyes requested, they tried to stay with a communal economy, but the internal cohesiveness was gone. Theodore, backed by most of the remaining Oneidians, complained about the loss of communal conviction and said that without it it was pointless to continue. Then Noyes, in December, sent another open letter in which he advised they reassess Oneida's future and devise a realistic way to dissolve the communal economy.[65]

Over the winter and summer of 1880 the discussion went back and forth. Finally, Theodore drew up a plan to form a holding company. When his father heard of the idea, he endorsed it, and, on the first of September, 203 adults created the Oneida Holding Company, Limited. Property would be distributed according to seniority and the amount of capital individuals had donated to the community when they joined it. The company issued 24,000 stock shares valued at $25 each. Every adult received 4.25 shares for each year in the society after the age of 16 years. Children were given $100 (per year of their age) and a $200 bonus when they turned 16 years old. All members were guaranteed lifetime work in any Oneida industry. If they wished, they could rent rooms in the Mansion House and use all of its facilities—kitchen, library, Family Hall, gardens, and so forth. In January 1881, they finalized the agreement.[66]

John Humphrey Noyes remained in Canada the rest of his life. In the fall of 1885, he became bedridden, and on April 13, 1886, with Theodore at his side, he died. Two days later they interred his body in the cemetery near the Mansion House. Theodore ran Oneida Limited for a year and then John R. Lord became its president. For a while, there was confusion and stagnation and many second-generation Oneidians departed. By 1890, only 100 members remained, either in the Mansion House or in the nearby town of Kenwood. Fortunately, in 1894, 23-year-old Pierrepont Noyes, another of John Humphrey's sons, took over. He closed down the trap and silk industries since they no longer made a profit. He modernized the silverware factory with a more efficient assembly-line method of mechanized production. He persuaded older managers to retire voluntarily and hired young people to replace them. He paid premium wages and built comfortable homes for the workers in the new town of Sherrill that he laid out south of the silverware factory. He started local social and athletic clubs and constructed a golf course and a baseball field. He donated money for churches and schools.[67]

In 2003, the Mansion House stood restored by Oneida Limited as a historic site. The bedrooms, kitchen, library, sitting rooms, and Family Hall have been carefully maintained. Some Oneida descendants still live there. Oved, after his visit in 1981, commented that he felt "imbued with a spirit of reverence for Oneida's heritage, which was clearly manifested in the attitude of descendants toward their ancestors' controversial past and the maintenance of the impressive mansion house."[68]

NOTES

1. Quoted in Oved, *American Communes*, p. 169. One of the better recent treatments of the Oneida Perfectionists is Spencer Klaw, *Without Sin: The Life and Death of the Oneida Community* (New York: Penguin Books, 1993). Of special value is his "Notes on Sources" where he identifies existing primary sources on the community (pp. 295–98). Other secondary sources include Maren Lockwood Carden, *Oneida: Utopian Community to Modern Corporation* (Baltimore: Johns Hopkins University Press, 1969; New York: Harper & Row, 1971); Robert Gayle V. Fischer, "Dressing to Please

God: Pants Wearing Women in Mid-Nineteenth Century Religious Communities,"
Communal Societies 15 (1995): 55–74; Robert S. Fogarty, ed., *Special Love/Special Sex:
A Oneida Community Diary* (Syracuse, N.Y.: Syracuse University Press, 1994); Law-
rence Foster, "Free Love and Community: John Humphrey Noyes and the Oneida
Perfectionists," in *America's Communal Utopias*, ed. Donald E. Pitzer (Chapel Hill:
University of North Carolina Press, 1997), pp. 253–79; Lawrence Foster, *Religion and
Sexuality: Three American Communal Experiments of the Nineteenth Century* (New York:
Oxford University Press, 1981); Lawrence Foster, *Women, Family, and Utopia;* Law-
rence Foster, "The Rise and Fall of Utopia: The Oneida Community Crises of 1852
and 1879," *Communal Societies* 8 (1988): 1–17; Dolores Hayden, "The Architecture of
Complex Marriage," in her *Seven American Utopias: The Architecture of Communitarian
Socialism 1790–1975* (Cambridge, Mass.: MIT Press, 1976); Louis J. Kern, *An Ordered
Love: Sex Roles and Sexuality in Victorian Utopias—the Shakers, the Mormons, and the
Oneida Community* (Chapel Hill: University of North Carolina Press, 1981); Seymour
R. Kesten, *Utopian Episodes: Daily Life in Experimental Colonies Dedicated to Changing
the World* (Syracuse, N.Y.: Syracuse University Press, 1993); Marilyn Klee-Hartzell,
"The Oneida Family," *Communal Societies* 16 (1996): 15–22; Robert H. Lauer and
Jeannette C. Lauer, *The Spirit and the Flesh: Sex in Utopian Communities* (Metuchen,
N.J.: Scarecrow Press, 1983); Lauer and Lauer, "Sex Roles in Nineteenth-Century
American Communal Societies," *Communal Societies* 3 (1983): 16–28; Spencer C. Olin,
"The Oneida Community and the Instability of Charismatic Authority," *Journal of
American History* 67, no. 2 (September 1980): 285–306; Robert A. Parker, *A Yankee
Saint: John Humphrey Noyes and the Oneida Community.* (New York: G. P. Putnam's
Sons, 1932); Robert D. Thomas, *The Man Who Would Be Perfect* (Philadelphia: Uni-
versity of Pennsylvania Press, 1977); Ellen Wayland-Smith, "The Status and Self-
Perception of Women in the Oneida Community," *Communal Societies* 1 (1981):
18–53.

2. Foster, "Free Love and Community," p. 254.

3. Quoted in Klaw, *Without Sin*, p. 23.

4. For a discussion of perfectionism and its goals, see Foster, "Free Love and Community," p. 272 n. 7 and *Women, Family, and Utopia*, pp. 77–80; Klaw, *Without Sin*,
pp. 29–33; Oved, *American Communes*, pp. 167–70. Other accounts of Noyes's experience at Yale are in Kern, *Ordered Love*, p. 18, and Thomas, *The Man*, pp. 14–17.

5. Carden, *Oneida*, pp. 1–9; Foster, *Religion and Sexuality*, pp. 78–79 and "Free Love
and Community," pp. 255–56; Hinds, *American Communities*, pp. 151–63; Klaw, *Without Sin*, pp. 37–38.

6. Foster, *Religion and Sexuality*, p. 79.

7. Ibid., p. 79.

8. Carden, *Oneida*, p. 11.

9. Foster, "Free Love and Community," p. 257; Thomas, *The Man*, pp. 87–90.

10. Quoted in Carden, *Oneida*, pp. 13–14.

11. Ibid., p. 15.

12. Quoted in Foster, *Religion and Sexuality*, pp. 81–82.

13. Ibid., p. 82; Klaw, *Without Sin*, p. 58.

14. Quoted in Klaw, *Without Sin*, pp. 55–57. See also Foster, *Religion and Sexuality*,
pp. 81–82; Foster, *Women, Family, and Utopia*, p. 82; Foster, "Free Love and Community," pp. 256–58; Thomas, *The Man*, pp. 98–105; Oved, *American Communes*,
p. 169; Carden, *Oneida*, pp. 16–17.

15. Quoted in Foster, *Religion and Sexuality*, p. 51. See also his "Free Love and Community," pp. 259–60, 274 n. 20 and *Women, Family, and Utopia*, pp. 85–86.

16. Quoted in Klaw, *Without Sin*, p. 43; Oved, *American Communes*, pp. 71–72; Parker, *Yankee Saint*, p. 43.

17. Quoted in Klaw, *Without Sin*, p. 44.

18. Quoted in Ibid., p. 44.

19. Quoted in Ibid., p. 45.

20. Thomas, *The Man*, pp. 95–98.

21. Klaw, *Without Sin*, p. 54; Parker, *Yankee Saint*, pp. 89–103.

22. Carden, *Oneida*, pp. 19–20.

23. Klaw, *Without Sin*, p. 59; Thomas, *The Man*, pp. 105–7; Parker, *Yankee Saint*, pp. 69–88; Oved, *American Communes*, p. 414.

24. Quoted in Klaw, *Without Sin*, p. 60. See also Thomas, *The Man*, pp. 105–7.

25. Lauer and Lauer, *Spirit and the Flesh*, pp. 82–83, 133–41.

26. Quoted in Klaw, *Without Sin*, pp. 65–66.

27. Quoted in Ibid., p. 67.

28. Quoted in Ibid., p. 69; Parker, *Yankee Saint*, pp. 134–42.

29. Quoted in Klaw, *Without Sin*, p. 72; Oved, *American Communes*, p. 173; Hinds, *American Communities*, pp. 176–80; Kern, *Ordered Love*, pp. 207–8.

30. Fogarty, *Special Love/Special Sex*; Foster, *Religion and Sexuality*, p. 88; Parker, *Yankee Saint*, pp. 160–71.

31. Nordhoff, *Communistic Societies*, p. 278; Carden, *Oneida*, pp. 42–43, 66, 96–97, 150–51; Foster, "Free Love and Community," p. 265; Constance Noyes Robertson, *Oneida Community: An Autobiography, 1851–1876* (Syracuse, N.Y.: Syracuse University Press, 1970), pp. 27–30; Oved, *American Communes*, p. 177.

32. Nordhoff, *Communistic Societies*, p. 282; Gayle V. Fischer, "Dressing to Please God," pp. 57–58; Oved, *American Communes*, pp. 420–23. Despite communalism, traditional family ties remained. See Klee-Hartzell, "The Oneida Family," pp. 1–14.

33. Quoted in Klaw, *Without Sin*, p. 83; Oved, *American Communes*, p. 175; Carden, *Oneida*, pp. 37–45; Foster, "Free Love and Community," pp. 265–66; Parker, *Yankee Saint*, pp. 14–60, 205–14.

34. Nordhoff, *Communistic Societies*, p. 40; Robertson, *Autobiography*, pp. 46–68; Carden, *Oneida*, pp. 37–49; Oved, *American Communes*, pp. 175–76, 434–42.

35. Quoted in Klaw, *Without Sin*, p. 85.

36. Quoted in Ibid., p. 99.

37. Quoted in Ibid., p. 99; Carden, *Oneida*, pp. 45–48, 65–71. Jeannette and Robert Lauer's study of women in Oneida found that they "were often the nineteenth-century version of today's superwoman" ("Sex Roles," p. 23).

38. Robertson, *Autobiography*, pp. 63–90; Carden, *Oneida*, pp. 65–71; Foster, "Free Love and Community," pp. 265–66.

39. Quoted in Klaw, *Without Sin*, pp. 105–6.

40. Parker, *Yankee Saint*, pp. 227–52; Robertson, *Autobiography*, pp. 188–211.

41. Carden, *Oneida*, pp. 71–77; Robertson, *Autobiography*, pp. 128–49.

42. Quoted in Klaw, *Without Sin*, pp. 113–14.

43. Nordhoff, *Communistic Societies*, p. 189.

44. Quoted in Klaw, *Without Sin*, p. 120; Robertson, *Autobiography*, pp. 128–49.

45. Quoted in Klaw, *Without Sin*, pp. 115, 120.

46. Quoted in Ibid., pp. 117, 180–85; Foster, "Free Love and Community," pp. 263–64 and *Women, Family, and Utopia*, pp. 98–99.

47. Quoted in Klaw, *Without Sin*, p. 118.

48. Quoted in Ibid., p. 119.

49. Quoted in Ibid., pp. 131, 136.

50. Foster, "Free Love and Community," p. 258; Klaw, *Without Sin*, p. 79.

51. Quoted in Klaw, *Without Sin*, p. 134. One historian claims that Oneida women had a "positive self-perception" that was reinforced by communal living. See Wayland-Smith, "Status and Self-Perception," p. 27.

52. Foster, *Religion and Sexuality*, p. 96; Oved, *American Communes*, pp. 411–23.

53. Quoted in Klaw, *Without Sin*, p. 203; Robert S. Fogarty, *Desire and Duty: Tirzah Miller's Intimate Memoir* (Bloomington: Indiana University Press, 2000), pp. 35, 63, 132–33, 196.

54. Carden, *Oneida*, pp. 61–65; Parker, *Yankee Saint*, pp. 253–66.

55. Quoted in Klaw, *Without Sin*, pp. 209–10; Foster, "Crises of 1852 and 1879," pp. 1–13.

56. Quoted in Klaw, *Without Sin*, p. 222.

57. Quoted in Ibid., p. 222.

58. Parker, *Yankee Saint*, pp. 267–83; Carden, *Oneida*, pp. 85–88.

59. Klaw, *Without Sin*, p. 238.

60. Quoted in Ibid., pp. 138, 240; Carden, *Oneida*, pp. 97, 100–101, 116–17, 158; Foster, "Free Love and Community," pp. 267–69. Spencer Olin believes that the schism represented "a classic Weberian conflict over legitimate domination, with the charismatic Noyes basing his authority on 'grace' and the legalistic Towner seeking to introduce the rule of law" (Olin, "Instability of Charismatic Authority," p. 299).

61. Klaw, *Without Sin*, p. 244; Parker, *Yankee Saint*, pp. 268–69, 281, 285; Carden, *Oneida*, pp. 101–3.

62. Quoted in Klaw, *Without Sin*, p. 246.

63. Parker, *Yankee Saint*, pp. 282–83, 292–93.

64. Quoted in Oved, *American Communes*, p. 184.

65. Foster, *Women, Family, and Utopia*, pp. 116–17.

66. Parker, *Yankee Saint*, pp. 287–91; Foster, "Free Love and Community," p. 268; Carden, *Oneida*, pp. 113–65; Foster, "Crises of 1852 and 1879," pp. 13–18.

67. Carden, *Oneida*, pp. 165–212; Parker, *Yankee Saint*, pp. 295–309.

68. Oved, *American Communes*, p. 190.

CHAPTER 5

The Hutterite Brethren

The Hutterite Brethren, or the Hutterites, originated in the Anabaptist movement of the Reformation, specifically in a radical faction of it located in the Austrian province of Tyrol. They took the name in memory of one of their leaders, Jakob Hutter, who was burned at the stake in 1536 for his beliefs. Their most distinguished characteristic was that they lived in a *bruderhof* (brother's farmyard) where they practiced *gutergemeinschaft* (communal property or "community of goods") and embraced *gelassenheit* (complete submission to God). Like the Separatists after them, they condemned war, refused to pay taxes, and insisted on adult baptism.

In what Gertrude E. Huntington has called "the golden years of the Hutterite movement," from 1565 to 1591 in Moravia, a typical *bruderhof* contained about 40 thatched-roof buildings clustered around a central square.[1] These structures included living quarters, workshops, a dining hall, kitchen, and schools. Led by a "first preacher" called the *Vorsteher* (the same title the Ephrata cloisterites gave Beissel), they raised cattle, sheep, and horses, grew wheat and corn, cultivated orchards and vineyards, and operated wineries, flour mills, and sawmills. Their craftsmen built carriages for the local nobility. Coppersmiths, dyers, and watchmakers practiced their trades. They produced fine ceramics, roof and wall tiles, and decorative tableware. Their physicians became so famous that one of them, George Zobel, was summoned to the Prague court to treat the Holy Roman Emperor Rudolph II.[2] Each meticulously clean, orderly *bruderhof* maintained two schools. One, taught by women, was for children ages 2 to 6; the other, taught my men, was for those ages 6 to 12. Young Hutterites were instructed in reading, writing, hygiene, and rules of conduct and were trained in vocational skills. They stayed at these schools all day and at night slept in children's houses so the parents could work full-time for the *bruderhof*.[3] Hutterites believed that holding all goods in common was "a precondition for living in a community, which is required of all true Christians."[4] This "community of goods," in turn, meant communal sharing; namely, living in brotherly love and complete submission to God's wish that all property be surrendered to the community. It also meant that every Hutterite had to accept joyfully all communal discipline. They believed that only by living in a community could one achieve salvation, "the natural climax of a lifetime shared with one's brethren in obedience and submission to God and the community."[5]

When war broke out in 1593 between the Hapsburg monarchy and the Ottoman Turks, the Hutterites found themselves in an intolerable situation. The Austrian authorities persecuted them for refusing to pay taxes to finance the war, and marauding Turks systematically attacked their *bruderhofs*. During the Thirty Years War (1618–1648) between Catholics and Protestants, both sides ravaged Hutterite communities and survivors scattered into Hungary, Romania, and eventually Russia. By 1770, most of them ended up at Vishenka, along the Desna River, some 120 miles north of Kiev, and lived on the estate of Count Peter Alexander Rumiantsev-Zadunaisky. Here, the count, in a 12-part contract, gave them the right to live communally, guaranteed religious freedom, and exempted them from military service and taking of oaths. He assured them a three-year reprieve from war taxation, and the right to keep the income from their communal work. In Vishenka the Hutterites lived communally by diversified farming supplemented by shops for pottery, weaving, metalworking. They operated a water-powered mill and distillery. When Count Rumianstev died in 1796, his two sons tried to make them into serfs by forcing them to farm crown lands. The Hutterites petitioned Czar Paul I, claiming that their original agreement with the count was a binding contract that could not arbitrarily be invalidated. The czar agreed, and in 1802 moved them off the Rumianstev estate to crown lands eight miles away at Radichev.[6] That year they laid out a 490-square-foot *bruderhof* surrounded by a hedge fence that contained 44 families, 99 males and 102 females. They soon replicated their prosperous communal life where bearded men in round hats and women in black caps, jackets, and skirts raised fine Hungarian cattle. They had a mill, distillery, and shops for pottery, weaving, leatherwork, tailoring, tanning, and cabinetmaking.

But within a decade a controversy developed over whether or not to continue the communal life. The communitarians, led by Johannes Waldner, demanded continued adherence to the old doctrines. The innovators, led by Jakob Walther, felt that the *bruderhof* should be dissolved. At one point he bluntly declared that he would "rather die" than live communally.[7] In 1817, he and 30 families left the *bruderhof* to live on private farms. At Radichev, the communitarians, about 20 families, faced new problems—scarcity of food, neglect of their schools, and growing illiteracy. In 1819, after a fire destroyed almost all of the buildings, Waldner admitted that they would have to abandon communal living altogether.[8]

When the Waltherites heard that the *bruderhof* had been dissolved, most of them returned to Radichev. From then on a compromise lifestyle developed. The two groups lived noncommunally and physically apart from each other on either side of the Desna River. Waldner served as the *Vorsteher* for both groups, while Walther took care of all financial matters. Eventually, they realized that the land could not sustain even private farms, since only 700 of their 2,000 acres were arable. In 1834, they petitioned St. Petersburg for permission to move to new crown lands where they could grow adequate crops. Their request was denied. Fortunately, in 1842, Johann Cornies, a sympathetic Mennonite and a government official, interceded on their behalf. He took charge of relocating 69 families to the Crimea, some 450 miles to the south in an area already settled by Mennonites. They named the place Huttertal.[9]

Cornies insisted that, as part of the agreement to move, Hutterites place their young men and women in Mennonite farms, ostensibly to learn modern agricultural practices, cattle breeding, and skilled crafts. He enrolled the younger children in the local schools and told them to lay out Huttertal as a Mennonite village with houses on both sides of the street and barns and other buildings placed in the rear.[10] The move brought enormous changes in their life. "In contrast to the isolation they had experienced for seventy years," Huntington has written, "they were now in contact with a thriving, German-speaking community of about 6,000."[11] The Hutterites were so cooperative that in 1848 the government allowed them to start another village nearby called Johannesruh, after Cornies. Later, they built three more villages 80 miles to the north at Hutterdorf (1856), Neu-Hutteral (1857), and Scheromet (1868).[12]

While in the Crimea some Hutterites tried to revive communal living, with mixed success. They elected *Vorstehers* who read sermons from *Das grosse Geschichtsbuch* (The Great Chronicle). This testament, filled with accounts of the torture and martyrdom of early Hutterites, portrayed a Manichaean world of conflicts between God and the Devil, the spiritual and carnal, a community of true believers and the corrupt outsiders. In 1859, a Hutterdorf *Vorsteher*, a blacksmith named Michael Waldner, convinced some villagers to reinstate the community of goods. His followers called themselves *Schmied-Michel*, which soon changed to *Schmiedeleut*, or the "blacksmith's people." In 1860, he took his followers to a location eight miles away at Scheromet. That year, at the other end of Hutterdorf, a preacher named Darius Walter started a community of a few families who called themselves *Dariusleut*, or "Darius's people." For the next 14 years the two communities lived peacefully in Hutterdorf alongside the noncommunal Hutterites.[13]

Unfortunately, beginning in 1864, government policies caused deep concern among Hutterites of both persuasions. That year the czar required that the Russian language be taught in the schools and, more alarming, in 1871 he introduced compulsory military service. After the czar denied their petition for an exemption from the draft, some Hutterites, communalist and noncommunalist, decided to emigrate to the United States. Most of them, however, remained in Russia because the government, although refusing draft exemptions, permitted their young men do alternative nonmilitary service.[14]

In April 1873, Paul Tschetter and his nephew Lorenz, both of them noncommunalist, arrived in New York City and went to Elkhart, Indiana, where they contacted a Mennonite publisher, John Funk, and hired him as a guide. The three men traveled to St. Paul, Duluth, Sioux City, Omaha, Lincoln, and Council Bluffs. The Tschetters were impressed with forests that could be used for lumbering and the black prairie soil that promised "excellent hayland."[15] In Washington, D.C., on July 27 they met with President Ulysses S. Grant and asked him to guarantee that, if they came to the United States, their young men would never be conscripted. After the Tschetters returned to Russia, they received a letter from the president. He said that while he could make no commitment on conscription, he could assure them that America would remain at peace for the next half century.[16]

Thus assured, in June 1874, 40 *Schmiedeleut* and *Dariusleut* families along with some noncommunal Hutterites sailed from Hamburg to New York City. From there they went by train to the Dakota Territory. In August, the *Schmiedeleut* purchased 2,500 acres of land on the Missouri River at Bon Homme, just west of the town of Yankton, for $25,000. They advanced $17,000 as a down payment and took a mortgage for the balance. The *Dariusleut* bought property 40 miles north of this site at Wolf Creek, near Silver Lake. A third group of 13 families, calling themselves *Lehrerleut*, or "instructor's people," after their *Vorsteher* who was a teacher, arrived in 1877 and built their first *bruderhof* at Elmspring, near Parkston, on 5,440 acres.

The 1880 census listed 443 Hutterites living in communal *bruderhofs*. Sandwiched between the *Schmiedeleut*, *Dariusleut*, and *Lehrerleut* were the scattered farmsteads of the noncommunal Hutterites, who called themselves *Prairieleut*. For a time there was considerable intermingling between the *bruderhofs* and the *Prairieleut*, and marriages, trading, and social activities took place regularly. But after the *Prairieleut* began to attend Mennonite conferences, both sides separated. During these pioneer years, roughly up to World War I, Americans largely ignored the communal Hutterites. Most *bruderhofs* were so far removed physically from their neighbors and were located in ravines and valleys that people just thought they were Mennonite settlements.[17]

By 1917, 2,000 Hutterites lived in 17 *bruderhofs* in South Dakota and 2 in Montana. They had proliferated rapidly because of their practice of starting a new colony when an existing *bruderhof*'s population reached 110. They believed it essential that each generation have the experience of living in a small, growing community. Each *bruderhof* concentrated on agriculture and on surmounting a range of physical hardships such as blizzards, floods, prairie fires, and insects. To help them through these tough years they contacted the Amana Society in Iowa and the Economy community in Pennsylvania and tried unsuccessfully to borrow money. Some of the Rappites, however, visited the Dakota *bruderhofs* and in 1884 negotiated a resettlement of 19 Hutterite families to Tidioute, Pennsylvania.[18]

Life in the American *bruderhofs* was different from life in the Ukraine. They became almost exclusively agricultural communities except for making tools and household utensils. They raised sheep, cattle, hogs, waterfowl, and pigeons. They operated water-powered flourmills and sold the flour and cornmeal to American farmers. They spun wool, made shoes, tanned leather, and made brooms from broomcorn. They raised waterfowl (geese, ducks) and pigeons for feather bedding and meat. The Bon Homme *bruderhof* was the most prosperous. In 1900, it had 400 cattle, 2,300 sheep, 200 hogs, 700 geese, 200 ducks, and 21 teams of horses to draw farm machinery. It used gasoline engines to operate churns and dairy machines and to pipe water from artesian wells.[19]

However, a critical issue surfaced with the outbreak of the Spanish-American War. Being pacifists, they opposed the war and in the summer of 1898 planned to build a *bruderhof* in Manitoba as a refuge for draft evaders. But when Congress failed to pass a conscription law, nothing came of this venture. But during World War I their pacifism became a very serious issue indeed. The Selective Service Act of May 1917 required that men between the ages of 21 and 31 years register for military duty. It allowed no exemptions, not even for conscientious objectors. The elders at first decided to act as if they would comply with the law. They permitted Hutterites to register but told them that if called for duty they should not wear a uniform, obey orders, or help the war effort in any way. Young men, when inducted and then refusing to follow orders, were beaten and tortured. Some were thrown fully clothed into a cold shower and then dragged outside along the ground. Others were submerged in tanks of water until they choked. They had to stand at attention in freezing weather. They were hounded by men on motorcycles across open fields like foxes until, exhausted, they collapsed. Most draftees, after such ordeals, were placed in stockades on bread and water diets.[20]

To protest such atrocities the elders sent a delegation to meet with President Woodrow Wilson. Instead, they talked with Newton D. Baker, Secretary of War, who told them that he could not, or would not, help. Matters worsened. In April 1918, Secretary Baker ordered the court martial of any soldier who refused an order. Soon afterward, four young draftees from the Rockport *bruderhof* were sentenced to 37 years in prison, reduced to 20 years, and sent to Alcatraz. For five days in the so-called hole, they had to sleep on wet concrete floors without adequate clothing, food, and water. Guards beat them with clubs and tied them, arms crossed behind, from the ceiling for hours at a time. They were locked in solitary confinement and permitted only one hour outside the cell each week, on Sunday. Four months later they were sent to Fort Leavenworth, chained two-by-two in a railroad car. There, they had to stand all night outside in the chilling cold. Two men collapsed and were hospitalized. The other two were put in solitary confinement on a starvation diet. For nine hours each day they stood at attention with hands tied behind their backs. By the time wives of the sick men had arrived at the hospital to visit their husbands, one was already dead. The other man died two days later.[21]

Meanwhile, back in South Dakota, local newspapers launched a vicious attack on these "German-speaking people." They called them cowards, traitors, and supporters of the kaiser. They said that Hutterites profited from selling agricultural products to the War Department at greatly inflated prices. They condemned them for not purchasing Liberty Bonds and for not contributing to the Red Cross. At the Jamesville *bruderhof* a local vigilante band stole 100 cattle and 1,000 sheep and used the $14,000 from the sale of the animals to buy war bonds. Vigilantes raided the Bon Homme colony.

The besieged Hutterites contacted the Canadian government which, in 1899, had guaranteed them exemption from military service. Ottawa informed them that the guarantees were still in effect. So, they purchased land in Alberta and Manitoba and sold their American properties at enormous losses. By 1922, they had laid out 15 Canadian *bruderhofs*. Only one colony, at Bon Homme, still remained in the United States; the others stood vacant—ghost farms on the prairie.[22]

In the Canadian provinces, three clusters of *Schmiedeleut, Dariusleut,* and *Lehrerleut* raised crops and built sturdy wooden houses and buildings. By 1940, the original 15 *bruderhofs* had grown to 52 colonies. During the economic depression of the 1930s, though, some of the Hutterites considered returning to the United States. They contacted the South Dakota legislature to find out what reception they might receive. The politicians, anxious to find any way to revive the state's stricken economy, promised to respect Hutterite communal ownership of property. They also assured the Hutterites that the *bruderhofs* would be exempt from state taxes, an exemption that lasted until 1955.[23] Most of the *Dariusleut* and *Lehrerleut*, however, wanted nothing more to do with Americans and remained in Canada. They purchased the lands of the *Schmiedeleut*, who took full advantage of the opportunity to relocate. Over the next 20 years the South Dakota legislature incorporated 15 new *Schmiedeleut bruderhofs*. In World War II conscription again came up, although this time the reaction was far less hysterical than during the First World War. The federal government provided draft exemptions for conscientious objectors. Instead of drafting young Hutterites, the War Department allowed them to serve in the Civilian Public Service program.

In Canada, Parliament constructed camps for the pacifists and placed them under the control of the Department of Mines and Resources.[24] Even so, the *Dariusleut* and *Lehrerleut* had to deal with unfriendly neighbors. Because the Hutterites had paid premium prices for land to build new colonies and were always able to outbid all competitors, many Canadians feared that they would eventually monopolize land ownership. Hutterite prosperity aroused jealousy among town merchants, who complained, wrongly, that they did all of their business through their own wholesale distributors. Acting on these pressures, the Canadian government, in 1942, passed a statute that outlawed land sales to Hutterites. In 1947, this was changed in the Communal Property Act restricting *bruderhofs* to 6,400 acres and prohibiting any new colonies closer than 40 kilometers to an older community. The law stood until 1970 when the government permitted a more flexible system of land acquisitions.

Such legal harassment forced the Canadian Hutterites to build new *bruderhofs* far away from the parent colony. For example, in Alberta the new *Dariusleut* community started at Pibroch in 1953, was 330 miles from its parent. And the *Lehrerleut bruderhof* organized at Huron, Saskatchewan, in 1969 was separated from its original community by 338 miles. Under these circumstances, many Hutterites decided to return to the United States. In Montana, the *Dariusleut*, between 1945 and 1998, built a string of 11 communities on the plains east of the Rocky Mountains and put up a *bruderhof* at Warden, Washington, near Spokane. Between 1959 and 1998, the *Lehrerleut* created 20 new *bruderhofs* in this state.[25]

Despite these frustrations, Hutterites in both countries prospered. Each *bruderhof* was the same, built on a geometric plan based on the points of a compass to represent a miniature model of the universe. It had a rectangular central square with living quarters on the east and west sides. Such geometry was essential because, as one Hutterite said: "You don't walk crooked to the earth, you walk straight, that is how buildings should be, straight with the compass and not askew."[26] Usually the living quarters were three-room houses with an "entrance room," a stairway to an attic that was used for storing tools and clothing, a table and chairs, a cupboard and dishes, and a washbasin. The two bedrooms had double beds, sofa beds, and cribs. One bedroom, called the parent's room, was designated as the mother's retreat, her niche. For larger families the elders added extra sleeping rooms on a formula of one room for every six children. Boys and girls slept in the same bedroom until the age of 12. They placed the communal kitchen, with the colony bell, at the north side of the square. It also served as a laundry and a bath and shower house. They located a two-room *Klein schul*, or kindergarten, close to the kitchen for children ages three to five years. It had a table and benches, a cupboard, a sleeping section inside and, outside, a fenced-in play area. The school was at the other end of the square, for the children over the age of five to attend during the week and for a Sunday school. In some of the larger colonies, such as the Rock Lake *bruderhof* in Alberta, there were two separate buildings, side by side, for a German and an English school. Barns, stables, chicken pens, and sheds were placed far on the north end of the colony away from the square. They placed structures such as a machine shop, garage, shoemaker's shop, and fuel tanks in the northwest section. The cemetery was in the southeast quarter of the property. Farthest away from the square, usually 500 yards, was the sheep pen.[27]

Although the size of a Hutterite colony varied, newer ones being the smallest in terms of population and acreage, the one founded in 1945 near Augusta, Montana, might be called a typical *bruderhof*. In the mid-1970s, it had 90 residents who farmed 4,500 acres with electricity, trucks, and machinery. The light, shallow soil yielded from 15 to 20 bushels per acre. The yearly harvest usually ran about 28,000 bushels of barley, 12,000 bushels of wheat, and 9,000 bushels of oats. They used another 11,500 acres for pasture and annually gathered some 36,000 bales of hay for winter feed. In addition to 40 dairy cows that provided the *bruderhof* with milk and butter, they owned 500 beef cattle. A thousand ducks and the same number of geese swam in the colony pond. They raised pigs in two mechanized buildings, for brood sows and for feed and fattening. Annually, they slaughtered 1,000 lambs, and the sale of the meat and the sheared wool provided an important source of revenue.[28]

Today Hutterites look much the same everywhere. Bearded men dress in black suits and suspenders and the women wear dotted scarfs and long skirts. Children speak a Hutterite dialect until they learn high German and English in school. High German is used in religious services for which sermons are readings from *The Great Chronicle*, the *Great Article Book*, and *Confessions of Faith*. Such readings are unchallenged doctrine: not even a preacher can impose his interpretation on them. Children memorize words and phrases from these books and repeat them in unison with the adults at precise "sacred times" during the day.[29]

All parts of the daily routine are rigidly patterned. The schedule starts with the ringing of the bell at sunrise, although some adults begin earlier. For example, bakers start at 3:30 A.M., women milk cows at 4:30, and mothers nurse their babies at 5:00. At 6:30 the bell announces breakfast and at 7:15 it clangs for work to begin. At 9:00 everyone pauses for a snack. At 10:00 the bell rings for the children to be served their snack in the kindergarten and the school. At 11:45 it tells everyone to come to an assigned place in the dining room where men and women, ranked by age, sit at tables on opposite sides of the room. Returning to work, they await a 2:30 bell that calls women to the kitchen to prepare supper. At 5:00 they carry food to the homes for the small children who had returned there to eat. At 6:00 they serve supper to the older children in the kitchen. At 6:30 the adults attend a church service and then go to supper with the same seating arrangement as at lunch. Afterward, they visit with each other or work on special projects until it is time for the evening church service.[30]

The service is held in the schoolhouse because there are no church buildings in a *bruderhof*. There, everyone gathers in a large, undecorated room lined with benches. The preachers and colony officers sit facing the congregation, men on one side and women on the other, according to age, with the younger people in front. After a quiet period the head preacher, still seated, announces the hymn and sings the first line. Only he has a hymnbook, or *Gesangbuchlein*, that includes songs about the Bible and events from Hutterite history. Everyone then imitates him line by line for the entire hymn. They sing in a loud, high voice that, they think, demonstrates the emotional purification of a pure people freed from sin. The sermon follows. It includes passages from Scripture and readings from the sacred books, which the preacher reads in a high-pitched monotone. The message is always the same: walk in inner peace, obey God's laws, love one's neighbor, avoid carnal temptations. For a benediction the head preacher recites a memorized prayer as everyone kneels with hands folded and faces uplifted. After church they go to the community kitchen for an evening snack and then the women prepare the children for bed at 9:00. Soon the adults retire. At the next sunrise the whole routine starts all over again.[31]

Singing is an important integrating force in Hutterite life. They sing daily, everywhere—in the home, at work, in services, in school, at weddings and funerals. They sing to inculcate feelings of obedience, self-surrender, and communal unity in a loud, shrill, nasal voice that one historian describes as having a "hypnotic, emotional catharsis," especially on the young.[32] Every Hutterite memorizes dozens of songs, some over 100 stanzas that often last for hours; and when a person is seriously ill they sing to him or her day and night.

Periods of designated leisure time in the *bruderhof*, if not taken up by singing, mostly involve conversation, again with modesty and restraint. Young people must be deferential and not express personal opinions on any matter. Frivolous talk is forbidden as a waste of time. In summer young people can go swimming in the colony pond. Other pastimes include visits to nearby *bruderhofs* and private hobbies such as making leather goods, embroidering, creating decorative crafts, or repairing electric motors. Hutterite men seldom hunt or fish.[33]

Women follow a tight weekly schedule. On Mondays they do the washing and mend and iron. Tuesdays are for housework, such as polishing floors and cleaning. Wednesday through Friday they cultivate the gardens. On Saturday the unmarried young women sweep and dust the schoolhouse for the Sunday church services. That afternoon everyone cleans up and gets ready for the next day. Women prepare food according to a precise pattern. They bake bread on Mondays and Wednesdays, rolls on Tuesdays and Saturdays. They select menus on Sunday and list exactly what will be served each day for breakfast, lunch, and supper. For example, a *Dariusleut* menu of April 1964 had a Monday breakfast of bacon and eggs, bread, and cheese. For lunch it was hamburger and onions, potatoes, buttered carrots, cherries, and plums. Supper included fresh bread with cheese, baked beans, fried potatoes, hamburger, and cold duck. Thursday's breakfast consisted of fried eggs, bread with cheese and celery. Lunch was fresh bread, beef, horseradish, potatoes, buttered beets, rice pudding. Supper was french-fried potatoes, ground carrots, boiled eggs, and fresh bread.[34]

Sunday is a special day for women. Events begin with a Saturday evening service for which they wear special dresses. There, the adults sing hymns and discuss religious topics or Hutterite history. On Sunday morning the bell rings at 7:30 for breakfast, where everyone, except the kindergarten children who do not go to the service, is dressed in clean clothes. Then the women change into "church clothes" to attend the 9:00 service. After church, at 10:30, they again change into informal "afternoon dresses" and prepare a Sunday brunch. Next, there is an afternoon rest until 4:30. At this time the unbaptized members meet with a teacher for Sunday school where they are tested on hymns they had to memorize and quizzed on the morning sermon. During this rest period, the baptized Hutterites, if they wish, visit among themselves or travel to a nearby *bruderhof*, provided they are back in time for supper.[35]

Discipline and authority within the *bruderhofs* are always the same. Baptized Hutterites make up the church, called the *Gemein*, that, by vote of the adult males, admits new members. Women participate in the meeting only by singing hymns, praying, and greeting visitors. They cannot vote on policy matters, become preachers, or hold any other office. A seven-man executive council makes the day-to-day decisions. The highest position in the colony, the head preacher, is chosen by lot from a list of nominees prepared by the council that annually reviews his performance. He serves a probation of several years during which he must show that he is conservative in religious matters and innovative in economic decisions. His responsibilities include transcribing his sermons in longhand and conducting all services, marriages, funerals, and baptisms. He records births, deaths, and marriages and maintains a ledger of any travel outside the *bruderhof*. He hears voluntary confessions and suggests appropriate penance for sins committed. He oversees the colony schools. In the larger communities there is a second preacher, a chief executive officer, who represents the colony to the outside world and helps the head preacher in all aspects of his duties. A colony boss, or steward, assisted by a couple of managers, directs the economic life of the colony, takes care of financial matters, and helps the head preacher in extracolony business matters. A farm boss directs all agricultural activities.[36]

Every *bruderhof* is gender segregated because Hutterites believe that men were created in God's image and reflect His glory. They do all the profit-making activities as cattlemen, pig men, shoemakers, shop mechanics, blacksmiths, carpenters, and so forth. Only a man can be a teacher in the German school. Their tasks are set up every Sunday by the steward, who develops a work plan and writes out specific job orders. For example, he might assign two men to a large diesel tractor for fieldwork and tell them what shifts to work. Often he appoints the older man as the "boss" and tells him to keep the machine in working order. During the harvest, the steward usually asks only married men to run the combines and adjusts their workloads for efficiency. Frequently, he and older men drive trucks and help repair machinery.[37]

One cardinal rule applies in all of these assignments: there must be enough work for every man to be constantly busy. This means that every individual performs different tasks throughout the year, and most have at least two specializations. The gardener in summer is the carpenter in winter. The shop mechanic becomes the tractor and combine repairman in the fall. If a person completes his job early, he goes to a central shop to find what unfinished jobs remain to be done. Humility is mandated. Any sign of resentment at work invites discipline at the *Gemein* and the man has to repent and apologize for negative conduct or comments.[38]

Women do only tasks directly related to the internal operation of the *bruderhof*. Some positions are permanent, such as the head tailoress, head cook, and head gardeners. The same two women run the kindergarten and take turns, one day at a time, in its supervision. All other tasks, done by teams, are reassigned each Sunday by the steward and are designated according to age categories. Women between the ages of 15 and 45 do the cooking and baking because of the physical demands of the job and the early rising. These women also milk the cows, clean up after meals, make pasta and noodles, and can fruit preserves and vegetables. Their other assignments include butchering chickens and ducks, helping with slaughtering the pigs, plucking feathers for bedding, and making soap. Unmarried women over the age of 15 scrub and clean the buildings. In addition to these colony duties, women must keep their homes in pristine condition, wash the family clothes, and care for their children.[39]

Men, women, and children share in a plan of community distribution of goods based on need. The head tailoress records what clothing will be made and what items will be given to the mother of each family. The mother, in turn, keeps a record of what she has received and decides who gets the clothing. The head tailoress also sends her yard goods, from which the women in the family make clothes. A family receives a specified number of yards of cloth for shirts, dresses, aprons, underwear, and diapers. For example, each year 10-year-old boys receive three yards and six inches of jacket material. Men over 14 years of age get four yards. The head tailoress also allocates bedding, mattresses and pillows, material for a comforter cover, and dishes and eating utensils.[40]

Hutterites believe that one must not have too much while someone else suffers. So, property "ownership" means only the right to use what the *bruderhof* provides. They categorize all goods according to three kinds of reciprocity: general, balanced, and negative. General reciprocity covers monthly allowances for which no individual accounting is required, such as a small cash allowance, an allotment of 12 bottles of beer four times a year, a quart of wine each month, and yard goods. This category also includes personal belongings such as a wallet, watch, tools, books, and magazines—all of which are purchased in a colony store. Balanced reciprocity requires that something be given back. For instance, a family might trade a portion of its allotment of goose feathers for cloth. They sometimes exchange work assignments. If a person is sick or attends a wedding or a funeral, someone else does the job and repayment is in goods or food. Balanced reciprocity also takes place regularly at mealtimes. If duck or chicken is served at Sunday dinner, they share it equally on a formula of one chicken for four adults. If some people eat the best slices one time, the next time the others get the best portions. The oldest person at the table always begins to eat first. They sharply criticize the third reciprocity, negative, as a violation of Christian charity. This is an effort to get something for nothing, to cheat.[41]

Hutterites insist that natural appetites must be strictly controlled. They prohibit any expression of carnal desire such as television, movies, dancing, excessive drinking, outside music, skating, and skiing. Austerity rules in their communal budgeting and determines how much to allocate to each family, usually it is at a poverty level of about $3,000 per year. In 1971, a *Schmiedeleut* colony in Manitoba in 1971 spent a total of $320,289 for livestock feed, building supplies, machinery, gasoline, seed, insecticides, and livestock medicines. But only 2.5 percent of this amount was for food and only 1 percent for clothing. Some money is set aside for property and school taxes. This austerity is possible because they maintain and repair all their machinery in shops where they cannibalize used equipment to fix tractors, trucks, and cultivators. They buy from local merchants and from wholesalers, wherever they can get the best prices. Hutterites, however, view retail merchandizing as sinful because they think profits make "the poor man the bondman of the rich." No man in the *bruderhof* can work as a merchant. They invest whatever surplus money a colony might have at year's end in savings banks, loan it to other colonies, or reallocate it to purchase additional supplies.[42]

The Hutterite family is the main agency of socialization. They consider children as gifts of God and set no limits on the number of babies a couple may have. They prohibit birth control and the average family is large, often a dozen children. Recently, however, some *bruderhofs* have relaxed the ban on contraception and family size is declining. Almost all adults marry, rarely with outsiders, and there is no divorce. The family house is the center of life for children under 3; for the older members it is a place to sleep. Privacy is unknown. No one knocks before entering a home, and inside the youngsters run unfettered back and forth in all rooms. They raise children in four distinct sequences. They are "house children" until the age of 3 and parents, siblings, and grandparents supervise them. Then, in the kindergarten until the age of 6, they are weaned from the family and taught cooperation and obedience. From 6 years until the age of 15 they attend the German and English schools. Childhood ends on an individual's fifteenth birthday. At that age the young Hutterite sits in the adult dining hall, at the lowest position at the table, and everyone considers him or her as "one of the people." From that time until baptism, when they become full members of the *Gemein*, they learn skills and trades and court the opposite sex. Baptism for girls is at the age of 20 and for boys about the age of 26. Only when baptized can they marry and, for the men, vote in the *Gemein*.[43]

The *bruderhof* closely watches all courting. Officially, preachers declare that carnal practices such as dating are forbidden; but this was an unenforced rule. Young men and women freely associate during visits between *bruderhofs*, during the social time after supper, and at work exchanges, funerals, and weddings. One 16-year-old girl discussed a de facto dating system. "If a boy wants a date," she said, "he goes out with one of our guys and tells him; then he calls out the girl he wants. . . . If she wants, she goes along with him. If not, she says no. . . . In all the colonies each boy gets a two-week vacation [during winter]," she went on, and "then they can go and visit whenever they please."[44]

At some point in this courtship the young man and his father go to a prospective bride's home to get her parents to agree to a marriage. Next, they receive the consent of the *Gemein*. Following that, there is an engagement service at which the couple drinks wine with the girl's parents in her home. Then they visit other families to serve them wine and receive wishes for a happy marriage. The day closes with an evening celebration in the kitchen called a *hulba* that often lasts past midnight. The evening before the Sunday wedding there is a special meal followed by more singing that often continues until the next day. At the Sunday morning ceremony the head preacher presents the couple to the *bruderhof* and marries them. This event is followed by a wedding feast with beer, wine, and soft drinks, and more singing. The rest of the afternoon is taken up with more snacks and visiting and ends with evening vespers. The new bride and groom usually take a home adjoining the young man's parents and just continue in their former jobs. For a bride from another *bruderhof*, however, there are many new work assignments and she has to adapt to new family relationships as an obedient and dependent wife.[45]

Adult Hutterites constantly reinforce their community bond by protocol. The Sunday and daily evening services teach them to set examples of self-sacrifice and humility. At work they never allow individual assertion of leadership or initiative and always discuss a subject until a consensus emerges. A person rises to a more prestigious place in a job by seniority, that is by increasing age. They suppress jealousy, competition, and envy by constant interaction with what they call one's "spiritual brothers and sisters." Only in the *Gemein* vote for colony offices is anything like ability or talent considered.[46]

Fear of rejection is the main mechanism of social control. If someone's conduct or language causes dissention, he or she appears before the council. If the problem persists, members of the *bruderhof* shun, but do not banish, the person. He or she may be asked to remain in the home for a period of time or to speak with no one but the head preacher. The individual sometimes is not allowed to attend church services or has to eat alone in the kitchen after everyone else has finished. Such discipline molds the Hutterite personality. A man is kind and cheerful, obedient to the colony regulations, and responsible at work. A woman is a submissive wife and attentive mother who must never appear upset or cranky.[47]

Adults become "older people" when they can no longer do the regular work in the *bruderhof*. For women this occurs between the ages of 45 and 50, although some women stay longer in the important positions of head cook and head tailoress. Some jobs are surrendered before others. Milking and hoeing are the first to be turned over to younger women. Next comes cooking and baking, although women continue to help in the kitchen as long as they are healthy. A widow moves to a home next to one of her children's family and assists in taking care of babies and the house children. For men, retirement involves convincing an older man to stop working, and no patterned stages apply to this change. Often, a man who is physically unable to keep up with his task is elected to the council. It is more difficult to remove the head preacher since no other "promotion" is available. Several years of gentle persuasion are frequently necessary to ease him out of office. The elderly usually make up about 25 percent of a community, and life expectancy is about the same as in the regular population. There is, however, a great deal more contact between the old and the young. And a strong emphasis on tradition brings the elderly high respect. Older Hutterites, it is said, never feel alone or economically deprived.[48]

Despite the integrated tranquility and cohesiveness of *bruderhof* life, there are some tensions. A few Americans resent the Hutterites' economic success. Some outsiders take offense at the Hutterite aloofness and consider it as hostility on their part, especially when *bruderhof* parents intervene to stop what they see as normal fraternization with outside children. Others complain that the Hutterites only allow visitors by special appointment, that they are just not friendly, and that they refuse to mix socially with the local community.[49]

Such insularity discouraged Hutterites from serious contact with other communal societies. Even the early connections with Amana and Economy were short lived. The only exception was their relationship with the Society of Brothers (after 1996 officially called the *Bruderhof* Communities), a German community of Anabaptist pacifists organized in the 1920s by Eberhard Arnold. In 1928, Arnold and his wife visited some of the Hutterite colonies in Canada. He impressed them with the fervor of his beliefs and devotion to communal living—and with the fact that he dressed like them with a beard, plain shirt, pants, and suspenders. In December 1930, they appointed him a missionary to establish the Hutterite way in Germany and backed him with financial support. But Arnold's preaching of pacifism made the Nazis confiscate the property of the two *bruderhofs* he established there. When he died in 1935, his followers moved first to England and then to Paraguay, where they constructed three *bruderhofs* with a total of 500 members.[50]

After World War II there were intermittent attempts to unify the Society of Brothers and the North American Hutterites. However, numerous visits to Paraguay by elders of the American and Canadian communities exposed them to disturbing practices of smoking, dancing, and attending movies. They were particularly upset with the society's allowing women to deliberate in the *Gemein* and with the absence of the traditional weighty sermon at the Sunday service. Society members, on the other hand, were unhappy with what they discovered about the northern communities: the purchase of war bonds, donations to the Red Cross, and the neglect of missionary work. One Paraguayan elder simply said: "We are a different kind of people." And the head of the American delegation, Samuel Kleinsasser, told him in return: "We cannot operate like you here."[51] When the elders returned, they reported that the Paraguayans were too worldly and asked the *bruderhofs* to end all further connections. The colony at Forest River, North Dakota, however, asked the Society of Brothers to visit it. The decision proved to be a disaster. One Forest River man complained that "they invaded . . . like an army, bringing thirty-six people, including nurses, teachers, lawyers, and four ministers, and took command of the place from the first day on."[52] Leaders from other *bruderhofs* came to Forest River to try to persuade the Paraguayans to leave and to get their Forest River brethren to support the elders' report. Failing that, they placed that colony on probation.

In the fall of 1956, the society, accompanied by 36 sympathizers from the Forest River community, relocated to Rifton, New York, and later to Farmington, Pennsylvania. There, and on additional land acquired nearby at Oak Lake, they invited all of the members of the society still in South America to join them. They did.

Disputes between the Hutterites and the Society of Brothers continued, however, and culminated in a botched 1974 effort at reconciliation. In Manitoba that year a delegation from the society met with 71 preachers of the North American *bruderhofs* and apologized for the disruption they had caused at Forest River. But the two groups, so separated from each other physically, remained as distinct, sometimes hostile, societies. For example, in the 1990s there was an acrimonious fight that seriously damaged the internal morale of the *Schmiedeleut.*

In 2003, the 2,500 members of the Society of Brothers lived in eight *bruderhofs* in Pennsylvania, New York, and Connecticut, and two colonies in England. They were more open to accommodation to the modern world. The Hutterites today number about 36,000 and live in 390 *bruderhofs* in South Dakota, Montana, Saskatchewan, and Manitoba. They are committed to the old ways of communal living, are devoted to the *Great Chronicle* and other books, and severely condemn worldly temptation. They live peacefully with their neighbors.[53]

NOTES

1. Gertrude E. Huntington, "Living in the Ark: Four Centuries of Hutterite Faith and Community," in *America's Communal Utopias*, ed. Donald E. Pitzer (Chapel Hill:

University of North Carolina Press, 1997), p. 323. In pages 319–27 of Huntington's "Living in the Ark," she presents an excellent summary of the origins and development of Hutterite beliefs. An English translation of the Hutterites own compilation of their history and doctrines can be found in Hutterian Brethren, eds. and trans., *The [Great] Chronicle of the Hutterian Brethren*, vol. I (Rifton, N.Y.: Plough, 1987). See also Jakob Hutter, *Brotherly Faithfulness: Epistles from a Time of Persecution (1535)* (Rifton, N.Y.: Plough, 1972). Other recent works are Rod Janzen, *The Prairie People: Forgotten Anabaptists* (Hanover, N.H.: University Press of New England, 1999); Yaacov Oved, *The Witness of the Brothers: A History of the Bruderhofs* (New Brunswick, N.J.: Transaction 1996); Werner O. Packull, *Hutterite Beginnings: Communitarian Experiments during the Reformation* (Baltimore: Johns Hopkins University Press, 1995). Older but useful monographs include Paul K. Conkin, *Two Paths to Utopia: The Hutterites and the Llano Colony* (Lincoln: University of Nebraska Press, 1964); Lee Emerson Deets, *The Hutterites: A Study in Social Cohesion* (Philadelphia: Porcupine Press, 1975); Leonard Gross, *The Golden Years: The Witness and Thought of the Communal Moravian Anabaptists during the Walpot Era 1565–1578* (Scottdale, Pa.: Herald, 1980); Arnold M. Hoffer, ed., *Hutterite Roots* (Freeman, S. Dak.: Pine Hill Press, 1985); John Hofer, David Wiebe, and Gerhard Ens, *The History of the Hutterites*, rev. ed. (Elie, Manitoba: Hutterian Educational Committee, 1988); John A. Hostetler, *A Hutterite Life* (Scottdale, Pa.: Herald, 1983) and *Hutterite Society* (Baltimore: Johns Hopkins University Press, 1974). The German Bruderhof communities (also known as the Society of Brothers and Hutterian Society of Brothers) is treated in two articles: Donald F. Durnbaugh, "Relocation of the German Bruderhof to England, South America, and North America," *Communal Societies* 11 (1991): 62–77, and Michael Tyldesley, "Gustav Landauer and the Bruderhof Communities," *Communal Societies* 16 (1996): 23–41. See also Benjamin Zablocki, *The Joyful Community* (Chicago: University of Chicago Press, 1980). The Hutterites in Canada is covered in John W. Bennett, *Hutterite Brethren: The Agricultural Economy and Social Organization of a Communal People* (Stanford, Calif.: Stanford University Press, 1967); Victor Peters, *All Things in Common: The Hutterite Way of Life* (Minneapolis: University of Minnesota Press, 1965); and Donovan E. Smucker, ed., *The Sociology of Canadian Mennonites, Hutterites and Amish: A Bibliography with Annotations* (Waterloo, Ontario, Canada: Wilfrid Laurier University Press, 1977).

2. Packull, *Hutterite Beginnings*, pp. 15–54, 62–63, 129–30, 173–78, 198–260, 266–77; Huntington, "Living in the Ark," pp. 319–20; Hostetler, *Hutterite Society*, pp. 29–52, 55–56.

3. Oved, *American Communes*, pp. 327–39; Hostetler, *Hutterite Society*, pp. 53–54; Huntington, "Living in the Ark," p. 347 n. 41.

4. Huntington, "Living in the Ark," pp. 322–23.

5. Ibid., p. 323; John Horsch, *The Hutterian Brethren 1528–1931* (Cayley, Alberta, Canada: Macmillan, 1977), pp. 33–37; Hostetler, *Hutterite Society*, pp. 53–54; Peters, *All Things in Common*, pp. 9–31.

6. Peters, *All Things in Common*, pp. 31–36; Hostetler, *Hutterite Society*, pp. 93–100.

7. Hostetler, *Hutterite Society*, p. 103.

8. Huntington, "Living in the Ark," pp. 323–26; Gross, *Golden Years*, pp. 200–204; Hostetler, *Hutterite Society*, pp. 100–104.

9. Peters, *All Things in Common*, p. 34; Hostetler, *Hutterite Society*, pp. 103–4.

10. Hostetler, *Hutterite Society*, p. 104.

11. Huntington, "Living in the Ark," p. 322.

12. Conkin, *Two Paths to Utopia*, pp. 39–40; Hostetler, *Hutterite Society*, pp. 105–7.

13. Hostetler, *Hutterite Society*, pp. 107–12; Huntington, "Living in the Ark," pp. 329–33; Oved, *American Communes*, pp. 347–49.

14. Huntington, "Living in the Ark," p. 333; Hostetler, *Hutterite Society*, pp. 112–13; Peters, *All Things in Common*, p. 35.

15. Hostetler, *Hutterite Society*, p. 114.

16. Ibid., p. 114; Peters, *All Things in Common*, p. 35; Oved, *American Communes*, pp. 349–40.

17. Janzen, *Prairie People*, pp. 31–61; Peters, *All Things in Common*, pp. 35–43; Hostetler, *Hutterite Society*, pp. 115–18; Oved, *American Communes*, pp. 350–53; Huntington, "Living in the Ark," pp. 333–35. The *Prairieleut* Hutterites chose to live outside of the "ark," or communal *bruderhofs*. The term refers to those saved from the flood by boarding Noah's ark in Genesis. See Rod Janzen, "The Prairieleut: A Forgotten Hutterite People," *Communal Societies* 14 (1994): 70.

18. Huntington, "Living in the Ark," pp. 335, 349 nn. 84 and 85; Oved, *American Communes*, pp. 351–53; Conkin, *Two Paths to Utopia*, pp. 49–55; Hostetler, *Hutterite Society*, pp. 122–26; Arndt, *Rapp's Successors and Heirs*, pp. 129–39.

19. Janzen, *Prairie People*, pp. 62–102; Conkin, *Two Paths to Utopia*, p. 54; Hostetler, *Hutterite Society*, pp. 124–26; Janzen, "Prairieleut," p. 77.

20. Hostetler, *Hutterite Society*, pp. 126–28; Oved, *American Communes*, 354; Conkin, *Two Paths to Utopia*, pp. 55–57; Huntington, "Living in the Ark," p. 336; Jacob Waldner, "An Account, by Jakob Waldner, Diary of a Conscientious Objector in World War I," ed. Theron Schlabach, trans. Ilse Reist and Elizabeth Bender, *Mennonite Quarterly Review* 48 (January 1974): 73–111; John D. Unruh, "The Hutterites during World War I," *Mennonite Life* 24 (July 1969): 130–37.

21. C. Henry Smith, *The Coming of the Russian Mennonites* (Berne, Ind.: Mennonite Book Concern, 1927), pp. 272–93; Conkin, *Two Paths to Utopia*, pp. 57–58; Hostetler, *Hutterite Society*, pp. 129–30.

22. Conkin, *Two Paths to Utopia*, pp. 59–64; Hostetler, *Hutterite Society*, p. 131; Oved, *American Communes*, p. 355.

23. Conkin, *Two Paths to Utopia*, pp. 65–66; Hostetler, *Hutterite Society*, p. 132; Oved, *American Communes*, pp. 355–57.

24. Peters, *All Things in Common*, pp. 51–54.

25. Ibid., pp. 51–71; Oved, *American Communes*, pp. 356–57; Hostetler, *Hutterite Society*, pp. 133–36; Conkin, *Two Paths to Utopia*, pp. 65–75.

26. Quoted in Hostetler, *Hutterite Society*, p. 154.

27. Conkin, *Two Paths to Utopia*, pp. 76–77; Hostetler, *Hutterite Society*, pp. 154–56; Peters, *All Things in Common*, pp. 78–80, 95–97; John Francis Melland, "Changes in Hutterite House Types: The Material Expression of the Contradiction between 'Being-On-The-Colony' and 'Being-In-The-World,'" (Ph.D. diss., Louisiana State University, 1985), pp. 45–59, 89–175.

28. Peters, *All Things in Common*, pp. 106–14; Huntington, "Living in the Ark," pp. 338–39.

29. Conkin, *Two Paths to Utopia*, pp. 89–90; Hostetler, *Hutterite Society*, p. 174.

30. Hostetler, *Hutterite Society*, pp. 156–59; John A. Hostetler and Gertrude Enders Huntington, *The Hutterites in North America* (New York: Holt, Rinehart and Winston, 1967), pp. 21–25.

31. Huntington, "Living in the Ark," pp. 338–41; Hostetler and Huntington, *Hutterites*, pp. 33–36; Hostetler, *Hutterite Society*, pp. 159–61; 166–73.

32. Hostetler, *Hutterite Society*, p. 170.

33. Peters, *All Things in Common*, pp. 103–5, 126–27, 130–31, 147; Hostetler, *Hutterite Society*, pp. 175–76; 195–96; Conkin, *Two Paths to Utopia*, pp. 88–89, 91–92.

34. Hostetler, *Hutterite Society*, pp. 203, 237–40, app. 13; Conkin, *Two Paths to Utopia*, pp. 83–84; 89; Hostetler and Huntington, *Hutterites*, pp. 31–34.

35. Hostetler, *Hutterite Society*, pp. 158–61; Peters, *All Things in Common*, pp. 125–26; Conkin, *Two Paths to Utopia*, pp. 84–85; Hostetler and Huntington, *Hutterites*, pp. 33–36.

36. John W. Bennett, *Hutterite Brethren: The Agricultural Economy and Social Organization of a Communal People* (Stanford, Calif.: Stanford University Press, 1967), p. 144; Hostetler, *Hutterite Society*, pp. 162–66; Hostetler and Huntington, *Hutterites*, pp. 27–30.

37. Hostetler and Huntington, *Hutterites*, pp. 40–43; Conkin, *Two Paths to Utopia*, pp. 78–81; Peters, *All Things in Common*, pp. 106–19.

38. Hostetler, *Hutterite Society*, pp. 182–84.

39. Hostetler and Huntington, *Hutterites*, pp. 31–33; Conkin, *Two Paths to Utopia*, p. 89; Bennett, *Hutterite Brethren*, pp. 111–14, 137–38, 145–46, 151–52.

40. Hostetler, *Hutterite Society*, pp. 190–94.

41. Ibid., pp. 194–200; Hostetler and Huntington, *Hutterites*, pp. 50–55.

42. Hostetler, *Hutterite Society*, pp. 194–97; Conkin, *Two Paths to Utopia*, pp. 88–89; Bennett, *Hutterite Brethren*, p. 189.

43. Hostetler and Huntington, *Hutterites*, pp. 57–87.

44. Quoted in Hostetler, *Hutterite Society*, p. 223; Conkin, *Two Paths to Utopia*, pp. 83–84.

45. Hostetler, *Hutterite Society*, pp. 237–40; Hostetler and Huntington, *Hutterites*, pp. 82–85.

46. Hostetler, *Hutterite Society*, pp. 244–47.

47. Ibid., pp. 225, 263–64, 267, 289–90; Hostetler and Huntington, *Hutterites*, pp. 105–7; Peters, *All Things in Common*, pp. 157–65.

48. Hostetler and Huntington, *Hutterites*, pp. 87–90; Hostetler, *Hutterite Society*, pp. 247–51, 262–68; Conkin, *Two Paths to Utopia*, p. 95.

49. Hostetler and Huntington, *Hutterites*, pp. 94–98; Peters, *All Things in Common*, pp. 171, 181–84; Conkin, *Two Paths to Utopia*, p. 95.

50. Peters, *All Things in Common*, pp. 173–78; Conkin, *Two Paths to Utopia*, pp. 95–98; Hostetler, *Hutterite Society*, pp. 279–81, 308; Durnbaugh, "Relocation of the German Bruderhof, pp. 62–77; Michael Tyldesley, "Gustav Landauer," pp. 28–35.

51. Quoted in Hostetler, *Hutterite Society*, p. 281.

52. Quoted in Ibid., p. 281.

53. Yaacov Oved, "Communes in the Twentieth Century," *Communal Societies* 19 (1999): 67.

CHAPTER 6

Nineteenth-Century Jewish Farm Colonies

While the Hutterite refugees from Russia were constructing their *bruderhofs* on the windswept Great Plains, Russian Jewish immigrants came to America to build their communal utopias.[1] Although there were Jewish utopian communities in the United States before the agricultural colony movement of the late nineteenth century, these later colonies were of unique significance. They pulled Jews away from their natural points of settlement in the urban Northeast and contributed, as Pearl W. Bartelt puts it, to "the Americanization of Russian Jewish Immigrants."[2] Nine of the longest lived were Sicily Island, Louisiana (1881), Crémieux, South Dakota (1881), Bethlehem-Jehudah, South Dakota (1882), New Odessa, Oregon (1882), Cotopaxi, Colorado (1882), Palestine or Bad Axe, Michigan (1890), and the New Jersey colonies of Alliance (1882), Carmel (1889), and Woodbine (1891).

This phase of Jewish communal utopianism started in 1881 with the assassination of Czar Alexander II. Jews were linked with the assassination and this connection led to a series of brutal pogroms and to Czar Alexander III's signing an edict forbidding them to own land or to farm. To escape this persecution Jewish intellectuals established *Am Olam* (Eternal People) to organize an emigration to the United States. But, they argued, to avoid anti-Semitism in America they would have to change their whole way of life. They believed that Russian hatred of the Jews was rooted in a perception of them as swindlers and parasites because unlike Russians, 90 percent of whom were farmers, they were urban merchants and bankers. So, an American promoter of *Am Olam* warned that they could not "well afford to run any risk of incurring the ill-feeling of their fellow citizens."[3] Consequently, Jewish agricultural communities were conceived, in the words of Uri D. Herscher, in "an attempt to 'repeal' the lengthy socio-economic history that had seen the evolution in Europe of a Christian policy designed to drive the Jews off the land, deny them agricultural experience, and confine them to commercial activities."[4]

Fund-raising associations and private philanthropy helped to underwrite the colonization. The most important were the Alliance Israelite Universélle (AIU) in Paris, the Mansion House Relief Fund in London, and the Jewish Colonization Association (JCA) and the Hebrew Emigrant Aid Society (HEAS) in New York. Support was provided reluctantly, though, because many European Jews harbored a suspicion if not hostility toward their Russian counterparts. For example, Baron Maurice de Hirsch, one of the most wealthy Jews in Europe and founder of the JCA, saw them as backward and uneducated. German Jewish newspapers called them disease-ridden, "dirty, loud, coarse . . . immoral, culturally backward." French Jews thought them ignorant, uncivilized, and "dangerous to society" and conjured up a picture of tens of thousands of persecuted Russian Jews fleeing to the West. To avoid this catastrophe they would have to be deflected to other countries not afflicted with anti-Semitism, and "European Jewry increasingly looked to America as the logical destination for the migrants."[5]

American Jewish leaders, most of them from Germany, were just as concerned about the arrival of these Russian Jews. They, too, regarded them as different, not at all like themselves—successful, educated, and modern in religious beliefs. They saw them as unhealthy, uncivilized, and fanatics in religious ritual observances. They feared a wave of American anti-Semitism rising against these Yiddish-speaking, impoverished immigrants flooding the urban slums. The *Jewish Messenger,* for instance, cautioned that while it was desirable for them "to leave that Empire, now that the riots have broken out . . . a better way, perhaps, would be to send American Jewish missionaries to Russia to civilize them there than give them an opportunity to Russianize us, in the event of such a colossal emigration."[6]

However, most American Jews put aside such apprehensions when they read accounts of the terrible suffering in Russia. And when they found out that *Am Olam* planned to settle the Russian emigrants not in the cities but in the countryside, they supported emigration. Such agrarian resettlement, said Louis Mounier, an American leader of colonization, would "remove 'a thorn in the side' of people who saw in the [immigrant Jewish] congestion of the large cities a danger to the Jewish cause."[7] Moritz Ellinger, a leader in the HEAS, told a gathering of Jewish leaders in Europe that he was fully aware of all the problems that emigration would bring. Still, "fully cognizant thereof, we recognize the fact that America . . . is the only land which has room enough, is free and generous enough, which offers an unobstructed field for all occupations and handicrafts." America, he predicted, "would form the Mecca of these persecuted people . . . in which they can hope to succeed in founding by their toil and labor homes worthy of freemen."[8] The New York weekly the *American Hebrew* predicted that Jewish farm communities would furnish new chances for "the able-bodied poor who find the avenues of petty traffic already too crowded for them." It described them as creating "the healthy, invigorating and independence-fostering avocation of the farmer" for the "thousands of poor Israelites who live and die as peddlers and small hucksters . . . from the slough of pinching privation and mind-debasing penury."[9] In Russia the *Am Olam* raised money for collective agricultural communities. Jewish leaders and organizations in England and France backed the idea financially. In the United States the idea of agrarian resettlement, after some misgivings, was supported by Jewish fund-raising organizations and newspapers.[10]

Herscher has identified certain features common to all these colonies. They were hastily planned. Their European organizers were almost naively romantic about America and viewed it as a land of "great and glorious liberty, whose broad and trackless acres offer an asylum and a place for . . . courageous souls, willing to toil."[11] Most significantly, these individuals were completely ignorant of the obstacles American farmers faced in the post–Civil War economy, such as the expense of mechanization; the devastation of floods, drought, insects, and disease; and the competition of a world market.

SICILY ISLAND

Herman Rosenthal, a Kiev merchant and intellectual, organized the first agricultural utopia. One of the founders of *Am Olam*, even before the pogroms he had wanted to move the East European Jews to America because he believed that "a class of half a million farmers and workers living by the sweat of their brows" would eradicate anti-Semitism.[12] In the winter of 1881, he came to the United States as *Am Olam's* planning agent. He convinced the AIU branch in New York to finance Russians who agreed to emigrate. Still, some members of AIU thought the idea preposterous and doubted that the Russians, all "peddlers," would ever become farmers. Nevertheless, that summer the AIU, the JCA, and HEAS paid for their passage and gave *Am Olam* a loan of $2,800 to purchase a farm. Rosenthal bought an abandoned plantation of 5,000 acres on Sicily Island in Louisiana, located 20 miles from the Mississippi River and about 400 miles north of New Orleans. It was accessible only by a three-day journey by steamboat and wagons from that city. The choice was a dubious one. The land was filled with swamps and marshes and alive with mosquitoes that carried malaria. Surrounded by other abandoned plantations, it was subjected to annual floods that destroyed crops and machinery.[13]

Twenty Russian families and several adult men, calling themselves the "American Chalutzim," arrived at New Orleans in February. They were warmly welcomed by the city's Jewish Immigrant Aid Society, a branch of the HEAS. Fifty-one men traveled to Sicily Island and were followed shortly by 34 women and 66 children. The newspaper the *American Hebrew* reported that the community ultimately had 12 merchants, 3 teachers, 1 lawyer, 1 carpenter, 1 bookkeeper, 1 typesetter, 1 cigarette maker, 6 clerks, 1 student, 1 tinsmith, 1 saddler, 1 professor, 1 tobacco manufacturer, 2 tobacco cutters, and only 11 farmers.[14]

Their charter announced a goal of moral and intellectual improvement, and stipulated that they would erect farmhouses and dwellings, establish a school for the children, and start a community library. HEAS supplied the money, lumber, machinery, furniture, and whatever else was necessary. It also hired a local German farmer as an advisor. The colony was to be administered by an elected seven-member board of directors that would keep financial records for the HEAS and settle all internal disputes. Any member who took a grievance to a Louisiana court would automatically be expelled. All personal assets were to be turned over to a general fund. Each individual was allowed to take colony supplies only for what was "necessary for his needs," unless by special authorization from a resident representative of the HEAS. They were forbidden to sell any item inside the colony and had to get prior approval of two-thirds of the members before starting any craft or business. No alcohol was allowed. Last, the charter promised that each farmer would be able to work the land without charge and after two years could purchase it with the money he earned.[15]

In the mild Louisiana winter they started to build their utopia by planting cotton, corn, and vegetables. A wealthy New Orleans Jewish merchant promised to pay them $2,000 for the first bale of cotton—the market price was $40. They constructed 10 houses, the first of 40 planned dwellings, for individual families or single men. They put up a general store and stocked it with items sent from New Orleans. Rosenthal started a school in a room of his home where students were taught English. Adults met almost every evening in English language classes. They issued a weekly newsletter in Russian that showed they were little concerned about religion and had no plans to build a synagogue. A later report on the colony after it disbanded stated that "Judaism was a mere by-word, the people were fed with ham and Sunday substituted for Sabbath."[16]

The optimism soon dwindled. By spring the temperatures soared and with the heat came the mosquitoes and malaria. Some young men, in robust health when they arrived, "were shattered like a broken pitcher from the asthmatic sickness" they contracted.[17] Economic problems added to their woes. They had counted on a fine cotton crop to bring in ready cash, but a spring flood ravaged the fields and damaged the buildings and machinery. They fretted about being surrounded by Black neighbors "whose pattern of life diverged widely from their own." By May they were completely discouraged. One member described their existence as "work, mostly useless, hope, despair, love, songs, poetry, happiness and misery—life as we lived it there in Louisiana." Rosenthal was more derogatory. He wrote: "A viler spot on God's earth it would be hard to find."[18] They easily found the two-thirds vote required by the charter to dissolve the community and to try again someplace else.

CRÉMIEUX

Rosenthal went back to New York and persuaded the philanthropist Michael Heilprin and a wealthy young Russian immigrant named Benoir Greenberg to relocate Sicily Island. Members of the *Am Olam* who had recently arrived in New York also joined in and convinced the AIU, JCA, and HEAS to back the relocation. Rosenthal found a place for sale at $1.25 per acre under the Homestead Act on the James River near Mitchell, South Dakota. This site, he said, would avoid the heat and pestilence that had destroyed the Louisiana community. More important, it would resemble the climate they had known in Russia. He called it Crémieux in honor of the recently deceased president of the AIU, Adolph Crémieux.[19]

In July 1881, many of the Sicily Island immigrants moved to Crémieux, and by autumn the community had 20 families. By the summer of 1882, it had 200 residents living on 15 square miles of land. Individual holdings were required by law under the Homestead Act, so the communal ownership plan of Sicily Island was impossible. But they did agree to work the fields cooperatively; to share machinery, seed, buildings, and livestock; and to distribute all profits from the harvests. Their cultural life was communal, however, and centered on two large houses whose living rooms were used for lectures, discussion, dances, and parties. They had a small orchestra, a glee club, and chorus. They invited American farmers to share in all the cultural events. As in Sicily Island, no religious services were held and they raised, and ate, hogs.

The climate was not, as Rosenthal had thought, a replica of Mother Russia. Rather, the first winter was long, dark, and severely cold; so frigid that kerosene froze in the lamps and well water turned to ice. Howling blizzards forced them to stay huddled inside for days. But they persevered, and in the spring they harvested crops of corn, flax, wheat, and vegetables. The fall harvest was another matter. A hailstorm flattened the flax crop and insects devoured the wheat. Market price for the grain steadily declined. By November, most colonists were deeply in debt, a condition they helped to bring on themselves by irresponsible spending.[20]

A later account published in the *Jewish Chronicle* accused them of sending men to Milwaukee where they "engaged in a reckless orgy of extravagant buying." They purchased horses for $800 a team and bought huge quantities of prime lumber to build more colony homes. The *Chronicle* said that they were simply incompetent. "Only after the livestock had arrived at the colony," it reported, "did they wake up to the fact that they had made no provision for its housing, and no preparation for its feeding." Furthermore, "only then did it dawn upon them that animals needed water, of which there was a woeful shortage."[21] The next harvest was lost to the Hessian fly, and water shortages all but exterminated the livestock. It became impossible for most colonists to pay the mortgages on their farms. By December 1885, as Crémieux backer George Price wrote, "they saw no way out of their misery and indebtedness . . . [and] sold their land and moved to various cities."[22] Rosenthal disposed of his property and purchased a grain elevator in Mitchell. He later moved to New York City to become head of the Public Library's Slavonic Department.

BETHLEHEM-JEHUDAH

In the fall of 1882, *Am Olam* sent 12 single men to build a colony three miles from Crémieux at a place called Bethlehem-Jehudah. They were followed by 20 other colonists, all of whom had just arrived in New York City from Russia. Only one young married couple was in the group. Led by a rabbi, Judah Wechsler, they wanted to demonstrate what single-minded, devout Jews committed to hard physical work could do on a collective farm. A Crémieux colonist described them as "brave youths . . . without inner conflict . . . looking toward their future with confidence."[23] They held all property in common, worked the farm communally, and lived in one building.

According to their constitution, Bethlehem-Jehudah was founded with the lofty goal "to help the Jewish people in its emancipation from slavery and in its rehabilitation to a new truth, freedom, and peace." It asserted that they would demonstrate to the world "that Jews are capable of farming." To that end the document prohibited any commercial activity and stipulated that members could "engage in other productive occupation" only after all the farmwork was done. Anticipating immediate success, they planned branch communities and set aside one-third of their income as a "colonization fund." From the start, however, they quarreled over work assignments and over what crops to plant. Rabbi Wechsler complained that they were torn by constant bickering and were totally devoid of self-discipline. Natural disasters hit— storms, insects, drought. The winters were as hard on these young men as they were on their neighbors at Crémieux. When the AIU found out about the dissension at Bethlehem-Jehudah, it withdrew its support and by 1885 the colony disappeared.[24]

NEW ODESSA

Michael Heilprin, aided by two millionaire Jewish bankers, Jacob Schiff and Jesse Seligman, helped another group of recent *Am Olam* immigrants from Odessa to begin a colony in Oregon. Called New Odessa, it was better planned than its predecessors and lasted four years. The immigrants arrived well financed by money from the AIU, and Heilprin was impressed with "the order and discipline which prevailed among them." He explained in a letter dated November 1883 that this group was hard working and, unlike the earlier colonists, had a "firm determination or ardent desire to devote themselves to agricultural pursuits." Members of such a community, he insisted, "deserve special attention." The group sent William Frey, a Gentile Russian nobleman and mathematician, to scout the Pacific Northwest for a site. By late 1882, he located 910 acres, most of it forestland, 250 miles south of Portland, Oregon, that was owned by a wealthy Jewish merchant then living in New York City. The man sold them the property in March 1883 for $2,800.[25]

Twenty-five colonists set out for Portland by way of the Panama Canal. By the spring of 1883, about 50 people had arrived, mostly young, single men. There were only 4 couples, 7 single women, and 4 children. The oldest member was just 38 years of age. They planted wheat, oats, peas, none of which earned a profit. Their major source of income came from lumbering after they signed a contract to supply finished lumber for a Portland railroad. They made about $8,000 from that operation during the first two years. They put up a two-story frame house and used the first floor as a communal kitchen, dining room, and meeting room. The second story was for sleeping quarters. They had a gristmill and a library.[26]

A reporter from the magazine the *Overland Monthly* described their communal life. Except for the married couples, everyone slept in a large upper room that had a section screened off for women. The furnishings were of handcrafted pine. Their meals were usually "bean soup and hard baked biscuits of unbolted flour called after the name of that wretched dyspeptic Graham."[27] There were no religious observances. The purpose of the community, as their charter put it, was the "mutual assistance in perfecting and development of physical, mental and moral capacities of its members."[28] Men and women were equal. They worked together cutting timber, in the kitchen doing the cooking, and in the laundry washing clothes.[29]

Visitors were impressed with their orderly routine. Everyone rose at six and went to a communal breakfast at eight-thirty. They worked from ten until four in the afternoon. Dinner was next, followed by strictly organized "intellectual activity." On Monday, Tuesday, Thursday, and Friday they studied mathematics, English, and philosophy. On Wednesday they discussed current events and issues. On Saturday they focused on community problems. Sunday evenings were marked for group singing that ended with "a session of mutual criticism" and the assignment of the next week's work schedule. Some visitors, though, criticized their secularism. Rabbi Wechsler wrote after his stay there in the fall of 1884 that "they do not observe the Sabbath . . . desecrate the Holidays [and] are completely disinterested definitely in Judaism."[30] Instead, they seemed devoted to Frey who preached a concoction of Communism, Comtism, vegetarianism, and multiple marriage partners. One individual, Herman Rosenthal, an outspoken critic of Frey, wrote that his speeches "were fresh dew to his disciples [but] a source of derision for those who did not accept this faith."[31] For a while, however, everyone pulled together.

By the end of 1884, the ambiance began to evaporate. A group of colonists led by Paul Kaplan, one of the original setters, broke with Frey. Part of the trouble was sex. There were few women in the community and frustration among some young men left them "moody, jealous, [and] isolated."[32] Kaplan also rejected Frey's idealism and said that the goals of the colony were too lofty and that they should abandon vegetarianism. Their mutual-criticism sessions turned into endless arguments. In 1885, fed up with the constant bickering, Frey and 15 followers left the colony. He later moved to London where, in the fall of 1888, he died at the age of 49.[33]

A reporter for the *San Francisco Overland Monthly* described 48 members "stagnating" together in one large building where they ate, slept, and discussed in a "large hall of rough boards and unplaned planks."[34] He commented that they had no rules or leaders, no code of conduct except "to be good," and no religion. The community dissolved in March 1887 after a fire destroyed this structure. One group of colonists went to New York City, where they lived as a commune and operated a steam laundry. Others pursued individual careers as physicians, lawyers, pharmacists, dentists, and scientists. As colonist Israel Mandelkorn put it: "What began as an experiment ended as an experience."[35]

COTOPAXI

In May 1882, the HEAS planted its fifth agricultural colony in Colorado when it sent 13 families and 50 individuals under the leadership of a Hungarian lawyer named Julius Schwarz to 3,220 acres of government land in Fremont County. The place, accessible by a railroad, was in a valley in a rich mining area atop the Rocky Mountains about 100 miles southwest of Denver. All land claims were registered in the name of the colonists, but HEAS retained the legal option of disposing of the land.[36]

They arrived on May 9, erected log cabins, and started a communal farm to grow cabbages, potatoes, beets, turnips, and berries. To earn money some men worked in nearby mines or for the railroad. Unlike the other communities, this one emphasized Jewish practices. Morris Tuska, an agent of the HEAS who came out to make a report, commented favorably that the "colonists keep their religion in accordance with the ancient customs." They conducted a ritually correct Passover, celebrated regular Sabbath services, and read the Torah. They ate kosher meat purchased in Denver. Tuska also noted that Schwarz was in control of his people and told HEAS that the colony was "a full and complete success." It would show beyond doubt that "the Jew can make as good a farmer as any other human being." Six months later Cotopaxi broke apart.[37]

As Schwarz himself later recounted, Cotopaxi failed because the colonists had no idea about how to farm. They owned just one team of horses. Only a few families had cows. A Jewish businessman who was the director of the nearby Fremont County's Place Mining Company wrote that farming by these people was "a lamentable failure." He described how they left the main income crop, potatoes, in the ground until it was destroyed by frost. "The training and tastes of our Russian co-religionists," he observed, "are against Western farming customs." He said that Schwarz was incompetent and "entirely ignorant of everything pertaining to either pioneer life or methodical business."[38] Moreover, instead of working the farm, they fussed over "every little religious feast or fast, engagement or marriage celebration." A team of outside inspectors working for the HEAS described the land as rocky and difficult to cultivate. The observer deplored the lack of adequate medical care, clothing, and food. HEAS, faced with the facts, told the colonists that if they wanted to quit they could do so. Nobody wanted to continue.[39]

PALESTINE (BAD AXE)

In the mid-1880s, some Russian Jews immigrated to Bay City, Michigan, and tried to make a living as traveling salesmen. One of them, Hyman Lewenberg, read about Cotopaxi and decided that he, too, would like to build an agricultural utopia. In 1890, while on one of his business trips, he gained the support of two wealthy bankers, Langdon Hubbard and his son, who owned large parcels of land in Huron County, about 50 miles west of Bay City near the village of Bad Axe. If Lewenberg would organize a group of settlers, the Hubbards would sell them parcels ranging from 20 to 60 acres.[40]

In July 1891, the Lewenberg colonists moved to the site and named it Palestine, as evidence of their determination to start a New Zion. They constructed six crude cabins, one of which they used as a synagogue. Most of them slept in tents, and by the time cold weather arrived some returned to Bay City for the winter. In late February 1892, Martin Butzel, a Detroit merchant, heard of the hard times at Palestine. Butzel, president of the Reform Hebrew Relief Society in his city, decided to help. He convinced Emanuel Woodic, a Prague immigrant turned successful farmer, to go to Palestine to evaluate the situation. When Woodic arrived that spring, he found 16 men, 7 women, 26 boys, and 8 girls. They had planted two-acre crops on 16 parcels of land and owned seven horses and two cows. Woodic went to Detroit and told Butzel about the conditions. The Relief Society advanced $1,200.[41]

Woodic returned to the colony and purchased livestock, seed, tools, groceries, and clothing. He remained through September, living in Bad Axe as a sort of farm advisor and arbiter of petty disputes. He instructed the men in plowing techniques, cultivating, and harvesting. Meanwhile, back in Detroit, Butzel was able to get $3,000 from the JCA's Baron De Hirsch Fund in New York City. In September he, too, went to Palestine to spend the appropriation for the colonists. His report to the Hirsch Fund praised their dedication. He wrote that "both men and women . . . through industry early and late, in all kinds of weather, seem to have accomplished all that could be expected in such a short time." Even though they suffered from inadequate food and terrible housing "these families seem willing to make sacrifices of all personal comforts and stick to farming."[42]

The situation improved with the 1893 spring harvest. It brought in enough money to build a modest frame synagogue and a school. They purchased kosher meat in the town of Saginaw. Nevertheless, the income was not enough to meet the annual mortgage payments, and in 1895 the Hubbards went to court for a lien on future crops and all the machinery. But when Butzel negotiated new loans for the colonists, the bankers dropped the suit and offered another contract. The lenders warned that if the colonists failed to meet the next interest payment, the land automatically would be forfeited.[43]

For two years the colonists held on, watched their purchases, and met the payments. However, when the 1897 harvest failed because of poor planning, they realized what was about to happen. They asked the Hirsch Fund to buy the land for them and allow them to continue to farm it. The fund sent out a representative. His account, like Butzel's 1892 statement, praised their perseverance. He wrote that some still had to sleep outdoors in all kinds of weather with only animals as companions. Without enough horses the men themselves pulled the plows. The obstacles they faced were "almost insurmountable," but he found it "surprising that they did not lose heart." The trustees of the Hirsch Fund, nevertheless, decided not to make the purchase because, obviously, nothing could save Palestine. They were correct.[44]

In January 1898, the Hubbards sent eviction notices. The Hirsch Fund trustees mailed the Hubbards $825 and asked them to allow the colonists another year to raise money. The bankers agreed. But the next January the colonists defaulted again and liquidation began. By the end of the year only eight families lived at Palestine, and they left the following winter. Herscher believed that the colony was doomed from the start, despite all the optimism, determination, and outside financial assistance, because the economy of the region, like much of the United States at the time, was depressed by the Panic of 1893.[45]

SOUTHERN NEW JERSEY COMMUNITIES: ALLIANCE, CARMEL, WOODBINE

Alliance

Alliance, the first of the New Jersey agricultural cooperatives, was started in May 1882 by the AIU and HEAS (after its dissolution in 1883, it was called the Alliance Land Trustor). This cooperative, not isolated from sponsors and new settlers, was closely supervised by the AIU and HEAS officers in New York City. The HEAS purchased 1,140 acres in Salem County, about 35 miles east of Philadelphia, and set aside 150 acres for a community compound on which they would fly the American flag. They turned the rest of the land into 66 homesteads of between 13 and 15 acres each. These were sold to 70 families for between $321 and $443, payable in a 33-year, interest-free mortgage. The next year HEAS bought another 80 acres, divided it into 6 more homesteads, and agreed to cover travel expenses of the settlers. It also agreed to construct three frame barracks for temporary housing and provide all food and clothing for six months. It planned to open a cigar factory and a shirt factory and pay an instructor to show the communards how to farm. It promised to give every family free "tools, furniture, cooking utensils, plants and farm utensils to the value of $100." The family, on its own time, could farm its homestead, but it had to agree to work four parcels communally.[46]

The first families, Russian storekeepers and traders, stayed in tents while the barracks were completed. Then they moved into the buildings, where they lived in a 12-by-14-foot room. A reporter for the *New York World* described it as "two rows of compartments [placed] on each side opposite one another with a narrow passage between them, the full length of the house." Each room had two beds, one for the husband, the other for the wife, and cradles for the children. A small wardrobe stood between the beds. Daily routine began at four in the morning and the adults, men and women together, worked communally to plant corn till breakfast at six. They returned to the fields until they stopped for a rest period from about noon until two in the afternoon. Then they went back to work until seven o'clock.[47]

In the spring of 1885, their harvest, for the first time, brought in a profit. At this point, feeling confident that the colony was on a sound agricultural basis, they decided to abandon the earlier communal work and allow every family to farm only its own plot. The change was enthusiastically welcomed. By 1887, Alliance sold their crops at peak prices in New York City and Philadelphia. With this money they built a school to teach their children English so that they could be enrolled in the public schools in the nearby town of Vineland. They were devoutly religious and respected Jewish rituals, ate kosher meat, and on the Sabbath abstained from work and attended services. They privately recited daily prayers. But a fight over rituals erupted that year between the traditional Hasidic Jews and the reformed groups. To avoid continual controversy they erected two synagogues, one for each persuasion.

Unfortunately, they made a number of financial mistakes. They spent excessive amounts of money for farm tools and machinery. They used their land as collateral to borrow funds to build more homes. When the Panic of 1893 struck, Alliance had to take out a second mortgage. But by 1897, they defaulted, and the holder, the Salem Building and Loan Association, moved to foreclose. The Hirsch Fund intervened, purchased the mortgage, and arranged a debt-payment plan for them. As a condition for this assistance, the Hirsch Fund trustees insisted that they convert to industrial production and become an agroindustrial community. Two Philadelphia manufacturers, Maurice and Joseph Fels, set up a canning factory. The conversion saved Alliance and it continued into the early 1930s as a Jewish agroindustrial community in which farming played a secondary role. Sydney Bailey, a former member of New Odessa who had moved there, remembered in his article "The First Fifty Years," published in 1932, that they soon paid off their debts. "We have a good name, and credit in the bank, befitting industrious and thrifty people," he wrote. He boasted that they were proud and prosperous, that "we [were] our own bosses," and led "a natural life." But by the end of the Great Depression, Alliance had dissolved, and at the site of the colony one found only a cluster of neglected farms and a few summer resort homes.[48]

Carmel

At the same time that Michael Heilprin was sponsoring New Odessa, he organized a communal agricultural colony of eight families at Carmel. Not much is known about its first years, except that its growth was retarded because of financial problems and by the mid-1880s it "became a haven for *Am Olam* radicals."[49] In February 1889, the families formed a 185-acre farm called the "Industrial Co-operation in Combination with Consumer-Patrons." Its purpose was to conduct "farm-work on co-operative principles, combining with it other manufacturing industries that are more or less connected with farming, such as dairy, canneries, manufacture of jellies, etc." It was governed by a "superintendency of the functionaries" elected annually. One of the colonists later remembered that there was no private profit and that work "was parceled out in accordance with ability to produce . . . and was paid for at the prevailing rate for that particular kind of work." They formed a cooperative sewing operation in a factory building. With financing of $15,000 from a new philanthropic organization, the Jewish Agricultural and Industrial Aid Society, they opened "Factory Number Two" as a clothing industry. They opened a third factory to manufacture ready-to-wear clothing for men, boys, and ladies. These industries became the main economic activity in the colony, and by 1901 only 50 of the 204 households cultivated farmland.[50]

Carmel had a library and sponsored cultural activities such as lectures and band concerts. Both religious and nonreligious settlers lived together without friction. They had a school for their children and night classes for the adults, both supported with money from the Hirsch Fund. One colonist bragged in a letter to the fund that "there is not any better place to educate the Russian Jewish emigrants than . . . in Carmel." He went on to say that the "vast majority of the young and old are good and hard-working people, willing to learn . . . they would do all possibilities to advance themselves to know the custom, style and language of the country."[51] But the community developed a reputation as a haven for atheists and anarchists committed to nihilism and free love. And by 1919, the number of Carmel families had declined from 220 to 156. One reason for the attrition was the distaste its young people had for farm life. As one Carmel man lamented, many of them "hankering after change, after new, different companions, lured by the city—go to the city at the first opportunity." By 1932, Carmel was largely abandoned, the factories shut down, and only a few farm families remained. One writer described it as "just a tangle of neglected old farms."[52]

Woodbine

Woodbine was started in 1891 as an agricultural and industrial colony. Learning from the troubles at Alliance and Carmel, its planners assumed that industrial revenues would supplement farm income. To organize Woodbine the Hirsch Fund trustees appointed a Committee on Agricultural and Industrial Settlements with Julius Goldman as its head. He investigated possible locations in southern New Jersey and eventually chose land in Dennis Township because, he told the Hirsch Fund, it was just 56 miles from Philadelphia and had land easily adapted to truck farming and fruit growing. In addition to Philadelphia, he noted that nearby stores and markets were found in Sea Isle City and Cape May. The West Jersey and Seashore Railroad would provide cheap transportation to all of these places.[53]

Trustees of the Hirsch Fund named themselves as the directors of the "Woodbine Land and Improvement Company" and offered $50,000 of stock for sale. They appointed Goldman president and in August 1891 purchased 5,300 acres of land for $37,500. Like Alliance, they set aside 800 acres for a central public square and divided the rest into family parcels of about 15 acres each. Some acreage was reserved for pasture. The company chose Herman Rosenthal to screen the colonists. He required every family to pay a membership fee of $200 and invest in some of the stock, after which it contracted for a 30-acre homestead at an average price of $1,100.[54]

Sixty families joined Woodbine the first year. The company paid them a weekly wage while they put in crops and planted fruit trees. The company also sent in all the lumber, tools, animals, and seeds necessary for the start-up. An 1893 report by a Mr. Francis B. Lee for the New Jersey State Board of Agriculture described Woodbine as having 170 town lots that "have been wrested from a natural wilderness." The houses, paid for by the company, cost between $850 and $1,300 and were "models of neatness and adaptability for the colonists' needs." He wrote that they were constructing a hotel, railway station, school, and synagogue. They had cleared 650 acres of land and developed over 100 miles of roads. They had a factory that made Jonasson cloaks and they planned to build other factories to make cigars, cutlery, and knitting.[55]

Then reversals set in. In 1894, the company decided that its financial assistance was no longer required because the factories could support Woodbine. The colonists protested, arguing that the factories had just opened and had not demonstrated that they could sustain the community. Other difficulties appeared. The colonists had cleared, but not planted, too much land at too heavy a toll in man-hours. A reporter for the New York Press wrote that the community was so filled with pine and oak that "the battle to be waged against the stumps and the ever springing brush, is one that is taking the heart out of many a 'farmer' bred to town ways, and has done much to bring about the present state of affairs." They had poorly planned housing and members had to live in shacks no larger than "a hen's roost." The reporter claimed that the 60 families had developed a ludicrous work plan. Children were expected to earn money in the factories, while the father stayed home and took care of the farm. It was preposterous, he wrote, to assume that "the children should support the parents while they were farm making."[56]

The Hirsch Fund trustees appointed John B. Weber, former Immigration Commissioner of the Port of New York, to look into matters. He recommended that Gentile workers be hired to expand the factories. With this new labor force Woodbine opened a broom and basket business, then a machine shop called the Woodbine Machine and Tool Company. They replaced the Jonasson cloak factory with another one known as Haas Brothers. They started Universal Lock Company. They opened an agricultural school in honor of Baron De Hirsch for boys over the age of 14. A catalog advertised it as giving "Jewish young men a course in agriculture, which is to teach young men practical agricultural work, and make them true tillers of the soil." In addition to agricultural training, the school offered courses in English, arithmetic, history, geography, chemistry, physics, botany, bookkeeping, and drawing. It remained open until 1917, and by then it had matriculated over 900 students.[57]

By 1901, Woodbine seemed to have survived. It was cultivating 1,800 acres of sweet potatoes and grapes that brought in large annual profits. It had developed a successful program for new arrivals in which they were supervised by experienced farmers who trained them in agronomy. It had 4 miles of streets and 12 miles of excellent farm roads. Its population of more 1,400 people included 160 Jewish and 34 Gentile families. It had a synagogue, a Baptist church, two school buildings, a power plant, and a bathhouse. It had an "improvement association," a fire department, a school system, and a board of health. In 1903, it incorporated as "First Self-Governed Jewish Community Since the Fall of Jerusalem." In 1907, the superintendent of Woodbine, Bernard A. Palitz, asserted that his colony would "convince the anti-Semite that the Jewish conception of social life is not commerce, that he loves the beautiful, the quiet and natural life of man and lives it when equal opportunities are offered to him." In his never-published promotional pamphlet, "The Borough of Woodbine," he exhorted Jews living "in the filth of the tenement house" to "come back to your natural calling, to the healthy life-prolonging occupation, to more light and purer air; harden your muscles and broaden your mind for the struggle that Israel is yet to meet before his mission is accomplished and his prophecies fulfilled."[58]

In 1929, Judah David Eisenstein, in his book *Otsar Zichronotai*, credited Woodbine with being "more important and of greater value than all the colonies founded by Russian émigrés in America." He said that other colonies such as Alliance and Carmel became communities of workers. Only Woodbine remained "to achieve the distinction [of becoming] a colony of genuine farmers."[59] In 1941, the trustees of the Hirsch Fund allowed Woodbine residents to purchase their own farms and turned over title of whatever remained to the borough government. Pearl Bartelt concluded in 1997 that "the town still exists, as well as many of the buildings and the cemeteries of the original colony, although its population is no longer predominantly Jewish."[60]

NOTES

1. Book-length studies of Jewish agricultural colonies in the United States are few in number and most focus on New Jersey. These monographs are Joseph Brandes, *Immigrants to Freedom: Jewish Communities in Rural New Jersey since 1882* (Philadelphia: University of Pennsylvania Press, 1971); Gabriel Davidson, *Our Jewish Farmers and the Story of the Jewish Agricultural Society* (New York: Fischer, 1943); Ellen Eisenberg, *Jewish Agricultural Societies in New Jersey 1882–1920* (Syracuse, N.Y.: Syracuse University Press, 1995); Reuben Philip Goldstein, *Social Aspects of the Jewish Colonies of South Jersey* (New York: League Printing Co., 1921). The only comprehensive treatment of Jewish communalism is a brief (123 pages) coverage by Uri D. Herscher, *Jewish Agricultural Utopias in America, 1880–1910* (Detroit, Mich.: Wayne State University Press, 1981). Much of the historical literature on the topic, therefore, is found in articles in scholarly journals or in chapters in books. In the latter category are four valuable publications: Pearl W. Bartelt, "American Jewish Agricultural Colonies," in *America's Communal Utopias*, ed. Donald E. Pitzer (Chapel Hill: University of North Carolina Press), pp. 352–74; Abraham Menes, "The Am Oylom Movement," in *Studies in Modern Jewish Social History*, ed. Joshua A. Fishman (New York: Ktav, 1977), pp. 155–79; and Oved, "New Odessa: A Jewish Colony of the Am Olam Group," in his *American Communes*, pp. 193–214. Articles include Davidson, "The Palestine Colony in Michigan: An Adventure in Colonization," *American Jewish Historical Society* 34 (1925): 61–74; Eisenberg, "The Limits of Gender Equality in 19th Century American Jewish Colonies," *Communal Societies* 13 (1993): 71–83; Violet Goering and Orlando J. Goering, "The Agricultural Communes of the *Am Olam*," *Communal Societies* 4 (1984): 74–86; David M. Gold, "Jewish Agriculture in the Catskill, 1900–1920," *Agricultural History* 55 (1980): 31–49; George M. Price, "The Russian Jews in America," trans. Leo Shpall, *American Jewish Quarterly* 48 (1958): 26–62, 78–133; Leo Shpall, "Jewish Agricultural Colonies in the United States," *Agricultural History* 24 (1950): 120–46; A. James Rudin, "Bad Axe, Michigan: An Experiment in Jewish Agricultural Settlement," *Michigan History* 56 (1972): 119–30; Lois Fields Schwarz, "Early Jewish Agricultural Colonies in South Dakota," *North Dakota History* 34 (1965): 217–32; Leo Shpall, "A Jewish Agricultural Colony in Louisiana," *Louisiana Historical Quarterly* 20 (1937): 821–30; Lois J. Swichkow, "The Jewish Agricultural Colony of Aspen, Wisconsin," *American Jewish Historical Quarterly* 54 (1964): 82–91; Bartelt, "Jewish Colonies," p. 367. For the history of agricultural colonies in America prior to the "great migration" of the 1880s, see Shpall, "Jewish Agricultural Colonies," pp. 120–24 and Brandes, *Immigrants to Freedom*, pp. 15–19. Other, smaller agricultural colonies of which there are historical records were Painted Woods, Dakota Territory (1882); the Arkansas Colony (1883); Beer Sheba Colony, Kansas (1882); Lasker Colony, Kansas

(1884); Rosenhayn, New Jersey (1882); Mitzpah, New Jersey (1891); and three other short-lived New Jersey colonies at Montefiore, Riga, and Ziontown.

2. Bartelt, "Jewish Colonies," p. 367.

3. Herscher, *Agricultural Utopias*, p. 24; Oved, *American Communes*, pp. 223–34; Menes, "Am Oylom Movement," pp. 155–62; Shpall, "Jewish Agricultural Colonies," pp. 127–32. For the impact of the pogroms on Jewish colonization in America see Goering and Goering, "Communes of the *Am Olam*," pp. 74–76; Brandes, *Immigrants to Freedom*, pp. 19–21; Louis Greenberg, *The Jews in Russia: The Struggle for Emancipation, 1881–1917* (New Haven, Conn.: Yale University Press), p. 2.

4. Herscher, *Agricultural Utopias*, p. 25; Davidson, *Our Jewish Farmers*, pp. 226–27; Bartelt, "Jewish Colonies," p. 353.

5. Eisenberg, *Agricultural Societies in New Jersey*, pp. 63–64, 67; Bartelt, "Jewish Colonies," pp. 354–55; Schwarz, "Early Jewish Agricultural Colonies," p. 221.

6. Quoted in Eisenberg, *Agricultural Societies in New Jersey*, p. 69.

7. Herscher, *Agricultural Utopias*, p. 24.

8. Quoted in Eisenberg, *Agricultural Societies in New Jersey*, pp. 70–71.

9. Quoted in Herscher, *Agricultural Utopias*, p. 23.

10. Bartelt, "Jewish Colonies," pp. 356–57; Brandes, *Immigrants to Freedom*, pp. 101–17.

11. Herscher, *Agricultural Utopias*, p. 31.

12. Eisenberg, *Agricultural Societies in New Jersey*, p. 38.

13. Brandes, *Immigrants to Freedom*, p. 47.

14. Shpall, "Jewish Agricultural Colonies," pp. 129–30.

15. Ibid., pp. 130–31; Shpall, "Agricultural Colony in Louisiana," pp. 825–30; Bartelt, "Jewish Colonies," p. 353; Goering and Goering, "Communes of the *Am Olam*," pp. 77–78.

16. Quoted in Eisenberg, *Agricultural Societies in New Jersey*, p. 40.

17. Herscher, *Agricultural Utopias*, p. 36.

18. Quoted in Ibid., p. 36; Shpall, "Jewish Agricultural Colonies," p. 131.

19. Goering and Goering, "Communes of the *Am Olam*," p. 69.

20. Shpall, "Jewish Agricultural Colonies," p. 133. These tribulations are recounted in Isidore Singer, ed., "Agricultural Colonies," in *The Jewish Encyclopedia* (New York: Funk and Wagnalls Co., 1901), 1:257; Goering and Goering, "Communes of the *Am Olam*," p. 80.

21. Quoted in Eisenberg, *Agricultural Societies in New Jersey*, pp. 42–43.

22. Ibid., p. 43.

23. Quoted in Ibid., p. 44.

24. Eisenberg, "Limits of Gender Equality," p. 79; Goering and Goering, "Communes of the *Am Olam*," pp. 80–81; Shpall, "Jewish Agricultural Colonies," pp. 132–33.

25. Avrahm Yarmolinsky, *A Russian-American Dream: A Memoir on William Frey* (Lawrence: University of Kansas Press, 1965), pp. 99–102. For a brief biographical sketch of Frey, see Oved, *American Communes*, p. 230 n. 5.

26. Oved, *American Communes*, pp. 225–26; Herscher, *Agricultural Utopias*, pp. 45–46; Shpall, "Jewish Agricultural Colonies," pp. 133–34; Goering and Goering, "Communes of the *Am Olam*," pp. 81–82.

27. Eisenberg, *Agricultural Societies in New Jersey*, p. 48.

28. Provisions of their charter are found in Shpall, "Jewish Agricultural Colonies," p. 135.

29. On gender roles, see Eisenberg, "Limits of Gender Equality," pp. 78–79.

30. Quoted in Eisenberg, *Agricultural Societies in New Jersey*, p. 51. A letter of Frey's describing communal routine at New Odessa is in Goering and Goering, "Communes of the *Am Olam*," p. 83. Other accounts of daily life are in Oved, *American Communes*, pp. 227–28.

31. Eisenberg, *Agricultural Societies in New Jersey*, p. 51.

32. Herscher, *Agricultural Utopias*, p. 46.

33. Ibid., pp. 47–48; Oved, *American Communes*, p. 228; Eisenberg, *Agricultural Societies in New Jersey*, p. 52; Bartelt, "Jewish Colonies," p. 359; Shpall, "Jewish Agricultural Colonies," p. 135; Goering and Goering, "Communes of the *Am Olam*," p. 85.

34. Quoted in Herscher, *Agricultural Utopias*, p. 47; Bartelt, "Jewish Colonies," p. 359.

35. Herscher, *Agricultural Utopias*, p. 48. For an analysis of the failure of the colony, see Goering and Goering, "Communes of the *Am Olam*," p. 85; Eisenberg, *Agricultural Societies in New Jersey*, p. 51; and Oved, *American Communes*, p. 229.

36. Shpall, "Jewish Agricultural Colonies," p. 135; Herscher, *Agricultural Utopias*, p. 55.

37. Herscher, *Agricultural Utopias*, p. 58.

38. Quoted in Ibid., p. 58.

39. Shpall, "Jewish Agricultural Colonies," pp. 136–37.

40. Bartelt, "Jewish Colonies," pp. 362–63; Davidson, "Palestine Colony," p. 62.

41. Davidson, "Palestine Colony," p. 65; Herscher, *Agricultural Utopias*, pp. 61–67; Rudin, "Bad Axe," pp. 119–20.

42. Quoted in Herscher, *Agricultural Utopias*, p. 68; Rudin, "Bad Axe," pp. 121–24.

43. Herscher, *Agricultural Utopias*, p. 68.

44. Ibid., p. 69; Davidson, "Palestine Colony," p. 72.

45. Herscher, *Agricultural Utopias*, pp. 69–70; Rudin, "Bad Axe," pp. 127–30.

46. Herscher, *Agricultural Utopias*, p. 74; Brandes, *Immigrants to Freedom*, pp. 4, 22–28, 51; Eisenberg, *Agricultural Societies in New Jersey*, p. 90 and her "Immigrant Origins and Sponsor Policies: Sources of Change in South Jersey Jewish Colonies," *Journal of American Ethnic History* 11 (Spring 1982): 27–40.

47. Eisenberg, "Limits of Gender Equality," pp. 74–75 and *Agricultural Societies in New Jersey*, pp. 90–91, 94–96; Bartelt, "Jewish Colonies," p. 360; Shpall, "Jewish Agricultural Colonies," pp. 141–43; Herscher, *Agricultural Utopias*, pp. 73–76, 76–78; Brandes, *Immigrants to Freedom*, pp. 55–59.

48. Herscher, *Agricultural Utopias*, p. 84; Eisenberg, *Agricultural Societies in New Jersey*, p. 171; Brandes, *Immigrants to Freedom*, pp. 59–60; Bartelt, "Jewish Colonies," p. 361; Shpall, "Jewish Agricultural Colonies," p. 143.

49. Eisenberg, *Colonies in New Jersey*, p. 109.

50. Ibid., pp. 109–10; Shpall, "Agricultural Colonies," pp. 143–44.

51. Quoted in Eisenberg, *Colonies in New Jersey*, p. 145.

52. Ibid., pp. 161–62, 171; Bartelt, "Jewish Colonies," p. 359.

53. Brandes, *Immigrants to Freedom*, p. 113; Herscher, *Agricultural Utopias*, pp. 84–88; Eisenberg, *Colonies in New Jersey*, p. 129; Shpall, "Agricultural Colonies," p. 145; Bartelt, "Jewish Colonies," pp. 33–64.

54. Brandes, *Immigrants to Freedom*, pp. 114–17; Herscher, *Agricultural Utopias*, pp. 88–91; Eisenberg, *Colonies in New Jersey*, pp. 129–31.

55. Herscher, *Agricultural Utopias*, pp. 92–93.

56. Ibid., p. 95.

57. Ibid., pp. 97–105; Brandes, *Immigrants to Freedom*, pp. 117–42; Eisenberg, *Colonies in New Jersey*, pp. 133–35.

58. Herscher, *Agricultural Utopias*, pp. 106–7; Eisenberg, *Colonies in New Jersey*, pp. 135–36.

59. Quoted in Herscher, *Agricultural Utopias*, p. 176 n. 5.

60. Bartelt, "Jewish Colonies," p. 364.

CHAPTER 7

California's Exotic Brotherhoods

During the half century after the Civil War, according to Robert V. Hine, the "course of utopia" moved westward to California. In these years some 17 communal utopias were started there. Many were socialist cooperatives with some degree of communal ownership of property. Four were religious, built by individuals who embarked on experiments, called "Brotherhoods," based upon Buddhism, Hinduism, mysticism, and Spiritualism. The most important of these communities were Fountain Grove and the Theosophical communities at Point Loma, Temple Home, and Krotona.

FOUNTAIN GROVE

In 1875, Thomas Lake Harris started his "Brotherhood of the New Life" at Fountain Grove, a secluded spot in the foothills two miles north of Santa Rosa. Harris, a vagabond religious mystic, was born in England in 1823 and came to Utica, New York, with his parents five years later. Raised as a strict Calvinist, at the age of 18 he rejected his family and its confining theology for Universalism. During his twenties, he held several Universalist pulpits, married, and fathered two sons. In 1850, his wife died, and for consolation he turned to spiritualism. Harris organized a millennial spiritualist community at Mountain Cove, West Virginia, where he felt in touch with the dead. Over the next three years he became deeply affected by the writings of the Swedish theologian and scientist Emanuel Swedenborg (1688–1772), especially his ideas about how to diminish the widening gulf between man and God. In 1854, he left Mountain Cove and became a Swedenborgian preacher to a small congregation in New York City. The following year he entered a celibate marriage with a second wife, Emily.[1]

Around 1857, he underwent a mystical experience. He told his church members that by practicing "Divine Respiration," a sort of yoga breathing exercise, he had communicated directly with God. The leadership of the Swedenborgian church, when they found out what he was doing, denounced him. He went to England for a year and visited the slums of Manchester and London to convert people to what he called the "Brotherhood of the New Life." Failing to attract any significant following, he returned to the village of Wassiac, in Dutchess County, New York, where he lived for a while with some of the Manhattan Swedenborgians. At Wassiac and nearby Amenia he organized a religious utopian community that in 10 years numbered 75 adults.[2]

Harris was an imposing personality, with a long flowing beard, overhanging eyebrows, and flashing blue eyes. In a monthly journal called the *Herald of Light* he contended that the millennium would be announced by the "pivotal man" (himself) who stood between the forces of good and evil.[3] He wrote about the doctrine of the "Two-in-One," that God the Father was both man and woman. He believed that Christ, too, was a "Divine Man-Woman" who concealed his bisexuality while on earth. Only a platonic relationship could exist between the sexes, a union that was achieved by a "Divine Respiration" that would unite a person with God and guarantee a sinless life. This spiritual union was to be the basis for a Universal Brotherhood through communal living. Humankind, living together as brothers and sisters and practicing the Respiration, would exist at "the very threshold of heaven." All private property would vanish because, he wrote, "possession of property held for individual ends, grapples man and fixes him in a selfish and fatal individualism and isolation from his fellows." In the Brotherhood members would have sexual intercourse only with angels, whom Harris called "spiritual counterparts."[4]

In 1868, he relocated his followers to 2,000 acres of excellent farmland on the shores of Lake Erie near the town of Brocton. The financial generosity of two new members of the colony—one gave Harris $250,000, another $100,000—enabled them to build a spacious main house called "Vine Cliff," plant grapes, and construct a large winery. Other buildings included a barn, a general store, restaurant, and hotel. In 1875, Harris decided to relocate the colony to California. There, he said, on the beautiful Pacific Coast, he would fashion "this new Eden of the West." There, the "mightier Muse" would flourish. There, as pivotal man, he would enjoy better experiences of the Divine Breath and have more revelations. That summer he purchased 700 acres two miles north of Santa Rosa for $21,000. And four years later he added another 1,000 acres. He and a handful of brothers began construction of "Fountain Grove," and soon it had a large frame home with a fountain surrounded by eucalyptus and fruit trees, hedges, gardens, and ponds. It conveyed a sense of serenity and tranquility he thought essential to probing "the mystery of Solitude" and gaining "the path into the spirit of Society."[5] The colony was located a quarter mile off State Highway 101 and was connected to San Francisco, 50 miles to the south, by railroad.

In 1881, by the time everyone had moved to Fountain Grove from Brocton, Harris lived in a palatial estate, called "Aestivossa," estimated to be valued at over $90,000. The mansion was a two-story building with a wide porch and sunrooms, high ceilings, paneled rooms, stained-glass windows, and luxurious carpets. On one side of the first floor was a spacious dining room and a kitchen. On the other side were sitting rooms and a library, one of the largest in northern California. The bedrooms were upstairs. At night gas lamps illuminated every room. Harris, his wife, and about a half dozen members lived in the main house, while others stayed across the road in a comfortable two-story apartment house with rooms paneled with polished redwood. Next to the apartment was a third, smaller house, built as a temporary shelter in 1875 while they constructed the main house, and it provided accommodations for new members. A quarter mile away from the living area Harris put up a winery, brandy house, and round barn.

He called Fountain Grove a "Theo-socialist community," and he elaborated on this definition in 54 books and pamphlets and in songs and poems he composed almost daily. He claimed that Christ was a "super Socialist" who wanted everyone to live together in equal social conditions. He wrote in *The New Republic: A Discourse of the Prospects, Dangers, Duties, and Safeties of the Times*, published in Santa Rosa in 1891, that the "Divine immanence" within all men and women made them "free and equal." The "virtue of the Divine Father-Motherhood," he stated, also made everyone sons and daughters, "free, coequal, interdependent," living under "the creed of the Social Christ." Harris did, however, approve of some aspects of capitalism. Profit was an appropriate goal of cooperative communities. As they multiplied in number, they would join together as a sort of trust, much the way in which industrial monopolies were created, to increase their common wealth.[6]

He organized Fountain Grove on a cooperative basis. All means of production, such as buildings and machinery, were held in common, but individuals could keep personal property and assets such as financial investments. Its most important industry was wine making, already important to Sonoma County. He planted 1,700 acres with cabernet, pinot noir, and zinfandel vines and annually pressed 70,000 gallons of wine. Yet, he said that wine making was not just an economic activity. It represented the fraternal love emanating from the souls of the brothers and sisters. According to Harris's idea of "infusion," "consecrated hands devoted to human service" made the wine and, consequently, it contained the "substance of Divine and celestial energy . . . to all who receive and partake of it."[7]

Everything made at Fountain Grove was supposed to embody the spirit of the community. All work, whether it was at the wine press, typesetting copy for Harris's books and pamphlets, sewing clothes, or tending livestock, was an expression of personal piety and universal love, a symbol of a willingness to serve humankind. Everyone at Fountain Grove "served humanity while he performed his individual task, for by the theory of infusion any object would inspire its subsequent holder with the inner light of its former owner."[8] Harris felt that production should never be cataloged or measured since it was, in essence, a spiritual gift.

Anyone who joined Fountain Grove just to relax and enjoy themselves was in for a surprise. As one of the faithful phrased it, an idler could not have "retained the Breath for an instant without [his] becoming subject to furious and fatal attack from the inversive Breath of the world and of the infernal spirits of evil below the world." Harris maintained discipline by arbitrarily assigning all tasks so that workers "will fit into the purpose of the king even as the sword fits into the scabbard; and in this unity of the social-will the dreamed-of paradise will rise on earth." Their spiritual attitude toward work was reflected in another name the members gave the colony: "The Use." "Everyone," one sister explained, "must have his or her 'use' or 'uses' according to his or her special genius."[9]

Harris legally owned everything as a trustee but required no transfer of property to him when individuals joined the colony. Even so, some members surrendered all of their possessions, while others kept control of their assets and regularly donated money to the community. If a person left Fountain Grove, he or she was allowed to recover these donations. Harris had observed in a letter written in the winter of 1871 that in the Brotherhood "there is no 'community'; every friend controls his own property and manages his own affairs." And, later, one brother remembered: "There never was . . . community of possessions in The Use, in any legal sense." "Every individual was duly invested with his own share of all properties, corresponding to his means," he said, "but of course all were essentially involved together in their increasing or lowering market values." Such discrepancies seemed not to bother him at all. As Hine explains it, to Harris "the extent of individual secular holdings was secondary as long as the brethren shared the fundamental unity of religious belief."[10]

A blithesome daily routine sustained Fountain Grove. They began each morning with a breakfast in the large communal dining hall where they joined hands and sang. They enlivened the evenings with more singing. Seated at a piano, Harris played the tunes as brothers and sisters sang such songs as "With Roses Wreathe the Drum," "Social Resurrection," and "Arrows of the Sun." At these gatherings Harris read his poems—light, fleetingly gay verse stanzas on love and nature peppered with metaphors of Eden, Adam and Eve, Cupid, and Mother-Glee. In 1886, he introduced square dancing. In groups of four couples they moved in three-fourths and six-eighths rhythm in flowing conviviality. "You would smile to see the full sisterhood, all in beautiful attire, and gliding through quadrilles as if they had wings on their feet," he wrote in an 1886 letter, "while the brethren, old and young, look on and wonder and smile and dance with them till the house quivers." In a poem "The Joy-

Bringer" he indicated that these pastimes were not mere frivolous amusements. "Dance while you may, dance while you may," he wrote, "For Heaven comes forth in social play."[11]

Men and women touched each other only at these dances because celibacy was required at Fountain Grove. Its rules of sexual conduct stemmed, as did all other aspects of life there, from Harris's personality. Perhaps his feelings about sexual intercourse were imprinted by an unhappy childhood. His mother, whom he dearly loved, died when he was nine years of age, and his strict Calvinist stepmother, whom he despised, was the reason he left home. In his writings he condemned sex as a paramount corruptor of society. He concluded that the only hope for "humankind . . . so diseased and disordered" by sex was "a period of complete separation between the sexes."[12] Only the spiritual connection of a man and a woman would bring the couple union with the male-female God. "God Himself is the only real Bridegroom," he declared, and "God Herself is the only real Bride." In a letter to Oneidian William Hinds dated August 22, 1877, he claimed that sexual temptation posed "no difficulty" for Fountain Grove, and only two births had occurred in 17 years.[13]

Such confidence in the suppression of sexual feelings notwithstanding, Harris constantly scrutinized relationships for any signs that sexual attraction might jeopardize the all-important mystical union with God and the broadening of one's love for humanity. Sometimes separation was the only way to stymie lust and destroy selfish love for another individual. Harris sometimes separated children from parents; that is, the children brought into the colony by their parents when they joined, since during the first 17 years of the Brotherhood only two infants were born there. Whenever he doubted the spirituality of the parents, as he did in two cases, he had the children live with other families rather than risk corruption by the natural parents. He then announced that they were fortunate to have two parents, their own and the community.

Still, Harris's ambiguous language about sex, and the lack of any colony newspaper as a source of information about relationships at Fountain Grove, led to serious misunderstandings by outsiders of what was going on there. It was easy to place a more conventional interpretation on statements such as: "Sing of love . . . of conjugal love. Be the poet of Maidens and Lovers, and Conjugal Consorts. Make thy poetic house a garden of Eden where the Adams and Eves of the Golden Age shall sing their endless marriage-hymn." He described the utopia as a place where "Hymen have his court, and every priest a Cupid be, Till golden babes are born to sport, Where lift the waves of Mother-Glee."[14]

In the beginning newspaper editors described him as a respectable squire developing a spa for wealthy easterners. They praised his library. They commended his coffee house and restaurant that gave free food and drink to any visitor. But in the spring of 1891, Margaret Oliphant, a relative of one of the members, published in New York City a two-volume *Memoir of the Life of*

Laurence Oliphant. In it she described Harris's sexual immorality. It was not long until parts of the book were serialized in the Santa Rosa newspapers. In December of that year June Alzire Chevailler, a Christian Scientist and suffragette who had stayed at Fountain Grove the previous summer, wrote a series of exposés for the *San Francisco Chronicle.* She claimed Harris had made sexual advances toward her, that he was an autocrat who made slaves of his followers. Encouraged by substantial public interest in these articles, Chevailler went to Santa Rosa and lectured about Fountain Grove to a packed town hall.[15]

Harris refused to respond to the charges, believing it impossible to squelch such rumors once they started. Anyhow, he was openly contemptuous of the press. However, because the growing hostility focused only on him, he reluctantly concluded that the only solution was to leave Fountain Grove. But just before he departed he made a decision that only exacerbated the situation. On February 27, 1892, at the age of 68, he married 64-year-old Jane Waring, his secretary for the past 17 years. The *San Francisco Call* sarcastically headlined: "No More a Celibate" and the city's *Chronicle* printed a story on its front page about the "wedded mystics."[16]

The couple left for a tour of Europe and afterward settled permanently in New York City. They lived comfortably, but celibate, on Harris's income from his interests in Fountain Grove. He tried to direct the community by mailing instructions to members still living there, but they largely ignored these epistles. With Harris gone, Fountain Grove withered as brothers and sisters just moved out. Harris completely abandoned all hope for the utopia and in 1900 sold out his interests, valued at $40,000, to five members who remained at the site. The sale had one catch. The men had to agree to a clause that whoever lived the longest would take possession of the property. In the 1920s, this person, Kanaye Nagasawa, inherited the profitable "Fountain Grove Winery." After his death in 1934, outside investors purchased the property.[17]

THEOSOPHY

On an autumn afternoon in 1874, Henry Steel Olcott, a New York attorney, sat in a Vermont farmhouse among a hushed audience awaiting the appearance of the famed spiritualist and medium Madame Helena Petrovna Blavatsky. Helena, born in 1831 in southern Russian, at the age of 17 had married a 70-year-old army general. But a year later she ran away and supported herself as a journalist, pianist, and circus performer. She visited monasteries in Tibet, went to Cairo to study magic with a Coptic magician, and in 1858 ended up in Paris, where she joined a spiritualist society. By that time she had declared herself a materialist "who did not believe in God" and then reversed herself to accept a pantheistic force in the universe and a divine Plan for it. She also had braided together various threads of Buddhism and Hinduism to create an eclectic version of how this Plan worked in the world. In 1873, she left France for New York City.[18]

Madame Blavatsky stepped on the Vermont stage that afternoon dressed in a Gypsy costume and announced that she was the "materialized spirit" of an Indian maiden. She danced with flowing scarves across the stage and disappeared. Next, an Egyptian juggler did a rope trick. He was followed by a wrinkled old woman who sat on a chair and spoke messages coming from the netherworld. Then Blavatsky suddenly reappeared and called forth the spirits: a singing former footman, a departed uncle, a Russian judge, and a soldier who, she said, had presented her with a military decoration. She showed the medal to the astonished audience. Olcott, on the spot, became her devoted disciple.[19]

In 1875, he and Blavatsky founded the Theosophical Society, a New York City organization for the study of spiritualism. *Theosophy*, meaning "divine wisdom," was a montage of ideas from Transcendentalism, Buddhism, Hinduism, and Spiritualism, all explained in Blavatsky's three most important books: *Isis Unveiled* (1877), *The Secret Doctrine* (1888), and *The Key to Theosophy* (1889). These ideas were revealed to her, Blavatsky said, through contacts with long-dead "Masters," who shared with her the eternal secrets of the universe by telepathic communication through astral currents. Theosophy's most original tenet was that the universe was directed not by a personal God of the Judeo-Christian heritage but governed by a transcendent "Eternal Principle" present everywhere. It created and sustained not just one but an infinite number of universes that constantly disappear and reemerge "within the totality of the encompassing Principle."[20] Blavatsky saw all life as a unified expression of the Eternal Principle that made possible a Universal Brotherhood of humankind. "There is no human being in whom intelligence is developed," she wrote, "that is not rooted in the One Life."[21] So united, it followed that an evil action by any person harmed all of humanity. Individuals progressed upward toward final union with the Principle according to karma, or the total effect of the person's actions in his or her present life.

The Theosophical Society had three objectives. Since it was based on the Universal Brotherhood of Humanity, it would admit everyone without discrimination against religion, race, or station in life. It would encourage the study of all religions, philosophies, and sciences to show how they were relevant to the divine Plan. Last, it would explore the mysteries of nature and the psychic powers of humans.[22]

In New York City, at an apartment at 47th Street and Eighth Avenue, the pair set up the "Lamasery," the society's headquarters. It was exotic. A mechanical bird and a golden Buddha sat on the mantelpiece. There were huge potted palms on the floor and stuffed owls, snakes, and lizards in the bookcases. A stuffed baboon with spectacles holding a journal article on Darwin's *Origin of the Species* gawked from the corner. Ordinary people, curious journalists, and Thomas Edison came to séances at the Lamasery where Blavatsky, always dressed outlandishly and chain-smoking cigarettes, performed her "phenomena." She made rapping sounds come from under a table. Pictures appeared on blank slates. Wind chimes tinkled from all parts of the room as she talked about the exotic world of Asia and the Middle East.[23]

Olcott ran the practical side of the society as its president and was the careful editor of Blavatsky's manuscripts. To increase membership he merged the society with a Hindu revivalist group in India called the Arya Samaj. In December 1878, he and Blavatsky moved the headquarters to Bombay, leaving behind a trusted lieutenant, William Quan Judge, as the head of the Theosophical Society of America. In India, Olcott took care of business matters and Blavatsky spent her time, as corresponding secretary, writing more books on the teachings of the Masters. In 1880, Olcott went on a lecture tour throughout India and Ceylon, collecting donations and founding new chapters of the society. Two years later he moved headquarters again, this time to Adyar, near Madras, and remained there until his death in 1907.[24]

Meanwhile, the British Society for Psychical Research in London conducted a scientific study of the Theosophists. During the investigation, one of Blavatsky's housekeepers claimed that the madame faked the mysterious happenings at the séances. An alarmed Blavatsky traveled to London to refute the charges. At the same time, in India Olcott tried to move the society away from Blavatsky's religious ideas and have it identify more with worldwide humanitarian reforms. She resented this maneuver and while in England attracted new followers dedicated exclusively to the cosmology of the Masters and the importance of the occult. Among the newcomers was Annie Besant, a former member of the Fabian Society and soon Blavatsky's most important disciple. From her London salon she met with the young poet William Butler Yeats and a law student named Mohandas K. Gandhi. Olcott, although initially opposed to Blavatsky's religious focus, came around in 1888 to agree with her. That year they formed the Esoteric Section of the Theosophical Society (ES) as an appendage of the Theosophical Society. But it was impossible to keep the two apart, and, three years before Blavatsky died in the London influenza epidemic of 1891, the religious ideas of the ES spread throughout the entire membership.

After Blavatsky's death Annie Besant became her designated successor in Europe and India. In America, Judge had taken firm control and claimed that he, like Blavatsky, was the sole recipient of messages from the Masters and that he alone was in charge of the ES. By 1894, there were two distinct organizations. Judge, in the United States, headed the "Theosophical Society of America" (TSA). In Europe and India, Besant controlled the lodges of the "Adyar branch of the Theosophical Society."[25]

Before Judge died in 1896, he appointed Katherine Tingley as leader of the TSA. She was born in Newburyport, Massachusetts, in 1852 and had married three times but remained childless. Beginning in 1887, she founded in New York City various philanthropic societies such as the Society of Mercy, the

Martha Washington Home for the Aged, and the Do-Good Mission. Meanwhile, she became attracted to spiritualism, met Judge, and joined the TSA. There was serious objection to Tingley's succession as "Outer Head" of the organization, and some lodges in New York City and Syracuse became independent.

The defections did not diminish Tingley's confidence. With Blavatsky dead and Olcott in virtual retirement in far-off Adyar, she decided to make the United States the center of a new World Theosophical Crusade. She went on a lecture tour to unify the lodges and to organize an international convention to meet in Chicago. Most significantly, she persuaded Besant to work with her and to lead Theosophy on a mission to build a Universal Brotherhood for social reform. In effect, the two women pushed Theosophy toward communalism as a vehicle for humanitarianism. Besant developed a variety of social programs for the poor in India. Tingley built a model community in America as a base from which to launch the universal crusade. They also changed the society's name to "The Universal Brotherhood and Theosophical Society."[26]

The Universal Brotherhood embraced doctrines more socially oriented than the occult Blavatskian tenets of the early years. Tingley insisted that social change and betterment was its paramount objective. They must make the United States a national cooperative state and use Edward Bellamy's *Looking Backward* as the blueprint of the new order. She correctly pointed out that Blavatsky initially had endorsed Bellamy's ideas and the Nationalist movement they sparked, as a visible manifestation of Theosophy's belief in a universal brotherhood. She recalled that Cyrus Field Willard and Sylvester Baxter, Boston newspapermen and original members of the society in 1883, had read *Looking Backward* and had corresponded with Bellamy about having the Theosophists and the Nationalists fuse to form an organization to spread the utopian plan of the book.

Events moved fast in that direction in 1888 with the organization of a committee to form the association and a December 15 meeting that elected officers. They published a joint declaration of mutual goals for the Universal Brotherhood "without distinction of race, creed, sex, caste, or color." Its principle was "one of the eternal truths that govern the world's progress on lines which distinguish human nature from brute nature." During the following year, "wherever a Theosophical group formed, a Nationalist club also soon opened its doors."[27] The merger of the Theosophical Society and the Nationalists never took place, however, because of the increasingly radical demands of the Nationalists for immediate, drastic change through political action. Nevertheless, Tingley felt that *Looking Backward* should serve as a guide book for the Brotherhood. After all, Bellamy had condemned the demoralizing impact of competition on the human spirit and, like the Brotherhood, wanted all means of production owned and controlled by the people. The book, like the Brotherhood, condemned class struggle and claimed that all humans were equal.²⁸ But Tingley was quick to emphasize concepts that were unique to Theosophy. The Universal Brotherhood claimed that every religion contained the same essential concepts of God, revelation, rules of moral conduct, and immortality of the soul. Theosophy maintained that Christ was a great teacher, as were Buddha and Krishna. None of them divine, they all taught the same eternal truths. Tingley placed special emphasis on karma and reincarnation, and many of her converts were firm believers in these doctrines. She also discounted the importance of the occult, saying that spiritualism was secondary to the social purposes of the Universal Brotherhood.²⁹

POINT LOMA

Tingley established the headquarters for the Universal Brotherhood on an estuary on the northern part of a peninsula called Point Loma. At noon one day in February 1897, she presided at the dedication of a magnificent temple. Dressed in a purple gown, she approached the cornerstone and christened it with oil, wine, and corn, while a small orchestra from San Diego played the Intermezzo by Mascagni. She placed a metal box into a hole in the stone, covered it with cement, and declared that the rock was "a fitting emblem of the perfect work that will be done in the temple for the benefit of humanity and glory of the ancient sages." Other speakers followed throughout the afternoon, quoting the Bhagavad-Gita, Upanishads, and Orphic Mysteries.³⁰

Tingley ruled Point Loma for 29 years. At its prime in the first decade of this century it was, according to Robert Hine, "as good an example of a religious utopia as can be found in California history."³¹ By 1910, 200 adults and 300 children lived in a 330-acre community that included three main buildings, groups of bungalows, an amphitheater, gardens, and orchards—all worth over $300,000. The Theosophists, some well educated and most from the middle class, paid an entrance fee of $500 and a monthly rent. A number of wealthy businessmen donated a great deal more than the stipulated fee. For example, entrepreneurs such as Albert B. Spalding, William Chase Temple, Clark Thurston, and W. Ross White endowed Point Loma with substantial sums of money. Like Fountain Grove, its members had private investments and owned property outside the community, but all land and buildings at Point Loma were in Tingley's name as trustee. She paid all the bills, even for visits from physicians, from a community fund. By its constitution she was "Leader and Official Head" for life and had the right to choose her successor, appoint all other officers, and establish bylaws. She named a cabinet that helped her manage the community and keep track of financial affairs. She and the cabinet supplied all members with food, education, medical supplies, and clothes. She assigned and rotated all jobs. Women did the domestic chores and made all the clothing, simple uniforms for both sexes. The men raised avocados, oranges, and honey for sale in San Diego.³²

Most members, married or single, lived in the central apartment called the Homestead, while others were housed in small bungalows. Everyone ate in a central refectory, where adults and children sat in separate rooms. Children lived apart from their parents, except for Sunday visits. From the age of five months until three years, they where kept in a nursery and then, until the age of five, in a dormitory where they learned communal rules and music. Boys over the age of five lived in group houses, circular bungalows that surrounded a central room where a teacher resided day and night. Girls lived in the Homestead.[33]

Tingley doubted that a Universal Brotherhood was attainable in the immediate future and hoped that the next generation, purged of poverty and crime and their souls cleansed through training and discipline, could accomplish it. Consequently, she placed paramount importance on the community school called Raja Yoga, or Kingly Union. There, children were trained in spiritual development, culture, and academics. Most of them came from outside Point Loma and paid a tuition fee often as high as $4,000. They were in class only a couple of hours each day and were taught arithmetic, history, English, and foreign languages. Afterward, they sang and played the piano and other musical instruments. They participated as actors in plays in the Point Loma amphitheater, an 11-row semicircular structure that seated 2,500 people. Teachers indoctrinated the children with the tenets of Theosophy and constantly watched for signs of evil conduct that might impede reincarnation to a higher life and thus frustrate progress of the Brotherhood.[34]

Tingley, in 1901, purchased an Opera House in San Diego and renamed it the Isis Theater. There, on Sunday evenings, Point Loma actors performed Greek tragedies and dramas. Ticket sales, at $.75 for general admission and up to $10.00 for box seats, brought in a sizeable income since audiences frequently numbered over a thousand.[35] Despite the financial success of the theater and substantial gifts from patrons, Tingley never balanced the books. By the time of her death in an automobile accident in July 1929, Point Loma was over $400,000 in debt. Her loss was fatal to the community. "Without a charismatic leader like Tingley," J. Gordon Melton writes, "it was never able to return to its former glory."[36]

Her successor, Gottfried de Purucker, started a fund-raising campaign, but the timing was catastrophic. The stock market crashed that October, and, during the ensuing Great Depression, Point Loma's financial condition became so serious that by 1940 creditors forced the sale of all real estate except the few acres of the central compound. Then, during World War II, when the army pressured it to turn over that facility for troop housing, Purucker sold everything and moved the community to Covina. In 1950, the international headquarters of Theosophy moved permanently to Pasadena.[37]

TEMPLE OF THE PEOPLE

In 1904, members of the Syracuse and New York City Theosophical Societies who had rejected Tingley's leadership moved to a 300-acre spot north of Santa Barbara and formed the Temple of the People.[38] Led by William H. Dower, a physician, and Mrs. Frances A. La Due, they maintained that they were carrying on Blavatsky's leadership by receiving revelations from the Masters. They said that they alone remained as the "channel" for such thoughts. The main part of the community, the Home Association, in the words of its brochure, was a place "wherein all the land will be owned all of the time by all of the people; where all the means of production and distribution, tools, machinery, and natural resources, will be owned by the people—the community—and where Capital and Labor may meet on equal terms and with no special privileges together." They believed that "all Theosophists should be Socialists."[39]

A board of three directors chosen by an annual meeting of all members (admission was open to anyone who came up with a $100 fee) ruled Temple of the People, and two of them were always Dower and La Due. The board assigned jobs and paid every member a $10 monthly allowance. Temple Home gave every resident the use of half-acre plots, where they planted oats, barley, sugar beets, vegetables, and flower seeds with much of the heavy farmwork done by Japanese laborers. Families lived in separate bungalows, and the children went to the public schools in the town of Arroyo Grande. Dower and La Due envisioned the temple as the hub of a ring of worldwide communities dedicated to their Theosophical mission. By 1905, they had identified 22 such satellite colonies, called "squares," throughout the United States.[40]

In 1908, they began publication of a monthly magazine called the *Temple Artisan*. It told of regular outings in which they dug for clams, swam in the surf, and enjoyed picnics on the beach. Still, internal divisions appeared. According to the *Temple Artisan*, the tension was only "between workers" and would soon be overcome by "the inflow of Lodge light and force ever welling from the real Temple Heart." Apparently, the force never appeared. The community failed to make money and payments on the mortgages became delinquent. In 1909, they reorganized and the board made residents pay a regular monthly fee. But this failed to raise enough money to satisfy the banks. The end came in 1912 when "the association abandoned the cooperative economic arrangements, cut its ties to the members' businesses, and sold some of the land to pay off all the outstanding mortgages." In 1913, the cooperative dissolved and sold all of the property except the central building called the Temple Home. It survived on 100 acres into the 1990s.[41]

KROTONA

In 1911, Albert P. Warrington, one of Besant's followers, purchased 23 acres halfway between Point Loma and Santa Barbara and organized the Krotona Institute of Theosophy.[42] Its 45 residents had a vegetarian cafeteria, a printing press, library, and a temple. It opened the Krotona School of Theosophy, which offered classes and seminars on Blavatsky's revelations. Warrington boasted that it would not be long before he would see at Krotona "a community fully exemplifying the life of the future under a truly scientific system of growth in all planes."[43]

He was naive. Financial problems mounted from the start and, despite donations of money and land by new members, in 1917 the mortgage balance stood at $41,000. Warrington became discouraged and resigned in 1920. L. W. Rogers succeeded him, but he, too, faced an increasingly divided community. Frustrated by all the rancor, Rogers asked Besant to intervene. She decided to sell some of the land to pay off the debts. Krotona lingered on as a marginal community until the 1960s, when it became active in reviving its School of Theosophy to offer regular classes and workshops annually from September through May.[44]

The communal aspects of Theosophy were the basis of Point Loma, Temple Home, and Krotona. Their leaders and members saw their communities as utopian models for a worldwide communal movement to realize universal brotherhood and achieve humanitarian reforms. Theosophy's internal contradictions and tensions, however, doomed their communalism. From the start there was an irresolvable conflict between the altruism of brotherhood and social reform and the intensely individualistic religious spiritualism. Ultimately, Theosophists' emphasis on the soul's journey through reincarnation to unification with the Eternal Principle won out, and most Theosophists abjured the brotherhood-humanitarianism commitment. In the words of Melton, they "abandoned the search for community for its more primary occult concerns." Even so, in 1997 he concluded, "Theosophy is alive and well. It is a worldwide movement . . . narrowly defined in several competing organizations that bear the name seeded by the several branches of the Theosophical Society."[45]

NOTES

1. Robert V. Hine, *California's Utopian Colonies* (Berkeley: University of California Press, 1983), pp. 12–15; Hinds, *American Communities*, pp. 422–24; Herbert W. Schneider and George Lawton, *A Prophet and a Pilgrim* (New York: Columbia University Press, 1942), pp. 3–20; Catherine McAllaister, *The Brotherhood of the New Life* (Fredonia: State University of New York at Fredonia, 1995), pp. 1–2. The historical literature on Fountain Grove is scant. Hine and Schneider are the only serious studies of Harris and the community; and Schneider, *A Prophet and a Pilgrim*, pp. 561–63, lists all of Harris's 54 books and pamphlets, and his appendixes have important documents on Fountain Grove. Articles on the colony are W. F. Barry, "Laurence Oliphant," *Quarterly Review* (London) 178 (October 1891): 392–413 and William S. Bailey, "The Harris Community—Brotherhood of the New Life," *New York History* 16 (July 1935): 278–85.

2. Hine, *Utopian Colonies*, pp. 24–25; Schneider and Lawton, *Prophet*, pp. 108, 113–14, 121.

3. Hine, *Utopian Colonies*, pp. 16–18; McAllister, *Brotherhood*, p. 2. For Hinds's personal impression of Harris after an interview, see *American Communities*, p. 429.

4. Hine, *Utopian Colonies*, p. 28; Schneider and Lawton, *Prophet*, pp. 145–207.

5. Hine, *Utopian Colonies*, p. 22; Schneider and Lawton, *Prophet*, pp. 276–310.

6. Hine, *Utopian Colonies*, p. 29; Schneider and Lawton, *Prophet*, pp. 310–22.

7. Hine, *Utopian Colonies*, p. 19; Schneider and Lawton, *Prophet*, pp. 160, 168, 280, 473.

8. Hine, *Utopian Colonies*, p. 19.

9. Ibid., pp. 19–20.

10. Ibid., pp. 27–28.

11. Ibid., pp. 22–23; Schneider and Lawton, *Prophet*, pp. 297–302.

12. Quoted in Hine, *Utopian Colonies*, p. 24.

13. Quoted in Ibid., p. 26; Schneider and Lawton, *Prophet*, pp. 180, 183, 301–2, 308.

14. Hine, *Utopian Colonies*, pp. 24–25.

15. Ibid., p. 312 n. 43.

16. Quoted in Ibid., p. 32.

17. Ibid., p. 32; Hinds, *American Communities*, pp. 430–31.

18. Marion Meade, *Madame Blavatsky: The Woman Behind the Myth* (New York: G. P. Putnam's Sons, 1980), pp. 15–97; Charles J. Ryan, *H. P. Blavatsky and the Theosophical Movement*, 2d and rev. ed. (Pasadena, Calif.: Theosophical University Press, 1975), pp. 3–42. Other valuable studies of theosophy and theosophical communities include Sylvia Cranston, *H. P. B.: The Extraordinary Life and Influence of Helena Blavatsky, Founder of the Modern Theosophical Movement* (New York: G. P. Putnam's Sons, 1993); Paul Kagan, *New World Utopias: A Photographic History of the Search for Community* (Baltimore: Penguin, 1975); G. Gordon Melton, "The Theosophical Communities and Their Ideal of Universal Brotherhood," in *America's Communal Utopias*, ed. Donald E. Pitzer (Chapel Hill: University of North Carolina Press, 1997), pp. 396–418; Joy Mills, *100 Years of Theosophy* (Wheaton, Ill.: Theosophical Publishing House, 1987); Arthur H. Nethercourt, *The First Five Lives of Annie Besant* (Chicago: University of Chicago Press, 1960); John Oliphant, *Brother Twelve: The Incredible Story of Canada's False Prophet* (Toronto: McClelland & Stewart, 1991).

19. Howard Murphet, *Hammer on the Mountain: Life of Henry Steel Olcott 1832–1907* (Wheaton, Ill.: Theosophical Publishing House, 1972), pp. 23–39; Meade, *Blavatsky*, pp. 113–22.

20. Melton, "Theosophical Communities," pp. 396–400; Hine, *Utopian Colonies*, p. 38.

21. Quoted in Hine, *Utopian Colonies*, p. 39.

22. Melton, "Theosophical Communities," p. 400; Ryan, *Blavatsky*, pp. 50–78.

23. Melton, "Theosophical Communities," p. 401; Meade, *Blavatsky*, pp. 125–89; Murphet, *Hammer on the Mountain*, pp. 54–68.

24. Murphet, *Hammer on the Mountain*, pp. 100–131, 178–202, 277–314.

25. Meade, *Blavatsky*, pp. 419–20, 446–49, 458–59; Hine, *Utopian Colonies*, pp. 34–35, 37; Nethercourt, *Annie Besant*, pp. 283–351; Ryan, *Blavatsky*, pp. 19–129.

26. Melton, "Theosophical Communities," pp. 401–2; Hine, *Utopian Colonies*, pp. 34–35; Ryan, *Blavatsky*, pp. 313–14.

27. Melton, "Theosophical Communities," pp. 397–98.

28. Hine, *Utopian Colonies*, pp. 40–41.

29. Melton, "Theosophical Communities," pp. 400–401.

30. Ibid., pp. 402–3; Hine, *Utopian Colonies*, p. 43.

31. Hine, *Utopian Colonies*, p. 43.

32. Melton, "Theosophical Communities," pp. 404–5; Emmett A. Greenwalt, *California Utopia: Point Loma, 1897–1942* (Berkeley: University of California Press, 1955), pp. 76–80.

33. Melton, "Theosophical Communities," p. 406; Hine, *Utopian Colonies*, pp. 44–48; Greenwalt, *Point Loma*, pp. 81–95.

34. Hine, *Utopian Colonies*, p. 49; Greenwalt, *Point Loma*, pp. 100–109.

35. Hine, *Utopian Colonies*, pp. 49–50; Greenwalt, *Point Loma*, pp. 87, 103–4, 168–69, 175, 185–88.

36. Melton, "Theosophical Communities," pp. 406–7; Hine, *Utopian Colonies*, p. 53.

37. Hine, *Utopian Colonies*, p. 54; Greenwalt, *Point Loma*, pp. 149–206.

38. Melton, "Theosophical Communities," p. 416 n.12.

39. Quoted in Hine, *Utopian Colonies*, p. 55.

40. Ibid., pp. 55–56; Melton, "Theosophical Communities," p. 408.

41. Melton, "Theosophical Communities," p. 408; Hine, *Utopian Colonies*, pp. 56–57.

42. Joseph E. Ross, *Krotona of Old Hollywood*, 2 vols. (Montecito, Calif.: El Montecito Oaks Press, 1989), pp. 103–9.

43. Melton, "Theosophical Communities," pp. 409–10.

44. Ibid., pp. 410–11; Ross, *Krotona*, pp. 110–232.

45. Melton, "Theosophical Communities," pp. 413–14.

CHAPTER 8

Twentieth-Century Religious Communities

KORESHAN UNITY

Dr. Cyrus Reed Teed, the founder of a religious communal utopia dedicated to "Cellular Cosmogony," was born in Teedsville, New York, in 1839. He was raised as a strict Baptist in the heart of the "burnt-over district" where Charles G. Finney's brimstone evangelism had flourished in the 1820s. Teed studied medicine with an uncle while working as a laborer on the Erie Canal and, during the Civil War, served in the Medical Corps of the Union Army. His experience with wounded soldiers convinced him that faith more than science helped them to recover. After the war he entered the New York Eclectic School of Medicine, received his degree in 1868, and opened a medical practice at Syracuse.[1]

One evening while in his laboratory, he later recalled, an exquisite woman surrounded by purple and gold illumination appeared and told him that God was male and female and had created a hollow-globe universe that renews itself by involution and evolution. She said that all life existed in the inner concave surface of this universe and that every human was reincarnated. The Bible symbolically contained the Divine Mind and could only be understood as interpreted by a prophet such as himself. She declared that humans must live communally, as did the primitive Christians, and eliminate capitalism and "wage slavery." The woman communicated more knowledge to him, he said, but it was so complicated that he could only present it to the world gradually.[2]

A small group of followers, mainly his wife, family, and close friends, began to meet at Teed's home. His neighbors, though, thought he was a crank, and he had to move from one small town to another to keep his medical practice.

He took the name "Koresh," the Hebrew name of Cyrus, and claimed that "Koreshanity," his new religion, supplanted all existing churches. His Cellular Cosmogony had humans living inside the shell of a hollow earth whose concave surface contained the universe. Its 100-mile crust had 17 layers, the outer 7 being made of precious metals. The last crust was pure gold beyond which nothing existed. The sun stood at the center of the hollow earth, half lit and half dark, a condition that explained day and night. Planets floated around the sun as "Mercurial discs," and stars were reflections of the light from these discs.[3]

In 1880, Teed formed the first Koreshan community in Moravia, New York, based upon the four essentials of his "Universology": communalization of society, abolition of private property, celibacy, and the coming millennium. Because of growing local hostility, however, he moved back to Syracuse. After his wife's death in 1886, Teed and four ladies moved again to an apartment in New York City at 135th Street and Eighth Avenue. There, he met a Mrs. Thankful Hale, a Chicago resident, who invited him to come to her city, all expenses paid, to speak to the convention of the National Association of Mental Science.[4]

His lecture, entitled "The Brain," featured a sketch of the organ, and he used it, according to a reporter from the *Chicago Herald*, "to illustrate the battery which generates the brain forces and how it can be applied to restoring invalids to health." He explained how "religion and science must be married" and how "death itself could be eliminated." He invited any sick members of the audience to come forth and be healed. The association was so impressed that it elected him its president and financed a series of public lectures in Chicago. He presented "The Brain" at the Central Music Hall, the National Union Building, and other locations, charging a $12 admission fee.

Later that year, still in Chicago, Teed founded the College of Life and began offering courses on Koreshanity. He established the Church Triumphant and the Society Arch-Triumphant, both dedicated to miraculous healing. He published a monthly periodical called the *Guiding Star*, later changed to the *Flaming Sword*. In 1888, he formed the Koreshan Unity community in a large brick house at 2–4 Collage Place. Sixty individuals, mostly females, lived there. By 1893, when it had grown to include 123 members, Teed moved it to a larger house in Washington Heights called Beth-Ophrah.[5]

Using Chicago as a base, Teed traveled across the country lecturing to religious utopian communities such as the Shakers, Harmonists, and the Brotherhood of the New Life at Fountain Grove. He opened Koreshan Unity branches in San Francisco, Denver, Baltimore, Boston, and other cities. When these ventures failed financially, the converts came to live in Chicago. At Beth-Ophrah the Koreshans, mostly women, adopted celibacy; renounced alcohol, tobacco, and gambling; and surrendered all possessions to Koresh. Teed divided the community into three classes. The "investigatives" were those single individuals who gave only financial support. The "maritals" were married couples who engaged in sex only for procreation. The "celibates," most of the members, were the highest category, and only they could be leaders of the Unity.[6]

In 1893, Koresh had another revelation in which he foresaw a golden age of Koreshan Unity arising in Florida. The disclosure was timely, because by then problems had started to pester the Chicago community. Beth-Ophrah manor house was overcrowded and Teed needed to find new accommodations. Newspapers, particularly the *Chicago Herald*, turned hostile. It claimed that the Unity had 4,000 members nationwide who secretly funneled the headquarters enormous amounts of money. Teed, they said, had sex with his female disciples, despite his vow of chastity, and was a virtual dictator. Irate husbands took Teed to court. Sydney C. Miller, president of the National Publishing Company, sued him for $100,000 for "poisoning his wife's mind." Miller alleged that Teed had "alienated her affection" after he convinced her that "a woman's body was her own" and that sexual love should cease. Miller claimed that Teed had persuaded her to turn over all her possessions to him, valued at over $5,000. Another husband, Thomas Cole, sued Teed for the same amount on much the same charges, only Cole added adultery, committed, he said, on June 20, 1890.[7]

In the autumn of 1893, Teed learned about land for sale on Pine Island near Punta Gorda, Florida. Unfortunately, when he arrived there on December 6, he discovered that the owner's asking price of $150,000 was beyond the financial capacity of the Unity. The next day he lectured in Punta Gorda on Koreshan cosmology, distributed copies of the *Flaming Sword* and other literature, and returned to Chicago. Copies of these publications fell into the hands of a grieving elderly widower named Gustave Damkohler. A German-speaking immigrant, in 1882 he had moved with his family to an isolated 320-acre tract along the Estero River just south of Ft. Myers. He cleared the brush and palmettos, built a one-room cabin, used boxes as furniture, and planted vegetables. Over the next 10 years, Damkohler buried his wife and five children on the farm. Then, at 78 years of age, blind in one eye, and living with his only surviving son, the lonely man eagerly read about the promises of Koreshan cosmogony. When he learned that Teed wanted to buy land, he sent the doctor a letter offering him the Estero homestead.[8]

On December 26, 1893, Teed and four women boarded a train for Florida. Damkohler and his son took the party by sailboat from Ft. Myers to the Estero farm, arriving late in the evening of January 1, 1894. Teed at once concluded that the area was "the vitellus of the cosmogonic egg, the vital beginning of the new order."[9] The group stayed six weeks in the small cabin and ate meals on a wooden shelf on the back porch. The women slept crosswise on the only bed, and in the loft Teed and the Damkohlers used mattresses of old sails. By early February Teed and Damkohler struck a deal. The German sold 300 acres of land for $2,000 and kept 20 acres for himself and his son. Koresh's party went back to Chicago, where Teed organized the relocation.[10]

Teed sent a 3-man work crew (a carpenter, a farmer, and a mechanic) to Estero, followed by an advance guard of 24 Koreshans. They built a tent encampment with cheesecloth screens, slept on the ground, and cooked meals over an open fire. During the day, they cleared more land, dredged the river, and dug drainage ditches. They put up a log house with a thatched roof with floors made of lumber hauled from a sawmill near Ft. Myers. By 1896, they had a sturdy 70-by-40-foot, three-story frame refectory. It had a kitchen and dining room on the first floor where men and women sat at separate tables, eating mainly fish and alligator meat. They installed an organ on the main floor and held evening singing sessions. Teed had his own special table at the east end of the room and used it as a lectern for sermons on the hollow earth. Living quarters for the women were on the upper two floors. Within three years, they erected a Master House for Teed and a school with a dormitory on the second floor. They had a sawmill and a post office. For recreation they swam in the Estero River and went to the Gulf of Mexico on beach picnics. Some evenings they organized "fire fishing" expeditions on the river, where they used lighted wire baskets of pine knots to make the mullet jump out of the water and into their small skiffs. In 1897, Teed opened a Geodetic Staff Headquarters in Naples with a "rectilineator" that, he stated, scientifically demonstrated that the earth was concave and that humans lived on its inner surface. The rectilineator was a survey device with a four-mile-long "air line" extended horizontally on the beach. Viewing the line with a hairline telescope, Teed claimed that the earth's surface could be seen to curve upward, not downward.[11] He published the details of these rectilineator demonstrations in 1899 as *The Cellular Cosmogony.*[12]

In 1903, Teed told the Koreshans still living in Chicago to come to Estero. When these 75 members arrived, more than 200 disciples were living in the community. That year Teed began a spurt of new construction. They replaced the log house with a one-story frame building and connected it to a new machine shop/laundry run by steam power. They put up a bakery that daily could bake 600 loaves of bread and erected Planetary Court with a center hall, a meeting room, seven bedrooms, and on the roof, a one-room cupola. Nearby was the Art Hall with a stage; several rooms for classes, lectures, and concerts; and a studio for displaying paintings done by the members. The Koreshans operated a blacksmith-plumbing shop, cement-making shop, and apiary. They built barns and storage sheds. They purchased a generator that produced electrical power to illuminate all the buildings. In 1904, they incorporated Estero as a city of 7,500 acres with a system of government where Teed, as prime counselor, had full executive, judicial, and legislative power.[13]

At Estero's "Pioneer University of Koreshan Universology" teachers instructed younger children in reading and writing, history, geography, and music and trained the older students in the manual arts. In the Art Hall the colony orchestra gave regular concerts for both Koreshans and Floridians; they played popular songs as well as compositions by Grieg, Verdi, Wagner, and Beethoven. At the Bamboo Landing next to the river they produced plays and enjoyed picnics and festivities honoring Teed's birth. A Shaker visitor was enthralled with the tree-lined ravine there that was crossed by "several artistic foot-bridges made of bamboo and other woods," and he admired the variety of tropical fruits found in their "delightful garden." Estero's library included books on agronomy, beekeeping, carpentry, history, and philosophy. They had their own publishing house equipped with presses brought from Chicago that continued printing the *Flaming Sword* as well as pamphlets and periodicals.[14]

But some members refused to acquiesce to Teed's autocratic rule and they left. They sued him, unsuccessfully, to get their property returned and charged that he misused colony funds for personal needs and for the benefit of a few favorites. A Ft. Myers newspaper editor wrote that Teed was a hypocrite who demanded celibacy for every male but himself. He scoffed at the bizarre science of Cellular Cosmogony and its concave world. Other rumors circulated about free love and drunkenness. Last, many voters in Lee County simply disliked the possibility of hundreds of Chicagoans voting as a block in local elections. Other Floridians objected to diverting tax funds for the upkeep of a road between Ft. Myers and Estero.[15]

In reaction to these developments, Teed formed a political party and ran Koreshan candidates in the 1906 county elections. He started a party newspaper called the *American Eagle*. On October 13, Ross Wallace, a Teed candidate for county commissioner, went to Ft. Myers and became involved in a fistfight with the town Marshall. As the Koreshans later told reporters, Teed, who was with Wallace, was involved in the skirmish and sustained severe head injuries. Afterward, he suffered painful attacks of neuritis and continued to weaken despite bed rest. He died on December 22, 1908. Koresh had told his followers that he was immortal, and they gathered around the corpse for three days, praying, waiting for him to revive. He remained motionless. The Lee County health officials found out about the vigil and ordered the corpse interred.[16]

After Teed's burial in a concrete mausoleum, Annie Ordway, who had served as director of the Chicago colony after Teed moved to Florida, took over but resigned in 1909 to create a short-lived Koreshan community in Seffner, Florida. In 1910, another contingent, calling itself the Order of Theocracy, moved to Ft. Myers and for 20 years operated a communal commercial laundry.

By 1940, only 35 people, all elderly and in poor health, still lived at Estero. Most buildings were dilapidated, the gardens were untended, and the generator worked sporadically. That year a dynamic, 38-year-old refugee from Nazi Germany, Hedwig Michel, joined the Unity and tried to revive communal life. Under her leadership, the Koreshans remodeled the general store, opened a restaurant in one side of the building, and managed a Standard Oil gas station on the road to Ft. Myers. They restored the botanical gardens and the Landing. They repaired the Planetary Court, which by then was rat-ridden and bug-infested, leaked in bad weather, and lacked toilets. It became a guesthouse for tourists. They reconditioned the generator and restored full electric power. Nevertheless, Michel eventually realized that the only way to preserve the Koreshan legacy was to have the state of Florida take it over as a historical park. In 1961, Governor Farris Bryant accepted the Koreshan gift and the 305-acre property, traversed by the Estero River, became the Koreshan State Historic Site.[17]

The state has restored much of the original settlement. Visitors in the twenty-first century can tour the Founder's House, General Store, Bakery, Planetary Court, Art Hall, the Machine Shops, and Generator Building. They can stand on the Bamboo Landing and go inside the Damkohler Cottage, both located on the banks of the river. They can walk a nature trail through pine flat woods and scrub oaks or fish from a boat ramp near the picnic area at the west end of the site. Adjacent to it Ranger, a 60-unit campground, conducts guided tours and presents interpretive programs on the Koreshan community. Michel's last project, completed in 1979, was the Koreshan Unity Foundation, Incorporated, a round wooden and glass structure located a half mile east of the colony across Highway 41, used as a repository for Teed's books, papers, and artifacts. There, a professional staff inventories the collections and makes them available to visitors.

THE CHRISTIAN COMMONWEALTH

In 1896, a religious utopia was built in western Georgia that focused on using Christian morality and compassion to solve the problems of the poor. The Reverend George Herron, a passionate Christian Socialist and author of eight books on the topic, was the inspiration of the Georgia colony. He hated capitalism with its greed, corruption, and exploitation of human labor and argued that there was no hope of reforming it. Instead, Christians must renounce all property, view atonement as the way to relieve the suffering of workers, and gather to build a holy Commonwealth.[18] An Indiana-born Congregational minister, Ralph Albertson, after he read Herron's books, published a series of articles in the Christian Socialist journal the *Kingdom* in which he called for just such a community as an asylum for unskilled workers. Within months, 25 families pooled their resources to finance one based upon "the standard of Christ, the teaching of the same Spirit that led Christ and his disciples to have all things in common."[19]

Albertson began construction in November 1896 at a 1,000-acre abandoned cotton plantation near Columbus, Georgia. The colonists signed a covenant that condemned capitalism and committed them to live in a cooperative brotherhood. Anyone could join, "beggar" or "professor," as Alberston put it, if he or she was willing to bear all difficulties as a cross for the benefit of humankind. It was to be totally egalitarian, all adults could vote and hold office. It would be motivated by a sense of love and harmony. Property was communal and Albertson permitted only a few personal possessions. Everyone received community clothing and housing.

In addition to a refectory they had 14 family cottages, a bachelors' dormitory, print shop, blacksmith shop, sawmill and flour mill, and barns. They cultivated 2,000 acres in oats, rye, and other grains and raised cows and horses on 300 additional acres. They thought work "the only reward they wanted and the displeasure of the community [was] the greatest punishment possible."[20] By 1898, they had a cotton mill that made mail-order towels. They had a library of 1,400 books, a school for the children, and evening classes for adults in topics such as literature and science. Sunday mornings were for nondenominational services and Bible study. Everything seemed so auspicious that in the winter of 1899 they planned another colony in western Florida. Then disaster struck.[21]

Heavy snow and drought destroyed their harvests, and food supplies had to be rationed. One ex-member wrote a pamphlet in which he charged that the colonists practiced illicit sex. Matters worsened when typhoid fever swept through the settlement. Albertson, one of its victims, was so debilitated that soon after his recovery he left the community. His defection caused a steady exodus of other colonists. So many people left the Christian Commonwealth that early in 1900 Albertson returned to forestall a total collapse, but to no avail. With all hope gone he decided to liquidate. They sent the county court a list of individuals entitled to proceeds of the community—anyone who had lived there for the preceding six months—and turned all matters over to the judge. Albertson later blamed the collapse on financial problems and disease. But other observers such as Frederick A. Bushee, writing in the *Political Science Quarterly* in 1905, believed that their difficulties stemmed from the poor quality of members who were allowed in by the open admissions policy and by the absence of effective leadership.[22]

ZION CITY

In January 1900, the Reverend John Alexander Dowie, a former Congregationalist minister who had been preaching in Chicago, founded Zion City, the first religious utopia to be created in the twentieth century. He began with the purchase of 6,500 acres of farmland for $50,000 located 40 miles north of the city. It was to be the new Zion, where members would live according to the precepts of Jesus and where Dowie, as its prophet, would prepare them for the Kingdom of God. In the meantime, before the millennium, he promised that he could heal them of illness through holy living based on the Bible.[23]

A communal theocracy, the city was based on the ideas Dowie had explained in a periodical called the *Leaves of Healing*. He claimed to be a "Dr." Dowie who cured the sick in a tabernacle, the "Little Wooden Hut" near the entrance to the Columbian Exposition at Jackson Park, one of three such healing tabernacles in Chicago. Dowie, with a full beard, looked like a five-foot four-inch 200-pound Moses. His meetings were widely reported in newspapers such as the *Chicago Tribune*, the *Chronicle*, and the *Record*. Hundreds of visitors thronged to the tabernacles to be cured of everything from convulsions to badly crossed eyes. Encouraged, Dowie opened the Zion Publishing House. In February 1897, he dedicated the Central Tabernacle on Michigan Avenue and Sixteenth Street with seating for over 3,000 adherents. Finally, a year later, he named his church the Christian Catholic Church and established its headquarters, "Zion," in the Imperial Hotel on Michigan Avenue and 16th Street.[24]

Dowie's message was always the same: total acceptance of the Bible and his own power of divine healing. Satan, he said, caused all disease. He condemned consumption of pork, oysters, tobacco, and alcohol. He attacked sweatshops, exploitation of bankers, and lynching of Blacks. He wanted a federally supported system of public education. When he and his wife were arrested in January 1895 for practicing medicine without a license, he began a "Holy War" against "doctors, drugs, and devils" and the editors of the city's newspapers, all of whom, he said, should be sent to the penitentiary. But realizing the crusade was hopeless, he decided that he would build his Zion away from Chicago.[25]

So, on Saturday morning January 6, 1900, a train with Dowie and 90 followers left for the promised land to the north. By the end of February over 1,000 "Dowieites" had arrived. That summer they consecrated a 72-foot observation tower to mark the center of an enormous Tabernacle. The event attracted 10,000 visitors on 11 trains from Chicago. Zion City was well planned. A plat map placed a recreation park at the eastern corner adjacent to Lake Michigan and a waterworks next to it. Factories were to be west of the park and farther west were the manufacturing and business sections. A boulevard ran between the factories and the businesses. In the middle of the city was the Tabernacle, at the center of a 200-acre "Shiloh Park." From the park wide streets extended into the residential areas to the south, west, and north. The city's first industry, manufacturing lace, was staffed with English craftsmen. What had started out as a tent encampment rapidly became a city of one- and two-story frame family homes and substantial brick businesses. There was a creamery, a feed store, and a post office. South of the city was a brickyard, a lumber mill, and farms with barns, tool sheds, and 50 teams of horses and wagons. In the fertile black soil the holy farmers grew vegetables, mainly potatoes, and harvested hay.[26]

Zion City was, as Dowie expressed it, a "theocracy of the heart" with the Bible as its "supreme law." In a published sermon he declared: "I deny the doctrine of Democracy. . . . It is the incarnation of accursed selfishness," he said, "the government of a man by himself and for himself . . . the government of a selfish brute."[27] Dowie as "general overseer" was the city's absolute leader.

In April 1900, the adults convened in the Tabernacle to adopt municipal regulations and to choose the Council of Overseers. The council served under

Dowie and ran the fire and police departments and the offices of the city engineer and municipal of finance. There was no contest for any office because Zion City had only one political party, the "Theocratic Party." Consequently, when the council met, it was always a rubber stamp for Dowie. It passed ordinances almost without discussion and always by unanimous approval. In August Dowie organized a 700-man missionary society called the "Ten Seventies" to go to Chicago and other cities, at church expense, and convert unbelievers to Dowie's call to perfection. Each unit of the Ten was led by an elder who divided it into seven companies of 10 men led by a deacon. The next month Dowie created the real basis of Zion City's theocracy, the Zion Restoration Host. As "Zion's Army" he ordered it to go out and wage war on evil. Its members—almost all of the adult male residents—took a solemn oath recognizing Dowie as "the Messenger of the Covenant, the Prophet foretold by Moses, and Elijah the Restorer." Dowie called himself Elijah III, the third manifestation of prophets Elijah and John the Baptist. The army pledged a submission to him that surpassed "all family ties and obligations." And, elevating church over state, they vowed that obedience to Dowie superseded "all relations to all human government."[28]

For a while this New Jerusalem prospered. Every month over 125 wagonloads of boards left the lumberyard on freight trains for Chicago. The brick factory expanded and a candy factory, a bakery, and laundry were built. When the Tabernacle was completed, it had a seating capacity for 5,000 persons. In March 1903, he installed a profit-sharing system, the "Zion Building and Manufacturing Association." It took over the construction and maintenance of all homes and buildings. He sold $20 shares of stock in it to raise a capital fund of $500,000. All profits beyond expenses would be divided by giving 10 percent to Dowie (an appropriate tithe), 20 percent to shareholders, and 70 percent to the employees of the association. He planned to have retail stores operate on the same profit-sharing formula in which the customer would, in Dowie's words, "share in proportion to the amount of his purchases." There would be no intermediaries in Zion City to skim the profits. Competition would be eliminated.[29]

Zion's daily activities centered on religion. There was a morning and evening prayer time when, on the blowing of a city whistle, everyone stopped what they were doing and bowed their heads for 2 minutes until the whistle sounded again. Every worker, city employee, and farmer spent 15 minutes in prayer before starting his or her job in the morning. Every home had a "family altar" that was inspected regularly by a "parish officer" appointed by the council who examined the moral condition of the family members. In each of the city's 13 wards, called parishes, Tuesday evening prayer meetings were held. They were two-hour events divided into three equal segments: for prayer and scripture reading, for testimony, and for social get-togethers. On Wednesday they went to a second prayer meeting. This time, in addition to praying and reading the Bible, they discussed social problems and planned for the future. On Sunday they attended services in the Tabernacle.[30]

Family life was based on Old Testament patriarchal principles. Council overseer John G. Speicher put it this way in a sermon entitled "Authority in the Home." He said that the father deserved absolute obedience as God's representative and was "responsible for what his children do unto the third and fourth generation." He, along with the mother, had to be certain that the home was "the most sacred thing outside of the Church of God." Dowie arranged all marriages. Couples had to pass an examination and answer questions on their habits and beliefs so that he could determine whether they were fit for wedlock. He had to be convinced that they were pure and compatible because, unless they were, perfection could never be reached. Dowie tolerated no vice, least of all lust and adultery. He declared: "I will have Zion pure." There would be no "filthy pictures and bad books."[31]

The paramount goal in training the children was religious perfection. Teachers indoctrinated pupils on the supremacy of God, the brotherhood of all men under God the Father, and individual free will. The Bible received as much attention as academic subjects. Dowie believed that schools, like the church and the home, had to be sanctified. They should prepare students "for service in the Master's Kingdom." They should "teach men how to pray so as to receive answers to their petitions." Their mottoes would be: "In the Beginning God" and "How to Pray."[32]

On January 6, 1902, they laid the cornerstone for a three-story central school with a huge domed auditorium. Four other, smaller frame schools were built in the residential sections. By 1905, 75 teachers were instructing over 2,000 students in grades 1 through 12. Classes opened with prayer and Bible reading. Each room was designated for a particular subject—reading, mathematics, science, art, and so on. School athletics had a religious tone to them. Dowie told the Zion City Athletic Association that it should discourage competition and insist on Christian cooperation. Athletes should try to illicit one another's love, even from members of the opposing team. All games had to open with readings from the Bible, a prayer, and a hymn. The association organized four baseball teams named the Elijahs, Ezekiels, Daniels, and Jobs and regularly switched players from one team to another to lessen "selfish ambition." Other Zion sports included touch football, cricket, basketball, cross-country, tennis, and golf. Religion permeated the youth's cultural and recreational activities. Their band concerts, ice-skating parties, and sleigh rides all were chaperoned by parish officers who began each event by leading everyone in prayer. A municipal choir of 1,000 members gave summer concerts on Lake Michigan to which throngs of visitors regularly came. No recreational event ever took place on Sunday, the Lord's Day.[33]

Any ungodly resident who desecrated the Sabbath by having fun had to deal with the police. The council, as a first order of business, passed an ordinance that created the Zion City Police under the direction of Dowie. In addition to supervising the Sabbath, the council enacted a variety of "blue laws" prohibiting drunkenness, smoking, swearing, gambling, fighting, spitting, and riding of bicycles on the sidewalks. The ordinances worked because in the spring of 1903 the magistrate of the municipal court, Joseph H. Lamonde, reported that only one-tenth of 1 percent of the people in Zion had been arrested. This righteousness was no doubt the result of constant spying on one another, because Dowie told his followers that it was their duty to tell church officials about any "hidden iniquities" they saw. Everyone, therefore, had to make public "anything which would imperil the purity and progress of Zion." If they did not tattle, then they themselves would be guilty of sin and would be held accountable.[34]

By the end of 1903, Zion City's economic structure began to crumble. Put simply, Dowie did not pay his bills. By November, 14 creditors sued him, seeking bankruptcy proceedings. The next month the U.S. district court in Chicago appointed receivers to investigate the city's financial condition. The upshot of this step was that Dowie voluntarily promised to pay all of his debts within one year's time. He called this arrangement a victory for the Lord. But two weeks later he left Zion City for Australia.

Overseer Speicher took charge. Without Dowie's charisma, though, discouragement spread like an epidemic. Fact was, as Speicher immediately recognized, industries were unable to hire all of the men living in Zion, and, so, many had to find jobs in Waukegan and Kenosha. Only the lace factory was producing on a regular basis and with just 350 workers. Most of the other factories had cut wages up to 50 percent. The candy factory closed in February 1904. The debt payments that Dowie had sent to the receivership crippled the city's finances; one installment in June 1904 alone was for $490,000.[35]

Dowie returned in July 1904, and for a few days the old enthusiasm revived. They held an elaborate "Feast" with parades, floats representing the industries, and a rousing sermon by the general overseer himself.[36] Seemingly oblivious to the failing economy, he insisted on planning for another Zion City in Mexico and went to Mexico City to lay the groundwork. Over the next few months, one overseer after another departed from Zion. Speicher, however, remained at his post.[37] By the time Dowie came back from Mexico in April 1905, the economy had stultified. Factory managers were unable to find money to buy raw materials or even to repair machinery. He told them that their complaints were evidence of a lack of faith and that the inconveniences were just temporary. They were not.[38]

In August the Building and Manufacturing Association dissolved. Dowie refused to recognize what was happening. He persisted in his plan to build the Mexican Zion. On Sunday, September 24, 1905, just before he was scheduled to leave for Mexico City again he led a five-hour service on the upbeat topic entitled "Going Forward." Toward the end of the service the 52-year-old prophet suffered a stroke that paralyzed his right side. Despite his incapacity he went to Mexico but returned for the Thanksgiving worship service.

But when he stood before his flock that November, everyone could see how ill he was. Three weeks later Dowie, his son Gladstone, and a personal attendant named Deacon Jasper H. DePew departed for a rest vacation in the Caribbean.

Over the following year a series of overseers replaced Speicher, all with Dowie's personal approval, and each one failed to halt the city's deepening economic depression. A malaise gripped the faithful. What had happened to the Lord's Prophet that he had not recovered? If illness was Satan's work, as he had preached, then perhaps Dowie was in the Devil's clutches. How could a man who healed others not heal himself? Finally, in April 1906, Overseer Wilber Glenn Voliva, the man then in charge, led a revolt. This 36-year-old former missionary leader of the Ten Seventies had seen during his four-month tenure in office that Zion City could not survive under Dowie's leadership. Voliva delivered a sermon titled "Disease Is the Result of Sin" with obvious implications about the prophet's spiritual purity.[39]

In Mexico City on April 2, Dowie received a telegram from Voliva and five other officers. It stunned him. Voliva had suspended him from "office and membership for polygamous teaching and other grave charges. . . . Quietly retire," Voliva ordered. The telegram ended by stating that "Zion and creditors will be protected at all costs."[40] Voliva then published a detailed exposé of Dowie's financial mistakes, his extravagant living, and his immorality—plans for a polygamous colony in Mexico where he would collect a harem. Voliva said he had affidavits that proved the validity of all the charges.

Dowie informed reporters from the *Chicago Tribune* that the allegations were false and ridiculous. He hired a lawyer to petition the Lake County Circuit Court to revoke Voliva's authority to govern; namely, the power of attorney Dowie had sent him on his appointment the previous January. He obtained an injunction that authorized him to enter Zion City to hold services in the Tabernacle. But by then Dowie was exhausted and had lost the will to fight. Anyhow, when he arrived at Zion, only a few old friends greeted him. And when he preached on April 29, only 200 people showed up, some just curious onlookers who left before he finished.[41]

The end of Zion City came in bankruptcy court in July 1906. The court determined that Dowie was only a trustee and not the proprietary owner of the city. He could, however, continue to reside in his private home there, which was known as "Shiloh House." The court appointed a receiver to resolve Zion's debts. The judge ordered that an election should take place in September to choose "the overseership of the church." When the 1,918 ballots were cast, Voliva received 1,900. At Shiloh House Dowie's health steadily deteriorated. He developed heart trouble and dropsy. Friends reported that at times he was delirious. On March 9, 1907, he died.[42]

Over the next four years some 1,500 people abandoned Zion City. An opposition political party was formed against Voliva calling itself the "Independents." It claimed to be the true heirs to Dowie's theocracy. Meanwhile, outsiders purchased some of the city's industries. For example, Marshall Field and Company of Chicago bought the lace factory. The remaining industries were incorporated into "Zion Industries" headed by Voliva. But in 1933, because of the Great Depression, this organization collapsed. Voliva ran the school until 1935 when it, too, closed because the money ran out. And, so, seven years before Overseer Voliva died in 1942, the theocratic utopia disappeared. Philip Cook, writing in 1996, described Zion, Illinois (the *City* had been dropped) as just another "mainstreet, U.S.A." There were the usual stores, a hospital, and even a golf course. There were no blue laws, but neither were there any liquor stores and taverns. "Visitors have little indication that Zion's beginnings were different from those of any other American community," Cook writes. It survives only as "a tourist oddity for history buffs and students of religious and utopian history."[43]

CATHOLIC WORKER MOVEMENT

Some American Catholics looked to communalism to help them through the dislocations of the Great Depression, many of them to Dorothy Day's Houses of Hospitality. Day, a Catholic convert and journalist, called attention to the terrible plight of the unemployed in articles in the *Commonweal* and *America*. She wrote about rent strikes by families desperate to avoid eviction and warned about the increasing popularity of the Communist Party's "hunger marches." In the winter of 1932, Peter Maurin, a French eccentric and social radical, persuaded her to start a newspaper to focus public attention on these dangerous developments. They collaborated as editors of a monthly newspaper, the *Catholic Worker*, whose first issue appeared on May 1, 1933. Day did most of the writing and looked after the fund-raising and circulation. Maurin contributed an occasional article, but mostly he traveled around eastern U.S. cities giving speeches on what he called his "Three-Point Program" and its goals. These were building Houses of Hospitality, distributing food to the unemployed, and starting communal farms to train workers in farming skills.[44]

Day established the first House of Hospitality in late 1933, St. Joseph's House, on East Third Street in Manhattan, where Maurin brought vagrants to be served soup and have a place to sleep. However, it was soon inadequate for the number of transients coming there, and Day moved to a large building that had been used for the editorial offices and print shop of the newspaper. On the average about 150 "guests" stayed there every night, and twice daily the soup kitchen fed about 1,200 people. Day described these developments in the *Catholic Worker*, and the publicity elicited a national response. She and Maurin received invitations to come to Boston, St. Louis, Chicago, Cleveland, and Washington, D.C., to start other Houses of Hospitality. By 1936, they had 12 such missions and within six years there were 32 in operation. They were of varying sizes. The one in St. Louis daily fed 2,600 people and sent meals to over 700 homes. The Chicago House sheltered over 300 individuals every night.[45]

Some houses were "worker groups" that held regular discussions on Christian love and other Social Gospel concepts. Others were more practical and assisted in organizing labor unions and rent strikes. Some of them concentrated on charity work, such as visiting the sick in hospitals or homes and bringing food to the desperately poor. Some had stable leadership, all appointed by Day, while others had a rapid turnover in guidance. None of the houses had a constitution, elected officers, and formal meetings, but they did follow three principles. One was voluntary poverty. This was the outward sign of internal purity when one accepted "simple sufficiency of food, clothing, shelter, and other goods, with nothing superfluous."[46] Voluntary poverty was seen as a "mysterious thing, a thing of the spirit." Citing Saint Thomas Aquinas, Maurin argued that living without material pleasures and goods "removes the obstacles that stand in the way of spiritual perfection." Or, as Day put it, it enabled one "to remember that we are our brother's keeper, and that we must not only care for his needs as far as we are immediately able, but try to build a better world."[47] Poverty engendered a "strong sense of sharp identification with the downtrodden that greatly intensified radical commitment while the sense of sharp departure from the whole cluster of American values surrounding abundance and consumption constituted a significant critique of American society."[48] Providing regular meals of soup, bread, and coffee was the second principle. Day wrote that these meals were "so important" because "in the breaking of bread [the participants] know Christ in each other."[49] Distribution of clothes was the third principle. It involved gathering secondhand clothing (in which the workers themselves dressed) and taking it to needy families.

Living in a house had its downside. Some individuals joined because of a sentimental feeling for the poor and found slum conditions unbearable after a while. Living in poverty created a heightened sensitivity to small differences of food, clothing, bedding, and space; and competition over such matters eroded the feeling of communal togetherness and shared sacrifices. One man complained in the *Catholic Worker:* "We hold on to our books, radios, our tools such as typewriters, and instead of rejoicing when they are taken from us we lament." The absence of bylaws and work assignments wrongly assumed that members would see what had to be done and do it. But in practice they did not, and arguments arose over who should perform what chore and for how long. One man wrote: "You could throw good examples at some people forever and they would just bounce off them like peanuts off a tank." Although most house residents worked hard, the slackers provoked irritation and resentment. Nevertheless, Mel Piehl concludes that "much difficult work was accomplished under this system [and it] argued against the cynics . . . who said it was impossible and bound to fail. . . . That it was done at a price," he observes, "proved the difficulties of utopia."[50]

The Catholic Church initially approved of the houses because most Catholics were from the working class and were hit hard by the depression. Besides, the church had already gone on record in favor of social reform legislation and charity work. For example, in 1919 the National Catholic Welfare Conference had printed the "Bishop's Program of Social Reconstruction." This document asked for minimum-wage laws, collective-bargaining statutes, social insurance, public housing, and worker ownership and management of industry. Catholic organizations such as the St. Vincent de Paul Society and the Sisters of Mercy had organized a national network of charitable institutions. Some parishes, such as St. James's and St. Stephen's in New York City, had an effective system of social services for their slum dwellers that included employment counseling, day care facilities, and recreational activities. "Parish benevolent unions, mutual aid societies, burial societies, and similar forms of primitive social security flourished during the late nineteenth and early twentieth centuries," Piehl writes, "and many of them were eventually combined into national associations like the Irish Catholic Benevolent Union and the German Catholic Central Verein."[51] It was no surprise, therefore, that both the church hierarchy and the *Catholic Worker* endorsed New Deal statutes such as the National Industrial Recovery Act (NIRA) and the Agricultural Adjustment Act (AAA). And it seemed for a while that the church and Day were acting in concert. Symbolic of this unity, in 1935 Day and 130 famous Catholics signed the National Catholic Welfare Conference's *Organize Social Justice* that condemned the Supreme Court's vacating of the NIRA. This event marked the apex of Day's feeling that she was in the vanguard of a national Catholic crusade for social and economic justice.[52]

After 1936, the consensus faded. When Congress sent the states the Child Labor Amendment, it failed eight short of approval because the church and Catholic newspapers opposed it as a threat to parental control of child rearing. But Day and the *Catholic Worker* supported it. Then, that same year, prestigious Catholic publications such as *America*, *Catholic World*, and *Our Sunday Visitor* began to print articles that reflected the rabid anti-Semitism of Father Charles E. Coughlin. When, in his weekly radio sermons, the priest charged that an international conspiracy of Jewish bankers had caused the depression, the *Catholic Worker* denounced him. Finally, in 1937 when Pope Pius XI issued the anti-Communist encyclical *Divini Redemptoris*, American bishops lined up to attack Day's political views as "subversive teaching and the audacity of subversive action." Day admitted that while she was aware of the dangers of Communism, she would not condemn house members who attended Communist meetings and that she would never stop supporting righteous causes just because the Communist Party favored them. Even more to the point, she wrote: "The Communist often more truly loves his brother, the poor and oppressed, than many so-called Christians."[53]

By the end of 1937, as Day moved far to the left of the church, internal division appeared inside the Houses of Hospitality. In New York and Boston a group of idealists calling themselves the Campoinites insisted on a frontal assault on capitalism. They organized demonstrations and confronted people on street corners. Day quickly moved from passive acceptance of what they were doing to opposition. She stopped mentioning them in the *Catholic Worker* and instructed her readers to return to the central mission of service to the poor. The Campoinites left the Worker's Movement and started their own organization and newspaper.[54]

Another internal problem was called the "family question." The houses had largely excluded couples with children, and "the problem of families had become a major issue in the movement." As put by one young worker, "We soon learned that marriage and our attempts at communal living were incompatible." He warned that since "the family seeks its own because it is a natural community [it] is the fundamental reason why a complete plan of communal living was bound to fail."[55] In response, in 1936 Day and Maurin planned a different sort of house, one based on agriculture. Both of them had written in the *Catholic Worker* about farm communities and had from time to time discussed plans for rural utopian villages. The April 1936 issue of the *Catholic Worker* announced that it had acquired a farm in Staten Island, and the May 1939 issue published an account of a successful farming commune there. It reported that "through the generosity of a reader" a second 28-acre farm 70 miles from New York at Easton, Pennsylvania, had been purchased. Day predicted that it was the first step in creating a community of families, each with three acres to cultivate. The following year she added 40 more acres to the Pennsylvania farm and constructed a common house for families as well as for single workers and guests. A third farm was organized at Trivoli, just north of New York City on the banks of the Hudson River.[56]

Altogether, Day established nine other subsistence agriculture communities near Boston, Pittsburgh, Minneapolis, Detroit, Cleveland, Chicago, St. Louis, and San Francisco. But they were filled with urban Hospitality House people who had no idea of how to run a farm. And they compounded their difficulties by allowing a constant stream of indolents in as guests. The result was that some farms became "a combination fresh-air camp, alcoholic recovery center, and lay retreat house." Conflicts arose between laborers, who were willing to do field work, and intellectuals, who only wanted to talk. All but a few of the "Houses of Hospitality on the Land" dissolved after World War II. The ones that remained were small truck farms within easy reach of Manhattan that survived by selling fresh vegetables to city markets.[57]

The urban Houses of Hospitality tried to deal with the family issue by quartering couples in nearby apartments and having them help in the soup kitchen on weekends. This accommodation might have worked, but the city units became divided over Day's unswerving pacifism. In 1940, she opposed the Selective Service Act and the U.S. entrance into the European war. As a result of her position some houses closed down, others stayed with her for a while, at least until after Pearl Harbor. A few just changed their names and continued with their charity work. By 1945, there were only 10 Hospitality Houses still running. Mel Piehl has concluded that in their heyday the Houses of Hospitality were examples of "enclaves that [were] expected to serve as alternative social models . . . [and] deserve a place in American history along-side other small but noteworthy American experiments such as the Shaker settlements, Brook Farm, and Oneida." And Timothy Miller has observed that "several new Worker farms were founded as part of the new wave of American communalism in the 1960s. . . . The paper and the Houses of Hospitality," he concludes, "continue to operate as the backbone of the on-going Catholic Worker movement."[58]

Day died in 1980 at Maryhouse, which she had started on East Third Street in Manhattan, and where she had lived for many years. In 1997, her followers commemorated the centennial of her birth in St. Patrick's Cathedral, where they heard John Cardinal O'Connor deliver a eulogy in which he announced that he was going to propose her for sainthood. If canonized, Day would be the second American woman saint alongside Mother Elizabeth Bayley Seton, who was elevated to that status by Pope Paul VI in 1975.[59]

THE PEACE MISSION

A messianic Black minister, Father Divine, led a religious communal re-sponse to the Great Depression called the Peace Mission. Born in Maryland in 1879, he became an itinerant preacher to poor Blacks in the state and, after 1900, throughout the South. He proclaimed that the spirit of God dwelled within everyone and that he was God's spokesman. In 1915, he settled in Harlem after Black ministers in the South rejected his claim of being God's agent on earth.

After four years there he moved to Sayville, Long Island, and became its only Black resident. Calling himself "Major J. Divine," he kept up a respect-able home and acquired a few disciples. His message by that time was a com-bination of Pentecostal Christianity, Eastern mysticism, and communal sharing. After the Crash of 1929, more Black guests began to show up at his free Sunday dinners to ask for help in finding a job. And by 1931, Robert S. Weisbrot has observed, large "crowds came regularly from Harlem and New-ark, venerating this mysterious provider as a heaven-sent deliverer."[60]

Father Divine steered away from salvation and damnation in his sermons and stressed instead a duty to help the poor and the outcast. But his White neighbors panicked. They feared that Major Divine was developing a "Negro colony" in their town and they had him arrested for disturbing the peace. A local magistrate fined him $500 and sentenced him to a year in prison, but his conviction was later reversed. Allegedly, when the magistrate died three days later, Divine sadly told reporters: "I hated to do it." Some newspapers, sensing a tabloid story, pictured him as a martyr and the judge's sudden death as mysteriously unexplainable.[61]

Encouraged by the press coverage, Father Divine formed the Peace Mission, mostly of Black women, widowed or divorced, who dedicated themselves to communal living, nonviolence, inner serenity, and helping the poor. By the mid-1930s, there were 150 mission centers and about 10,000 followers, predominantly from the urban ghettos; but some came from the educated, prosperous middle class. A few Whites joined the movement. Each center had a large banquet table where hundreds of members could share well-planned meals that were seen as symbolic of the timeless need for God's love and human fellowship. The meals provided the opportunity to praise Father Divine and to hear someone read his special message. Sometimes he attended and preached. Either in printed form or delivered personally, the sermon was always the same: help the powerless and bring them closer to God.[62]

Members lived communally at a mission, although Divine did not require it. Some were large "kingdom extensions" with separate living quarters for the sexes, kitchens, dining rooms, meeting halls, and a special room set aside for Father Divine. Others were simply renovated brick homes in the heart of the slums. Divine developed an informal administrative structure in which he appointed individuals to supervise the missions, conduct sessions for legal advice, distribute pamphlets and leaflets on his message, and plan new missions into White neighborhoods.

Divine kept his message simple and focused on basic points. One was that all members should live and eat together, free. Nonmembers could lodge at a center for only $1 a week. There could be no tobacco, alcohol, or cosmetics. The missions operated restaurants, groceries, barber shops, laundries, fish markets, and small businesses and shared all income from these activities. They usually sold their products and goods at a lower price than the local retail merchants and counted on volume sales and turnover to make a profit. For example, their restaurants were famous for providing a complete meal for just $.15. The Harlem Mission, the largest, owned 3 apartments, 9 homes, 20 flats, and a number of assembly halls and dormitories. The Peace Mission soon grew "from a modest commune to a far-flung network that reportedly handled over $15 million in business annually by the later part of the decade."[63]

Divine's other objective was building rural social resettlement communes. Like their secular counterparts in the New Deal, they would be agrarian homesteads for the urban poor. In 1935, he planned a large cooperative in upstate New York called the "Promised Land." It was racially integrated, on excellent farmland, and within a couple of years was a successful agricultural cooperative selling produce in New York City at a substantial profit. There were other communities and, Weisbrot writes, "within a few years the centers were thriving and even supplying Father Divine's urban cooperatives with agricultural products."[64]

The elimination of racial injustice and segregation was Divine's third concern. He campaigned against lynching and helped draft proposals to Congress to pass laws making it a federal crime. In 1940, he sent to Congress a petition with 250,000 signatures. He developed a "Righteous Government Platform" that demanded federal civil rights statutes to end discrimination in public facilities, to stop racial separation in neighborhoods, and to desegregate the schools.[65]

From World War II until Father Divine's death in September 1965, the Peace Mission changed. As he drastically reduced his participation because of age and poor health, his assistants neglected his preaching and contacts with the mass of his followers. They erected an elaborate administrative hierarchy of trusteeships, presidencies, and other offices. They created three new orders of uniformed members with special names, codes of conduct, and functions. Without Father Divine's personal touch, membership steadily declined. By the late forties, only the Peace Missions in Harlem, Philadelphia, and Newark remained open. Developments other than a bloated bureaucracy and the lack of charismatic leadership accounted for the deterioration. The National Association for the Advancement of Colored People (NAACP) and the civil rights movement preempted its position on Black civil rights. Moreover, the fifties and sixties were prosperous years, and the appeal of communal living and economic cooperation no longer was as compelling as it had been during the depression.[66]

Even though Divine required celibacy for his orders in 1946, nine years after his first wife, the "First Mother Divine," died he married a 21-year-old Caucasian, Edna Rose Ritchings. He anointed her the Second Mother Divine, claimed she was a "spotless virgin bride," and said that the marriage was only a spiritual union. She eventually took charge of running the Peace Mission and kept it active through the 1990s. She tried to preserve the legacy of Father Divine's initial purpose, which was one of being "a distinctive part of the process by which Black religious leaders moved from an era of absorbing spirituality to one of vital commitment to the struggle for equality."[67]

KOINONIA FARM

In the 1940s, the charismatic minister Clarence Jordon built a biracial utopian community in western Georgia for sharecroppers and small farmers. A native of Talbot County, Georgia, he earned a Ph.D. in New Testament Greek from Southern Baptist Theological Seminary in 1939. His first church was an all-White mission in the Black area of Louisville called the Sunshine Center. There, he came into contact with the city's segregated churches and soon urged Baptist officials to have the center integrated. They told him to drop the idea, shut down the center, and open a rescue mission for the poor Whites in another part of town. Jordan agreed and laid plans for "The Lord's Storehouse," as he named it, and started gathering donations of food, clothing, and fuel. Although not enough contributions came in to permit him to open the Storehouse, a number of young men and women, mostly students, met regularly with him to discuss racial equality, pacifism, and communal sharing. Within a year, they adopted the name "Koinonia," a Greek word for fellowship.[68]

In 1941, while looking for a place to build a communal fellowship, Jordon met Martin England, a South Carolinian with a divinity degree from Crozer Seminary who had also attended Southern Baptist Theological Seminary. England, like Jordon, believed that the early Christian model of communal living was the true path to salvation and the only means to deal with the social and racial problems of the world. The two men became close friends and published a promotional brochure in which they announced that they were going to embark on an "agricultural missionary enterprise" to help sharecroppers and poor farmers of both races by providing instruction in scientific farming methods and rules of successful business operation. Above all, they promised a racially integrated, biblically based Christian farm community. It is impossible to say how many people were favorably impressed by the brochure, but a wealthy businessman and pacifist named Arthur Steilberg read the pamphlet and contacted the two men. He offered to finance their rural utopia and advanced the down payment on the land.[69]

In 1942, Jordan and England purchased 400 acres of eroded acreage in Sumter County, Georgia, near the town of Americus. Only Jordan, England, and their families lived there at first. Neither man knew anything about agriculture, and their efforts to cultivate the land were pathetic. Without machinery or animals, the two men pulled the plow. Jordon had so little knowledge of farming that he had to watch his neighbors from the roof of his house every morning to see what they were doing. If they were fertilizing, he would fertilize. If they ploughed, he ploughed. When they weeded, he weeded.[70]

For all outward appearances, Koinonia seemed to be just another two-family farm. However, when they invited local Blacks to join them, hostility immediately broke out. Georgians had no tolerance for Whites who asked Blacks to sit with them at mealtime. Deacon Ludrell Pope, who lived at Koinonia during these early years, told Deborah Altus in a February 1996 interview that neighbors tried to run them out by threats of violence. When, during World War II, they learned that one of England's children, a philatelist, was collecting stamps from Japan, they believed Koinonia was a secret spy operation for Prime Minister Hideki Tojo! For a while White members of the farm attended the Rehobeth Baptist Church, located a few miles away, became Sunday School teachers, sang in the choir, and spoke as guest preachers. But when the Baptists found out that Blacks were living at the colony, they expelled the Koinonians.[71]

This experience, and the arrival of new members by 1950 that pushed the farm's population to over 60, caused them to turn inward and to develop formal rules of "total community." They adopted an admissions policy requiring applicants to serve a probation of from three to nine months during which they would study Jordan's communal ideas and demonstrate a total commitment to living as the early Christians. After that they could request formal admission, and, when admitted, they surrendered all goods and personal possessions to the farm. Distribution of money and clothes was according to need. Margaret Wittamper, who moved there with her minister husband in 1953, told Deborah Altus in February 1996 that the 10 families were fully communal. "You gave everything," she said. Everyone was equal without distinction of race or prior religious beliefs. They held a religious worship at 5 o'clock every afternoon in which they denounced all violence and condemned any signs of resentment or revenge. Decisions were made by consensus. Each morning the adults agreed on what work had to be done and decided other matters, such as what money needed to be borrowed or what machinery had to be purchased or repaired. They kept formal minutes of these meetings and often spent an inordinate amount of time on trivial matters such as what kind of linoleum to put on the floor of a building. They ended all discussions with prayers. In the evenings they met for more prayers and Bible study.[72]

Koinonians had no formally elected leaders at these meetings and rotated chair responsibilities; most of the time Jordan just assumed the duty. The position of a work coordinator, who kept track of all jobs, also was a revolving assignment. This person made sure that the men moved from one team to another in doing the field work and manual labor. The women cooked, cleaned the buildings, and watched the children, who, when old enough, attended the county school. Koinonia had separate family houses, but everyone ate the noon meal in a refectory where the single members had their sleeping rooms. Women prepared evening meals in the refectory kitchen and carried them back to the family homes. Some families, though, had their own kitchens and never bothered with the catered evening meals. A temporary setback happened in 1954 when a drought caused a crop failure. Assistance from the Pennsylvania Society of Brothers, though, pulled the Koinonians through the crisis. Afterward, Koinonia developed a prosperous poultry business and showed some nearby farmers how to start their own operations. They created a "cow library" where poor families could borrow a milk cow without charge.[73]

In 1954, when the United States Supreme Court, in *Brown v. Board of Education of Topeka*, ended segregated schools in the South, two Black students tried to enroll in classes at the University of Georgia School of Business. They asked Jordon to endorse their applications. He went to Atlanta and told university officials that they should be admitted because the young men could not get the courses they needed anywhere else. He made it clear, however, that his recommendation was not to be taken as an endorsement of the integration of Georgia's public schools. Shortly after he returned to the farm, however, he discovered that Governor Marvin Griffin had telephoned the Sumter County Courthouse to inquire about "this Jordon fellow" and his intentions in regard to the desegregation order. When Atlanta newspapers got hold of the story, they branded Jordan an "integrationist."[74]

Soon afterward, Koinonia began to experience uninterrupted violence. Neighbors fired gunshots at their buildings and their roadside market and, later, demolished it by dynamite. They cut their wire fences and dumped garbage at the entrance to the colony. When Whites assaulted Koinonia men, the county sheriff arrested the Koinonians for battery. The farm's children suffered physical and verbal abuse at school. Insurance companies canceled the colony's property coverage. Local banks closed their checking account and refused them new loans for farm operations. Local garages declined to do repair work on their machinery. Businessmen stopped buying their produce and eggs. One man who continued to deal with the farm found his store bombed and totally demolished. Koinonia's once-lucrative truck and egg market dried up, and they had to slaughter 3,000 laying hens.

Still, some Georgians were sympathetic. A group of graduates of Goshen College who had founded a community in Evanston called the Reba Place Fellowship came to help out. Two Hutterite men from the Forest River *bruderhof* lived for a while at the colony. On the other hand, the continuous violence caused most members to leave. Blacks departed first. Jordan went on a fruitless speaking tour to gather public support and to recruit new disciples.[75]

In 1963, when only two families remained at the farm, Jordon offered it for sale. When no one responded, he tried to give it to any church group who wanted it, but none did. Through the financial support of a wealthy lawyer named Millard Fuller, however, they reincorporated as "Koinonia Partners" and started a house-building service and a garment business. They published the "Cotton-Patch" edition of the Bible in which Jordan retold the Scripture in the vernacular. After his death in 1969, the members focused their attention on building affordable homes for low-income families in Sumter County. They constructed 194 homes there with volunteer labor and donations.

In 1976, Koinonia Partners started a worldwide housing program now known as "Habitat for Humanity." Located in Americus, Habitat is an ecumenical Christian ministry that raises donations for a "Fund for Humanity." Today, with the money and volunteer labor, they build new houses and repair older ones. They support land acquisition and underwrite infrastructure costs. In 1995, Habitat had over 11,000 projects in the United States and 164 ventures abroad.[76]

During the past twenty years, with the racial controversies and violence behind it, new members have gradually joined Koinonia. At the beginning of the twenty-first century, it is not an intentional community in the sense of a communal ownership of possessions. It is rather a loosely knit community of people with mutual interests. They interact economically by sharing mills and workshops. They share a goal of eliminating poverty and inequality. As one resident put it, they attempt "to address the economic sources of poverty with our products, businesses, and farm" and provide jobs in "this extremely economically depressed region" of Georgia. Toward that end, Koinonia created two sister communities in the state. In 1979, they opened Jubilee Partners in Comer to resettle hundreds of refugees from around the world. It has twenty adults and ten children who live on 258 acres of land. The other one, New Hope House in Griffin, ministers to people in prison and their families.[77]

Koinonia Partners is listed in the *Communities Directory* as a "Christian community and service organization committed to compassionate living, racial reconciliation, nonviolence, and good ecology." Its twenty or so members offer outreach programs that include prison work, community development, and hospitality. Its economy is based on cultivation of pecans and grapes on 800 of the community's 1,500 acres. The community sells "Products from the Farm" in a mail-order catalog. Money also comes in from the sale of Jordan's books and tapes. It runs a child development center as a preschool/day care facility for local children up to the age of 5 years. It has a youth program for children ages 5 to 16 that tries to challenge local teenagers to succeed, to encourage study habits, and to have them recognize the harmful effects of substance abuse. It offers a three-month residency program to outsiders in which 6 to 10 individuals live in the community and share its work, group building, and worship—on Wednesday morning at 8:15 and Sunday afternoon at 5:00 in a chapel. It also welcomes tourists, either as individuals or groups, provided they contact it in advance of the visit.[78]

ABODE OF THE MESSAGE: A SUFI UTOPIA

The *Communities Directory* described the Abode of the Message as a "thriving spiritual community of 41 adults and 16 children living on 430 acres in the Berkshire Mountains."[79] Actually, the site was a part of the former location of the Mount Lebanon Shaker village, which their leader, Pir Vilayat Inayat Khan, purchased in 1975 for $350,000. He was the son of Hazrat Inayat Khan, the founder of the Sufi Order in Europe in 1910, and the elder Khan's successor as the spiritual leader of the order. Income from this order, contributions mainly, provided the down payment on the property and during the early years helped pay the mortgage and other expenses. Building started in the spring of 1975 when a 20-man work crew arrived. By the fall they had erected dwellings for 75 people. By winter there were 100 adults, some from England and Germany, and 25 children living there. In November 1995, Abode member Charles Gruber told Timothy Miller that "there was a high level of educated people who come to the Abode. . . . Here were medical doctors, teachers, business people, engineers, computer people, and psychologists."[80]

Gruber described Khan as a "standout in a crowd," as a man with "an Oxford accent . . . but . . . not British."[81] He did not live at the Abode but, as its president, kept in touch with the community through two vice presidents. Until 1981, these officers were Taj Inayat, Khan's "spiritual partner" and mother of his children, and a Manhattan physician named Stephen Rechtshaffen. They took care of the day-to-day running of the Abode. When they left the Abode, Kahn replaced them with Boston attorney Akbar Scott and his wife, Aziza. Weekly "family meetings" governed the colony along with all sorts of committees. All decisions were made by consensus. If that were not possible, the matter was taken to an executive board made up of the heads of the committees. It was chaired by the two vice presidents. Kahn, though, gave final approval to all determinations.[82]

Each day began at 6:30 with meditation followed by breakfast. Work was done between 8:00 and noon. Then there was lunch and midday prayers followed by more work until meditation and supper at 6:00. Twice each week members attended classes, usually "how-to" instruction in music and dancing, or had discussions of selected readings. On Sundays they had a religious service during which they expressed gratitude for the Sufi message of peace and cooperation and read books on the world's major religions. The Abode's central idea was "that the whole of humanity is like one body, and any organ which is hurt or troubled can indirectly cause damage to the whole body."[83]

They went through three stages in trying to find a viable economic system that would blend shared work with individual initiative. For the first five months they used a cumbersome credit arrangement. Everyone earned a credit for each hour of work and had to do community service, called "karma yoga," for which they received no credit. Then they adopted profit sharing in which individuals went outside the Abode to work and used some of the income to pay for housing and food, donating the rest of it, usually about 40 percent of the total, to the community. But this method tended to encourage some people to leave the Abode altogether and discouraged those who stayed from doing the karma yoga. So, in 1978, they decided just to pay every person a salary for jobs done at the community, except for voluntary work in the dining hall and garden, and charge them a monthly fee of $235.[84]

All projects were organized under the name of "Winged Heart Corporation." They included Reza Quality Bakery that supplied regional supermarkets and Mount Lebanon Natural Foods, a distributing company that reached the same retail outlets. They had the Heart and Wings Volkswagen Repair Shop. The Winged Heart Energy Systems installed woodstoves and composting toilets. They ran an excavating service called Earthworks. Rechtshaffen opened the Springs Health Center in the town of Lebanon Springs, three miles from the Abode, and practiced holistic medicine. They started an Earth Light Apprentice Program in which participants learned carpentry, herb gardening, and cooking and baking of natural foods. They opened a community bookstore. They had the Omega Institute, a school for instruction in Sufi principles that in the early years was located in rented buildings near the colony. They opened the Mountain Road Children's School eight miles from the community in a large Dutch Colonial home with 16 rooms. Five full-time adults and two assistants offered some 50 students a preschool program, a kindergarten, and instruction in grades one through six. Older children attended the public junior and senior high schools.[85]

Physically, the main compound consisted of a communal dining hall/laundry (for eating three meals each day), apartments, and homes. The kitchen was managed by members who took turns at the job. Meals were vegetarian in the beginning, but soon they allowed fish and chicken. They prohibited red meat, white flour, and granulated sugar. Alcohol was allowed but had to be consumed privately and was never served in the dining hall. They proscribed illegal drugs, however. Communal work included four hours every week in the dining hall and four hours every month in the 10-acre community garden.[86] Sexual relations were casual. "There was a tendency for people to couple up at the Abode," Gruber said, and "there was also a tendency for people to uncouple." The approach was, in his words, as "an experiment in the works." For example, a person with whom a woman named Khabira was coupled was reported to have said: "I think it's time we talk about triangles." Whereupon someone remarked: "That sounds like a good idea, I've always been interested in Pythagoras!" Gruber at times was blunt. "I think people came into the community [because] it was a great chance to get laid." Khabira, however, had another perspective. She thought that the "women were looking for their soul-mates."[87]

On a hill overlooking the central complex stood a stone, wood, and glass sanctuary of four sitting Buddhas placed back to back to symbolize simplicity, humanity, unity, and understanding. Near the sanctuary members placed small huts and kitchen facilities and held a month-long summer retreat for visitors. The Abode had family concert series in which members presented an evening's entertainment of music and reading of poetry. A classical choir practiced weekly and in 1983 performed a Christmas concert in a nearby Catholic church. Four times a year they celebrated the seasonal solstices and equinoxes. And each June they commemorated Abode's founding with an open house to which they invited outsiders.[88]

Unlike many other religious utopian communities, the Abode demanded no high level of commitment. One could live there without being a Sufi. Members only had to show respect for the Sufi principles and be committed to a spiritual life. It was easy to leave. Some, like Khabira, departed because she and Charles "found that we were much more into being a couple and having our own place." Gruber remembered that by November 1978, when he left, it had become "time to take all this studying we had been doing and apply it to the outside world. . . . It just felt," he concluded, "like it was time to try for something different." In 1995, the Abode advertised itself as a "retreat center for those who seek the opportunity to withdraw from the world for a period so they may commune with their innermost being." Gruber somewhat wistfully recalled that the community had "really changed." The land had been opened up for sale to put up private homes and the Abode "went from a completely communal thing to the idea of mixing the communal with the private on sacred ground to be able to afford to survive." He and his wife, Khabira, still return there to lead classes, to enjoy Sufi dancing, and to participate in a "healing circle."[89]

PADANARAM SETTLEMENT

Daniel Wright, the founder and leader of Padanaram, was born in 1917 at Douglas Acres just outside Des Moines and was raised in the Church of the Brethren, but left it after he converted to a radical fundamentalist theology. He opposed World War II as a conscientious objector and for 20 years traveled about the Midwest as a revivalist. While he was pastor of a church in Indianapolis, he had a profound religious experience. "I saw the end community [sic]," he said in a July 1997 interview with Miller, "was the salvation of the human family and that it took teamwork and loving their neighbor as themselves and I realized that it had to be upon a religious base also."[90]

So, in September 1966, Wright and a dozen members of his congregation moved to an 80-acre farm in the rolling hills of Martin County, Indiana, near the town of Williams. They called it Padanaram, from the Book of Genesis. The group included five men who were "carpenters, stone masons, and mechanics," three women, and several young children. They lived in an 80-year-old, rundown house without toilet facilities. Sleeping quarters were overcrowded, and the group's neighbors viewed them with suspicion.

By 1972, however, they had constructed a log-cabin community of two large dormitories or "lodges"—one for the men, one for the women—and houses for married couples. They had a communal dining room in which the sexes ate at different times. They had a school for grades one through six taught by several women, all certified teachers, who were supervised by a male principal. They opened a preschool and kindergarten for the younger children. They grew vegetables and raised cattle and hogs. They constructed a lodge for married couples and had acquired 2,700 acres of forestland. By the late seventies, Padanaram had a logging and sawmill business that annually grossed over $100,000. Using standing timber from groves as far away as 50 miles, they hauled lumber on community trucks to nearby lumberyards.[91]

Padanaram revolved around Wright's tenet that life was a constant battle between Carnality and Wisdom. He believed that most humans, through weakness, loose the struggle and succumb to impulses that lead to aggression, sexual gratification, competition, disease, war, and death. But Carnality could be overcome by Wisdom, or the path to God, and that this resulted in a love of humankind. However, God revealed Wisdom only to a limited number of humans. Those individuals who received Wisdom had to live together in a communal quest for continual moral improvement. Wright saw communal life as a "school" in which each person, although sometimes slipping into Carnality, would regain the path of Wisdom with the tolerant assistance of other members of the community.[92]

Wright's most controversial idea was his sex-role ideology. According to one scholar, Jon Wagner, Wright believed females were fundamentally different from, and inferior to, men. "Man is the head, woman is a heart," he said, and "they are not alike mentally, emotionally, or physically."[93] A woman's nature was much more carnal. They were more sexual and used sex to try to manipulate men. Since women could never gain as much Wisdom as men, they must always be subservient to them. Wright had a list of printed gender rules. "No woman can hear or tell the truth. . . . No two women can be friends. . . . No man can be equal with a woman. . . . No man can trust a woman and trust God."[94]

According to Wagner, Padanaram was a patriarchy, but what kind of patriarchy is open to question. Its members resented his 1982 study of their community as a distortion of what they considered a "mildly patriarchal community."[95] They had a weekly communal assembly over which Wright presided. By consensus the men discussed and decided political and economic questions. As a matter of fact, one adult male named Steven in 1996 conceded to Miller that "we never vote—on anything. . . . We're patriarchal," he stated, "so that in every area, Wisdom surfaces." Even so, when a man spoke in the assembly, the women had to remain silent. They even had to sit at the back of the room so as not to distract the men in their deliberations.[96]

Padanaram women saw their role as positive. Rachel Summerton, for example, told Miller that she felt as a "cooperative equal" to the men. She praised the lack of competition between men and women because "we just sort of found our cooperative places together." She said that at the colony women were "much more liberated than the so-called 'liberated women' because in a communal atmosphere the women have everything they could want." She elaborated. "You can have a family and you can go over to the nursery and nurse your baby and you can have as many children as you and your husband want to and yet, you still have your work area."[97]

Daily work was gender based. Men did the logging and milling, drove the trucks, ran the equipment, butchered the cattle and hogs, and kept the account books. Women cooked, washed clothes, canned food, and cleaned the buildings. Only when it was time to harvest the vegetable garden did the sexes work together. Wright frequently referred to the way Padanaram functioned as a community in a sports metaphor. Although everyone had different roles, all worked together "like a football team to make a touchdown." To deal with individuals who were lazy they imposed the discipline of shunning. Steven conceded that these lazy people "feel that discontentedness with how their behavior is and pretty soon they just leave."[98]

Their attitude toward marriage reflected Wright's gender ideology. The community condemned any sex outside of marriage as evil. Intercourse was allowed only in a totally morally committed relationship between a man and woman in a "communal marriage." But this was not the same as a legal marriage in mainstream America. That institution, Wright taught, was corrupt because in it women controlled and manipulated men through "romantic love." Husbands fell into a destructive worship of the flesh and became obsessed with sex. The wife used this emotion to make the husband do what she wanted him to do. In a Padanaram marriage, without ceremony or contract, the partners had different but loving responsibilities. The husband, or "hussy-band" in Wright's terms, restrained an unruly wife, called the "hussy," which meant that he had to teach her and take care of her, but never brutalize or exploit her. The wife was to be faithful, obedient, and supportive of her husband.[99]

Whether married or single, Wright insisted on clear-cut communal roles for the sexes. Men, being more intelligent, had to guide women gently away from their "feminine traits" such as selfishness, impulsiveness, and competitiveness. Both single women and wives had to be obedient to men because all women were placed on earth by God to help them serve Him. Women must accept the fact that "philosophy," as one of them put it, was exclusively for men. Women had to recognize that they were unable to understand or speak the truth because they were locked into "emotions and cycles." A woman, if she followed these rules, would be blessed with security and the comfort and love of a prosperous community.

Both men and women, though, had to watch out for the "special love" of parents for their children. This emotion was based on selfishness and natural inclinations. It eroded the commitment to the group. However, children were permitted to live with their parents until, as teenagers, they went to adult single men's or women's lodges. Even while in the nuclear family they were subjected to the authority of the community, or "Superma and Superpa." This meant that if necessary any adult could discipline or correct any child.[100]

By 1996, Padanaram had grown to include over 100 individuals. But, Steven observed, they "don't proselytize or recruit members, so whatever has come down the road and joined, that hasn't been our selection. . . . We view that [process]," he said, "as divine providence . . . we will take in anyone willing to work." New children had been born, the school had expanded and was described favorably in local newspapers as "experimental." Wright suggested that the strict rules about the roles of men and women had softened but were still in place. Because of its highly profitable business operations, the community had become a stable, cohesive almost harmonious fellowship of like-minded people.[101]

Padanaram in the late 1990s was a village trust managed by a board of seven men. Its members pay no rent. Its 1994 publication, *Padanaram Settlement*, described it as "a twentieth-century Communitarian settlement" in which the "villagers live in many wood lodges and have their own apartment dwellings."[102] Wright called the sawmill "a technological marvel" and in the interview with Miller he said that it was "a several million dollar investment" that "grossed maybe seven million dollars a year." Steven boasted: "Everything is paid! We owe nothing!"[103] Today, Padanaram concentrates on five simple principles: the Golden Rule, hold all things in common, distribution according to need, one who has much from him much is required, and those who do not work do not eat. Its school is in a rough-sawn wooden structure that stresses openness and informality. In addition to an academic curriculum, the children are involved in extensive outdoor activities such as camping, fishing, and horseback riding. Their economic success has fostered a buoyant optimism about the future. They confidently declared in 1994 that humanity will live together "in security, peace, and righteousness. . . . All men," they asserted, "can be their brother's keeper."[104]

NOTES

1. James E. Landing, "Cyrus R. Teed, Koreshanity and Cellular Cosmogony," *Communal Societies* 1, no. 2 (1981): 1–17 was revised and published in 1997 as a chapter in Pitzer's anthology, *America's Communal Societies*, as "Cyrus Reed Teed and the Koreshan Unity," pp. 375–95. See also Carl Carmer, *Dark Trees to the Wind: A Cycle of New York State Years* (New York: William Sloane Associates, 1949), pp. 266–68; Howard D. Fine, "The Koreshan Unity: The Chicago Years of a Utopian Community," *Journal of the Illinois State Historical Society* 68 (1975): 213–14; Sara Weber Rea, *The Koreshan Story* (Estero, Fla.: Guiding Star Publishing House, 1994), pp. 1–2.

2. Cyrus Reed Teed, *The Cellular Cosmogony . . . Or . . . The Earth a Concave Sphere* (Philadelphia: Porcupine Press, 1975), pp. 7–8; Carmer, *Dark Trees*, pp. 264–66; Landing, "Cyrus Reed Teed," pp. 376–77; Elmer Talmadge Clark, *The Small Sects in America* (New York: Abingdon, 1949), pp. 147–50; Fine, "Koreshan Unity," pp. 214–15; Rea, *Koreshan Story*, p. 3. Damkohler's son never accepted Teed's cosmogony, and in the spring of 1902, he and his father moved to Juneau, Alaska.

3. Koresh, *The Illumination of Koresh: Marvelous Experiences of the Great Alchemist Thirty Years Ago, at Utica, N. Y.* (Chicago: Guiding Star, 1899), pp. 5–8, 10–12; Carmer, *Dark Trees*, p. 267; Landing, "Cyrus Reed Teed," pp. 378–80.

4. Landing, "Cyrus Reed Teed," p. 380; Carmer, *Dark Trees*, pp. 267–70; Rea, *Koreshan Story*, p. 4.

5. Fine, "Koreshan Unity," pp. 215–17; Landing, "Cyrus Reed Teed," pp. 380–84; Rea, "Koreshan Story," pp. 7–9; Carmer, *Dark Trees*, p. 270.

6. Fine, "Koreshan Unity," p. 218; Landing, "Cyrus Reed Teed," pp. 284–86; Rea, *Koreshan Story*, pp. 8–11.

7. Fine, "Koreshan Unity," pp. 222–232.

8. Ibid., pp. 224–25; Carmer, *Dark Trees*, pp. 271–72; Rea, *Koreshan Story*, pp. 14–21.

9. Quoted in Landing, "Koreshanity," p. 9; Rea, *Koreshan Story*, pp. 21–24.

10. Landing, "Cyrus Reed Teed," p. 386; Carmer, *Dark Trees*, pp. 272–73; Fine, "Koreshan Unity," pp. 8–9.

11. Landing, "Cyrus Reed Teed," pp. 388–89 and "Koreshanity," p. 10.

12. Rea, *Koreshan Story*, pp. 25–30.

13. Landing, "Cyrus Reed Teed," pp. 388–89 and "Koreshanity," pp. 11–12.

14. Landing, "Koreshanity," p. 12; Carmer, *Dark Trees*, pp. 273–78; Rea, *Koreshan Story*, pp. 31–55.

15. Rea, *Koreshan Story*, pp. 55–56; Landing, "Cyrus Reed Teed," p. 390 and "Koreshanity," p. 12; Carmer, *Dark Trees*, p. 278.

16. Timothy Miller, *The Quest for Utopia in Twentieth-Century America* (Syracuse, N.Y.: Syracuse University Press, 1998), pp. 24–25; Rea, *Koreshan Story*, pp. 57–58; Landing, "Cyrus Reed Teed," p. 390 and "Koreshanity," pp. 12–13; Carmer, *Dark*

Trees, pp. 278–80; Ross Wallace, "Cause of Dr. Teed's Tragic Death," *Flaming Sword* (February 15, 1909): 58–59.

17. Landing, "Cyrus Reed Teed," pp. 390–92; Rea, *Koreshan Story*, pp. 58–72; Carmer, *Dark Trees*, pp. 380–90.

18. For an extensive discussion of Herron's ideas, see James Dombrowski, *The Early Days of Christian Socialism in America* (New York: Octagon Books, 1966), pp. 171–93.

19. Ibid., pp. 132–43; Miller, *Quest for Utopia*, pp. 9–10; Oved, *American Communes*, pp. 275–77.

20. Oved, *American Communes*, pp. 277–79.

21. Ibid., pp. 279–80; Dombrowski, *Christian Socialism*, pp. 144–64.

22. Frederick A. Bushee, "Communistic Societies in the United States," *Political Science Quarterly* 20, no. 4 (1905): 625–26; Dombrowski, *Christian Socialism*, pp. 164–70; Oved, *American Communes*, pp. 281–82.

23. Miller, *Quest for Utopia*, pp. 67–68; Philip L. Cook, *Zion City, Illinois: Twentieth Century Utopia* (Syracuse, N.Y.: Syracuse University Press, 1996), pp. ix–xi. For a full list of books and articles on John Alexander Dowie and Zion City, see Cook, pp. 268–73.

24. Cook, *Zion City*, pp. 1–14.

25. Ibid., pp. 15–39.

26. Ibid., pp. 54–90.

27. Quoted in Ibid., p. 108.

28. Ibid., pp. 145–46.

29. Ibid., pp. 79–90.

30. Ibid., pp. 116–19.

31. Ibid., 124–25.

32. Ibid., 125–30.

33. Ibid., 131–38.

34. Ibid., 113–14.

35. Ibid., pp. 154–65, 251 n. 24; Miller, *Quest for Utopia*, p. 68.

36. Cook, *Zion City*, p. 164.

37. Ibid., pp. 182–83.

38. Ibid., pp. 185–87.

39. Ibid., p. 197.

40. Quoted in Ibid., p. 198.

41. Ibid., pp. 199, 204, 257 n. 1.

42. Ibid., pp. 207–15; Miller, *Quest for Utopia*, p. 69.

43. Cook, *Zion City*, p. 216.

44. Miller, *Quest for Utopia*, pp. 142–43; Mel Piehl, *Breaking Bread: The Catholic Worker and the Origin of Catholic Radicalism in America* (Philadelphia: Temple University Press, 1982), pp. 3–57; Nancy L. Roberts, *Dorothy Day and the Catholic Worker* (Albany: State University of New York Press, 1984), pp. 17–31. Dorothy Day's own version of her upbringing, the birth of her child, and her conversion to Catholicism in 1928 is in *From Union Square to Rome* (New York: Arno Press, 1978). Also valuable as autobiography is her *On Pilgrimage* (New York: Catholic Worker Books, 1948) and *The Long Loneliness: An Autobiography* (New York: Harper & Row, 1952). See also David J. O'Brien, "The Pilgrimage of Dorothy Day," *Commonweal* (December 19, 1980): 711.

45. Dorothy Day, *House of Hospitality* (New York: Catholic Worker Books, 1939),

Loaves and Fishes (New York: Harper, 1963), pp. 19, 85–86, and "House of Hospitality," *Commonweal* 15 (1938): 683; Miller, *Quest for Utopia*, pp. 113–36; Piehl, *Breaking Bread*, pp. 95–97, 109–12.

46. Piehl, *Breaking Bread*, p. 98; Peter Maurin, *The Green Revolution* (New York: Academy Guild Press, 1961), pp. 8–11, 50–52.

47. Piehl, *Breaking Bread*, pp. 99–100.

48. Ibid., p. 100.

49. Quoted in Ibid., pp. 98–99.

50. Ibid., p. 101.

51. Ibid., p. 35.

52. Ibid., pp. 119–20; Abigail McCarthy, *Private Faces, Public Places* (New York: Curtis, 1972), p. 24; Social Action Department, National Catholic Welfare Conference, *Organized Social Justice* (New York: Paulist Press, 1935), pp. 2–23.

53. Day, *From Union Square*, pp. 143–51; Piehl, *Breaking Bread*, pp. 121–22; Raphel M. Huber, ed., *Our Bishops Speak* (Milwaukee: Bruce, 1952), pp. 98–101; Roberts, *Dorothy Day*, pp. 118–21.

54. Piehl, *Breaking Bread*, pp. 123–24; Day, *Long Loneliness*, p. 234.

55. Piehl, *Breaking Bread*, pp. 128–29.

56. Ibid., pp. 129–30; Miller, *Quest for Utopia*, p. 143; James F. Montague, "History of a Farming Commune," *Catholic Worker* 6, no. 10 (May 1939): 2, 5, 8; Rosalie Riegle Troester, *Voices from the Catholic Worker* (Philadelphia: Temple University Press, 1993), p. 249.

57. Piehl, *Breaking Bread*, pp. 129–32.

58. Ibid., pp. 242–43; Miller, *Quest for Utopia*, pp. 143–44; Roberts, *Dorothy Day*, pp. 173–78.

59. Miller, *Quest for Utopia*, p. 144.

60. Robert S. Weisbrot, "Father Divine and the Peace Mission," in *America's Communal Utopias*, ed. Donald E. Pitzer (Chapel Hill: University of North Carolina Press, 1997), p. 434. See also Weisbrot, *Father Divine and the Struggle for Racial Equality* (Urbana: University of Illinois Press, 1983), pp. 9–37; Jill Watts, *God, Harlem U.S.A.: The Father Divine Story* (Berkeley: University of California Press, 1992).

61. The conviction was later reversed. Weisbrot, *Father Divine*, pp. 34–47, 46–49, 51–53; John Hoshor, *God in a Rolls-Royce; The Rise of Father Divine: Madman, Menace, or Messiah* (New York: Hillman-Carl, 1936), p. 85 first stated that Father Divine said that he "hated to do it." But Robert A. Parker, *The Deification of Father Divine* (Boston: Little, Brown, 1937), p. 28 claims he did not.

62. Weisbrot, "Father Divine," p. 436.

63. Ibid., p. 438.

64. Ibid., p. 440 and *Father Divine*, pp. 58–90.

65. Weisbrot, *Father Divine*, pp. 438 and 145–75.

66. Ibid., pp. 441–44 and 176–221.

67. Ibid., "Father Divine," p. 445; Miller, *Quest for Utopia*, p. 84.

68. Tracy Elaine K'Meyer, *Interracialism and Christian Community in the Postwar South: The Story of Koinonia Farm* (Charlottesville: University Press of Virginia, 1997), pp. 11–35; Andrew S. Chancey, "Race, Religion, and Agricultural Reform: The Communal Vision of Koinonia Farm," in *Georgia in Black and White*, ed. John C. Inscoe (Athens: University of Georgia Press, 1994), pp. 247–49; Millard Fuller with Diane Scott, *No More Shacks!: The Daring Vision of Habitat for Humanity* (Waco, Tex.: Word

Books Publisher, 1986), pp. 25–32; Dallas Lee, *The Cotton Patch Evidence* (New York: Harper & Row, 1971), pp. 1–34.

69. K'Meyers, *Christian Community*, pp. 35–41; Chancey, "Race, Religion," pp. 251–52; Lee, *Cotton Patch*, pp. 19–34.

70. Chancey, "Race, Religion," p. 253.

71. Timothy Miller, ed., "The 60s Communes Project," Archives, University of Kansas; K'Meyers, *Christian Community*, pp. 51–61; Chancey, "Race, Religion," pp. 253–56; Lee, *Cotton Patch*, pp. 35–52; Chancey, "Race, Religion," pp. 253–54.

72. Miller, "60s Communes Project."

73. K'Meyers, *Christian Community*, pp. 63–77; Chancey, "Race, Religion," pp. 253–56.

74. K'Meyers, *Christian Community*, pp. 83–88; Chancey, "Race, Religion," pp. 260–62.

75. K'Meyers, *Christian Community*, pp. 88–98, 127–65; Lee, *Cotton Patch*, pp. 105–54; Chancey, "Race, Religion," pp. 259–61.

76. K'Meyers, *Christian Community*, pp. 169–70, 177–78; Lee, *Cotton Patch*, pp. 105–54; Miller, *Quest for Utopia*, pp. 172–73.

77. K'Meyers, *Christian Community*, pp. 165–82; Lee, *Cotton Patch*, pp. 197–200.

78. *Communities Directory: A Guide to Cooperative Living* (Langley, Wash.: Fellowship for Intentional Community, 1995), p. 266.

79. *Communities Directory*, p. 212.

80. Miller, "60s Communes Project"; Oliver Popenoe and Cris Popenoe, *Seeds of Tomorrow: New Age Communities That Work* (San Francisco: Harper & Row, 1984), pp. 64–65.

81. Miller, "60s Communes Project."

82. Popenoe and Popenoe, *Seeds of Tomorrow*, p. 69.

83. Ibid., p. 64.

84. Ibid., pp. 66–67.

85. Ibid., pp. 67–68, 72.

86. Ibid., p. 70.

87. Miller, "60s Communes Project."

88. Popenoe and Popenoe, *Seeds of Tomorrow*, pp. 70–74.

89. Miller, "60s Commune Project"; *Communities Directory*, p. 212.

90. Miller, "60s Communes Project" and his *The 60s Communes: Hippies and Beyond* (Syracuse, N.Y.: Syracuse University Press, 1999), pp. 11, 125–26, 154–55; *Padanaram Settlement* (Williams, Ind.: Padanaram Press, 1994); Rachel E. Wright-Summerton, "Survey of Letters to Padanaram Settlement, 1967–1991/92," *Communal Societies* 15 (1995): 121–30; Jon Wagner, "A Midwestern Patriarchy," in *Sex Roles in Contemporary American Communes*, ed. John Wagner (Bloomington: Indiana University Press, 1982), pp. 211–12.

91. *Padanaram Settlement*, pp. 1–6; Wagner, "Midwestern Patriarchy," p. 212.

92. Wagner, "Midwestern Patriarchy," pp. 212–15.

93. Ibid., p. 218.

94. Ibid., p. 221.

95. Miller, *60s Communes*, pp. 126, 302 n. 128.

96. Miller, "60s Communes Project."

97. Ibid.

98. Ibid; Wagner, "Midwestern Patriarchy," p. 224.

99. Wagner, "Midwestern Patriarchy," pp. 218–19.
100. Ibid., pp. 219–20.
101. Miller, "60s Communes Project."
102. *Padanaram Settlement*, p. 6.
103. Miller, "60s Communes Project."
104. *Padanaram Settlement*, pp. 23–24.

Selected Bibliography

Andelson, Jonathan G. "The Community of True Inspiration from Germany to the Amana Colonies." In *America's Communal Utopias*, edited by Donald E. Pitzer, 181–203. Chapel Hill: University of North Carolina Press, 1997.

Andrews, Edward D. *The People Called Shakers: A Search for the Perfect Society*. New York: Dover, 1963.

Arndt, Karl J. R. *Economy on the Ohio, 1826–1834: George Rapp's Third American Harmony*. Worcester, Mass.: Harmónie Society Press, 1984.

———. "George Rapp's Harmony Society." In *America's Communal Utopias*, ed. Donald E. Pitzer, 57–88. Chapel Hill: University of North Carolina Press, 1997.

———. *George Rapp's Harmony Society 1785–1847*. Rev. ed. Rutherford, N.J.: Farleigh Dickinson University Press, 1972.

———. *George Rapp's Successors and Material Heirs, 1847–1916*. Rutherford, N.J.: Farleigh Dickinson University Press, 1971.

———. *George Rapp's Years of Glory: Economy on the Ohio, 1834–1847*. New York: Peter Lang, 1987.

Bartelt, Pearl W. "American Jewish Agricultural Colonies." In *America's Communal Utopias*, ed. Donald E. Pitzer, 352–74. Chapel Hill: University of North Carolina Press, 1997.

Barton, H. Arnold. "The Eric-Janssonists and the Shifting Contours of Community." *Western Illinois Regional Studies* 12, no. 2: 16–35, 1989.

Bennett, John W. *Hutterian Brethren: The Agricultural Economy and Social Organization of a Communal People*. Stanford, Calif.: Stanford University Press, 1967.

Berry, Brian J. L. *America's Utopian Experiments: Communal Havens from Long-Wave Crises*. Hanover, N.H.: University Press of New England, 1992.

Boyle, John A. *The Harmony Society: A Chapter in German American Culture History*. New York: AMS Press, 1973.

Brandes, Joseph. *Immigrants to Freedom: Jewish Communities in Rural New Jersey since 1882*. Philadelphia: University of Pennsylvania Press, 1972.

Brewer, Priscilla J. *Shaker Communities, Shaker Lives*. Hanover, N.H.: University Press of New England, 1986.

Carden, Maren Lockwood. *Oneida: Utopian Community to Modern Corporation*. Baltimore: Johns Hopkins Press, 1969.

Carmer, Carl. *Dark Trees to the Wind: A Cycle of New York State Years*. New York: McKay, 1949. Reprint, New York: W. Sloane Associates, 1956.

Clark, Elmer Talmadge. *The Small Sects in America*. New York: Abingdon, 1949.

Communities Directory: A Guide to Cooperative Living. Langley, Wash.: Fellowship for Intentional Communities, 1995.

Conkin, Paul K. *Two Paths to Utopia: The Hutterites and the Llano Colony*. Lincoln: University of Nebraska Press, 1964.

Cook, Philip L. *Zion City, Illinois: Twentieth Century Utopia*. Syracuse, N.Y.: Syracuse University Press, 1997.

Cranston, L. L. *The Extraordinary Life and Influence of Helena Blavatsky, Founder of the Theosophical Movement*. New York: G. P. Putnam's Sons, 1993.

Day, Dorothy. *The Long Loneliness: An Autobiography*. New York: Harper, 1952.

Desroche, Henri. *The American Shakers: From Neo-Christianity to Presocialism*, trans. John K. Savacool. Boston: University of Massachusetts Press, 1971.

Dobbs, Catherine R. *Freedom's Will: The Society of the Separatists of Zoar*. New York: William-Frederick Press, 1947.

Dombrowski, James. *The Early Days of Christian Socialism in America*. New York: Octagon, 1966.

Eisenberg, Ellen. *Jewish Agricultrual Societies in New Jersey, 1882–1920*. Syracuse, N.Y.: Syracuse University Press, 1995.

Elmen, Paul. *Wheat Flour Messiah: Eric Jansson of Bishop Hill*. Carbondale: Southern Illinois University Press, 1976.

Fine, Howard D. "The Koreshan Unity: The Chicago Years of a Utopian Community." *Journal of the Illinois State Historical Society* 68 (1975): 213–27.

Fogarty, Robert S. *All Things New: American Communes and Utopian Movements, 1860–1914*. Chicago: University of Chicago Press, 1990.

———. *Dictionary of American Communal and Utopian History*. Westport, Conn.: Greenwood Press, 1980.

———, ed. *Special Love/Special Sex: An Oneida Community Diary*. Syracuse N.Y.: Syracuse University Press, 1994.

Foster, Lawrence. "Free Love and Community: John Humphrey Noyes and the Oneida Perfectionists." In *America's Communal Utopias*, ed. Donald F. Pitzer, 253–78. Chapel Hill: University of North Carolina Press, 1997.

———. *Religion and Sexuality: Three American Communal Experiments of the Nineteenth Century*. New York: Oxford University Press, 1981.

———. *Women, Family, and Utopia: Communal Experiments of the Shakers, the Oneida Community, and the Mormons*. Syracuse, N.Y.: Syracuse University Press, 1991.

Goldstein, Philip Reuben. *Social Aspects of Jewish Colonies of South Jersey*. New York: League Printing Co., 1921.

Greenwalt, Emmett A. *California Utopia: Point Loma, 1897–1942*. San Diego, Calif.: Point Loma Publications, 1978.

Hawley, Victor. *Special Love/Special Sex: An Oneida Community Diary*, ed. Robert S. Fogarty. Syracuse, N.Y.: Syracuse University Press, 1994.

Herrick, Tirzah Miller. *Desire and Duty at Oneida: Tirzah Miller's Intimate Memoir,* ed. Robert S. Fogarty. Bloomington: Indiana University Press, 2000.

Herscher, Uri D. *Jewish Agricultural Utopias in America, 1880–1910.* Detroit: Wayne State University Press, 1981.

Hinds, William Alfred. *American Communities and Cooperative Colonies.* 1878. Philadelphia: Porcupine Press, 1975.

Hine, Robert V. *California's Utopian Colonies.* Berkeley: University of California Press, 1983.

Hoffer, Arnold M., ed. *History of the Hutterite Mennonites.* Freeman, S. Dak.: Pine Hill Press, 1974.

Horsch, John. *The Hutterian Brethren 1528–1931.* Cayley, Alberta, Canada: Macmillan, 1977.

Hostetler, John A. *Hutterite Society.* Baltimore: Johns Hopkins University Press, 1977.

Hostetler, John A., and Gertrude Enders Huntington. *The Hutterites in North America.* New York: Holt, Rinehart and Winston, 1967.

Huntington, Gertrude E. "Living the Ark: Four Centuries of Hutterite Faith and Community." In *America's Communal Utopias,* ed. Donald E. Pitzer, 319–51. Chapel Hill: University of North Carolina Press, 1997.

Inscoe, John, ed. *Georgia in Black and White: Explorations in the Race Relations of a Southern State, 1865–1950.* Athens: University of Georgia Press, 1994.

Janzen, Rod A. *The Prairie People: Forgotten Anabaptists.* Hanover, N.H.: University Press of New England, 1999.

Kanter, Rosabeth Moss. *Commitment and Community: Communes and Utopias in Sociological Perspective.* Cambridge, Mass.: Harvard University Press, 1972.

Kern, Louis J. *An Ordered Love: Sex Rules and Sexuality in Victorian Utopias—The Shakers, the Mormons, and the Oneida Community.* Chapel Hill: University of North Carolina Press, 1981.

Kesten, Seymour R. *Utopian Episodes: Daily Life in Experimental Colonies Dedicated to Changing the World.* Syracuse, N.Y.: Syracuse University Press, 1993.

Klaw, Spencer. *Without Sin: The Life and Death of the Oneida Community.* New York: Penguin Press, 1993.

Landing, James E. "Cyrus R. Teed, Koreshanity and Cellular Cosmogony." *Communal Societies* 1, no. 3 (1981): 1–17.

McAllaister, Catherine. *The Brotherhood of the New Life.* Fredonia: State University of New York at Fredonia, 1995.

Meade, Marion. *Madame Blavatsky: The Woman behind the Myth.* New York: G. P. Putnam's Sons, 1980.

Melcher, M. Fellows. *The Shaker Adventure.* New York: Shaker Museum, 1975.

Melton, G. Gordon. "The Theosophical Communities and Their Ideal of Universal Brotherhood." In *America's Communal Utopias,* ed. Donald E. Pitzer, 396–418. Chapel Hill: University of North Carolina Press, 1997.

Miller, Timothy. *The Quest for Utopia in Twentieth-Century America 1900–1968.* Syracuse, N.Y.: Syracuse University Press, 1996.

———. *The 60s Communes: Hippies and Beyond.* Syracuse, N.Y.: Syracuse University Press, 1999.

Morhart, Hilda Dischinger. *The Zoar Story.* Dover, Ohio: Seibert Printing Company, 1967.

Morse, Flo. *The Shakers and the World's People.* New York: Dodd Mead, 1980.

Murphet, Howard. *Hammer on the Mountain: Life of Henry Steel Olcott 1832–1907.* Wheaton, Ill.: Theosophical Publishing House, 1972.

Nelson, Ronald E. "Bishop Hill: Swedish Development of the Western Illinois Frontier." *Western Illinois Regional Studies* 1, no. 2 (1978): 109–20.

Nordhoff, Charles. *The Communistic Societies of the United States.* London: John Murray, 1875.

Ohio Historical Society. *Zoar: An Ohio Experiment in Communalism.* Columbus: Ohio Archaeological and Historical Society, 1952.

Oved, Yaacov. *Two Hundred Years of American Communes.* New Brunswick, N.J.: Transaction, 1988.

———. *The Witness of the Brothers: A History of the Bruderhof.* New Brunswick, N.J.: Transaction, 1996.

Padanaram Settlement. Williams, Ind.: Padanaram Press, 1994.

Parker, Robert Allerton. *A Yankee Saint: John Humphrey Noyes and the Oneida Community.* New York: G. P. Putnam's Sons, 1935.

Peters, Victor. *All Things Common: The Hutterian Way of Life.* Minneapolis: University of Minnesota Press, 1965.

Piehl, Mel. *Breaking Bread: the Catholic Worker and the Origin of Catholic Radicalism in America.* Philadelphia: Temple University Press, 1982.

Popenoe, Oliver and Cris. *Seeds of Tomorrow: New Age Communities That Work.* San Francisco: Harper & Row, Publishers, 1984.

Rainard, Lyn. "Conflict Inside the Earth: The Koreshan Unity in Lee County." *Tampa Bay History* 3 (1981): 5–16.

Randall, Emilius. *History of the Zoar Society.* Columbus, Ohio: Press of Fred J. Heer, 1904.

Rea, Sara Weber. *The Koreshan Story.* Estero, Fla.: Guiding Star Publishing House, 1994.

Rideman, Peter. *An Account of Our Religion: Doctrine and Faith of the Brothers Whom Men Call Hutterians.* London: Hodder & Stoughton, 1950.

Robertson, Constance Noyes, ed. *Oneida Community: An Autobiography, 1851–1876.* Syracuse, N.Y.: Syracuse University Press, 1970.

———. *Oneida Community: The Breakup, 1876–1881.* Syracuse, N.Y.: Syracuse University Press, 1972.

Ross, Joseph E. *Krotona of Old Hollywood, 1866–1913.* Montecito, Calif.: El Montecito Oaks Press, 1989.

Ryan, Charles J. *H. P. Blavatsky and the Theosophical Movement.* Pasadena, Calif.: Theosophical University Press, 1975.

Shambough, Bertha M. *Amana, the Community of True Inspiration.* New York: B. Blom, 1971.

Shpall, Leo. "Jewish Agricultural Colonies in the United States." *Agricultural History* 24 (July 1950): 120–46.

Smucker, Donovan E., ed. *The Sociology of Canadian Mennonites, Hutterites and Amish: A Bibliography with Annotations.* Waterloo, Ontario: Wilfrid Laurier University Press, 1977–1991.

Sneider, Herbert Wallace. *A Prophet and a Pilgrim.* New York: AMS Press, 1942.

Snyder, Eugene Edmund. *Aurora, Their Last Utopia.* Portland, Ore.: Binford & Mort Publishing, 1993.

Stein, Stephen J. *The Shaker Experience in America: A History of the United Society of Believers.* New Haven, Conn.: Yale University Press, 1992.

Sutton, Robert P. *Les Icariens: The Utopian Dream in Europe and America.* Urbana: University of Illinois Press, 1994.

Thomas, Robert D. *The Man Who Would Be Perfect.* Philadelphia: University of Pennsylvania Press, 1977.

Troester, Rosalie Riegle. *Voices from the Past.* Philadelphia: Temple University Press, 1993.

Tyler, Alice Felt. *Freedom's Ferment: Phases of American Social History from the Colonial Period to the Outbreak of the Civil War.* New York: Harper & Row, 1962.

Wagner, Jon. "Eric Jansson and the Bishop Hill Colony." In *America's Communal Utopias,* ed. Donald E. Pitzer. Chapel Hill: University of North Carolina Press, 297–318.

———. "Living in Community: Daily Life in the Bishop Hill Colony." *Western Illinois Regional Studies* 12, no. 2 (1989): 61–81.

———. "A Midwestern Patriarchy." In *Sex Roles in Contemporary American Communes,* ed. Jon Wagner, 211–40. Bloomington: Indiana University Press, 1982.

Wayland-Smith, Ellen. "The Status and Self Perception of Women in the Oneida Community." *Communal Societies* 8 (1988): 18–53.

Weisbrot, Robert. "Father Divine and the Peace Mission." In *America's Communal Utopias,* ed. Donald E. Pitzer, 432–48. Chapel Hill: University of North Carolina Press, 1997.

———. *Father Divine and the Struggle for Racial Equality.* Urbana: University of Illinois Press, 1983.

Wergland, Glendyne R. "Lust, 'A Snare of Satan to Beguile the Soul': New Light on Shaker Celibacy." *Communal Societies* 15 (1995): 1–24.

Wetzel, Richard D. *Frontier Musicians on the Connoquenessing, Wabash, and Ohio.* Athens: Ohio University Press, 1976.

Wheeler, Wayne. "Eric Jannssonism: Community and Freedom in Nineteenth-Century Sweden and America." *Western Illinois Regional Studies* 12, no. 2 (1989): 7–15.

Williams, Aaron. *The Harmony Society.* Reprint. New York: Augustus M. Kelley Publishers, 1971.

Yarmolinsky, Avrahm. *A Russian-American Dream: A Memoir on William Frey.* Lawrence: University of Kansas Press, 1965.

Zablocki, Benjamin. *The Joyful Community.* Chicago: University of Chicago Press, 1980.

Index

About the Author

ROBERT P. SUTTON is Professor of History at Western Illinois University. He is the author of *Immigration of the Icarians to Illinois* (1987), and the translator of Etienne Cabet's *Voyage en Icarie* (1996).